Leipziger Altorientalistische Studien

Herausgegeben von
Michael P. Streck

Band 7, 2

2019
Harrassowitz Verlag · Wiesbaden

Michael P. Streck

Supplement to the Akkadian Dictionaries

Vol. 2: D, T, Ṭ

with the collaboration of Janine Wende,
Bert Kouwenberg, Nadezda Rudik, Johannes Hackl,
Frank Simons and Elyze Zomer

2019
Harrassowitz Verlag · Wiesbaden

Bibliografische Information der Deutschen Nationalbibliothek
Die Deutsche Nationalbibliothek verzeichnet diese Publikation in der Deutschen Nationalbibliografie; detaillierte bibliografische Daten sind im Internet über http://dnb.dnb.de abrufbar.

Bibliographic information published by the Deutsche Nationalbibliothek
The Deutsche Nationalbibliothek lists this publication in the Deutsche Nationalbibliografie; detailed bibliographic data are available in the Internet at http://dnb.dnb.de.

For further information about our publishing program consult our website http://www.harrassowitz-verlag.de

Printed on permanent/durable paper.
Printing and binding: Hubert & Co., Göttingen
Printed in Germany

ISSN 2193-4436
ISBN 978-3-447-11026-6

Table of Contents

Introduction

1. Volume D/T/Ṭ of the Supplement to the Akkadian Dictionaries

For the goals and organization of SAD cf. in general the introduction of volume B/P. In the following, some additional information pertaining to volume D/T/Ṭ will be given.

The reader is kindly referred to the website of the project (http://altorient.gko.uni-leipzig.de/etymd.html) where all results published in the present volume are accessible online. In addition, the website also offers much material for the other letters of the alphabet. New material and corrections for the letters B/P, not published in the pertinent volume, are marked in yellow on the website.

For the present volume, Michael P. Streck was mainly responsible for including material from new text editions, whereas Nadezda Rudik, Elyze Zomer and, above all, Janine Wende mainly sifted through the secondary literature. Old Assyrian material was kindly sent to us by Bert Kouwenberg, and Late Babylonian material was provided by Johannes Hackl. In weekly sessions, first drafts of the lemmata were discussed by Streck and Rudik or Wende, and the results were subsequently published on the website of the project.

At the end of each lemma, responsibilities for the first drafts of the articles are indicated by the following abbreviations: EZ = Elyze Zomer, JH = Johannes Hackl, JW = Janine Wende, MPS = Michael P. Streck, NJCK = Bert Kouwenberg, NR = Nadezda Rudik. First drafts of all lemmata not claimed by any author remain the responsibility of Streck.

The final manuscript of the present volume was revised and corrected by Streck. English corrections were made by Frank Simons (= FJMS). The manuscript was formatted by Janine Wende.

In addition to the corpus used for volume B/P (cf. LAOS 7/1 p. xii–xiv) the following publications were used for volume D/T/Ṭ:

Old Akkadian:	CUSAS 27: Šu-ilišu archive and misc.
Old Babylonian:	Cohen 2018: List of sheep body parts.
	CUSAS 29: OB Dūr-Abī-ešuḫ.
	CUSAS 36: OB letters.
Middle Babylonian:	CUSAS 30.
Neo-Babylonian:	SAA 21: Rituals.
Late Babylonian:	dubsar 3: LB letters.
	dubsar 7: Texts from Ur.
	CUSAS 28: Documents of West Semites.
Assyrian:	CUSAS 34.
Old Assyrian:	AKT 8–10.
Middle Assyrian:	StAT 5: Texts from Assur.
	BATSH 18: Texts from Dūr-Katlimmu.
Literary Texts:	Wasserman 2016 (= ALL): Love Lyrics.
	Wasserman 2018: OB incantations.
	Streck/Wasserman 2018: OB Ištar Louvre.
	SB KAL 5–7, 9.

ORA 7: SB Hymn to Marduk; Lament of Nabû-šuma-ukīn.
MesCiv. 13: SB oracle questions.
Jiménez 2017: SB disputation poems.

In addition to the *secondary literature* used for volume B/P, the following publications may be mentioned (selection):

Beaulieu 1999: LB Uruk cult inventory.
Cherry 2016: Aram. loanwords.
Jursa 2010: LB economy.
Richter 2012: Hurrian.
Sjöberg 1998: Emar Sa vocabulary.
Streck 2017: times of the day.
Such-Gutiérrez 2018: OAkk Adab.
Zawadzki 2006 and 2013: textiles in LB cult.

2. Statistics

The following table provides the numerical breakdown for the volume D/T/Ṭ of SAD.

	D	T	Ṭ	Total
Number of entries in AHw	361	860	133	1,354
Number of entries in CAD	380	1,116	143	1,639
Number of entries in SAD	229	446	61	736
New words in SAD in total	43	91	9	143
New nouns	38	76	7	121
New numerals		1		1
New verbs	2	10	1	13
New adjectives		2		2
New adverbs	3	1	1	5
New prepositions		1		1
New verbal stems in total	11	4	4	19
New Gt-stems	1	1	1	3
New Gtn-stems	2			2
New D-stems	2		1	3
New Dt-stems		1		1
New Dtn-stems		1		1
New Štn-stems	1			1
New N-stems	2	1	2	5
New Ntn-stems	1			1
New ŠD-stems	1			1
New R-stems	1			1

3. Addition to the History of Akkadian Lexicography

In the following, I will give an addition to the short history of Akk. lexicography presented in LAOS 7/1 p. vii–x.

In 2017, while cleaning up some old storage places in Yale university, Benjamin Foster found several boxes of lexical files. He suggested that they were the work of Carl Bezold, apparently updated by Albrecht Goetze here and there. He kindly sent the files to Leipzig where they are now kept in the Altorientalisches Institut. Most of the estimated 25,000 file cards are small, only 7.5 x 4.8 cm. They are written in German and contain a mix of references from cuneiform texts and from secondary literature (see fig. below). That they have been updated by Goetze, Bezold's student, is clear from the fact that two of them were written on the back of an official letter addressed to Frieda Goetze, Beethovenstraße 44, the house of Goetze's family in Heidelberg, and another one mentions "Prof. Götze" on the back. Still others contain Hittite material on the back, which also points to Goetze.

Which file cards are they? The 200,000 file cards prepared by Bezold for his Assyrian thesaurus and later sent to Leipzig were burnt in 1943 (LAOS 7/1 p. viif.). However, Bezold and his wife Adele also compiled supplementary file cards, described by Borger[1] as follows: "Daneben hatte er eine Ergänzungskartei mit Sekundärliteratur und Zitaten aus von ihm nicht verzettelten Texten. In diese Kartei hatte Adele Bezold die bis dahin erschienenen Spezialglossare eingearbeitet … Die Ergänzungskartei verblieb in Heidelberg, aber Frau Bezold hat diese noch einmal abgeschrieben und ihre Abschrift ebenfalls nach Leipzig geschickt … Am 4. Dezember 1943 wurde das Leipziger Institut durch eine Bombe vernichtet. Von Bezolds Materialien blieb dabei nichts übrig … Die ursprüngliche Ergänzungskartei (zehn Kästen mit kleinen Zettelchen) wurde kürzlich im Heidelberger Seminar 'ausgegraben', seit fast einem halben Jahrhundert wohl von niemandem angerührt".[2] Apparently, these supplementary file cards do not exist any more in Heidelberg (information courtesy B. Faist).

It is suggested here that the file cards now stored in Leipzig are Bezold's original supplementary file cards. How and when did they reach Yale? There is no information about this, but one may suggest that they were sent there after they were rediscovered around 1980. It is an irony of history that Bezold's file cards now repose once more in Leipzig, after an absence of more than 70 years.

[1] Borger 1984, 91f.

[2] These are the file cards referred to by von Soden 1957, 485: "Seine [scil. Bezold's] heute noch in Heidelberg befindlichen Sammlungen erfaßten aber nur einen ziemlich kleinen Teil der Literatur".

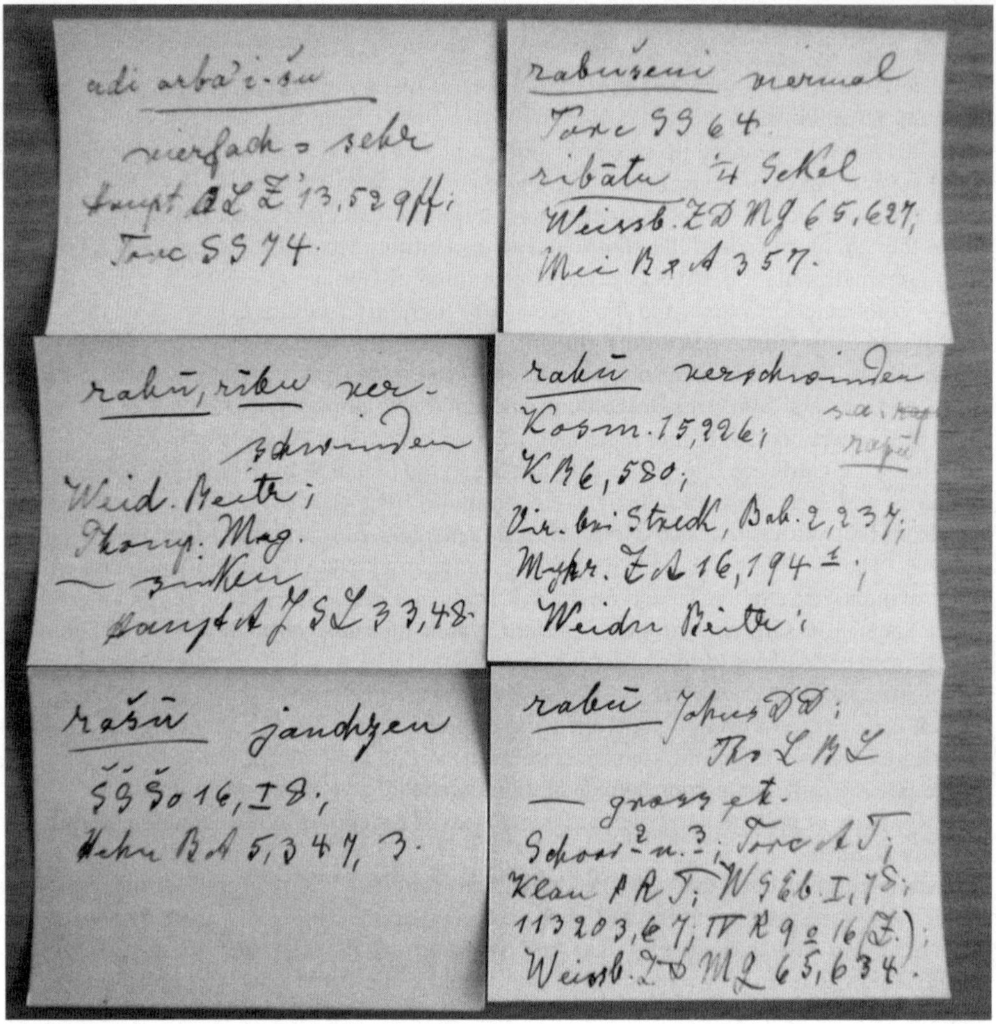

Fig. 1: Specimina of Bezold's supplementary file cards now reposing in the Altorientalisches Institut, Leipzig (photo: M. P. Streck).

Bibliography

Abraham K. 2004: Business and Politics under the Persian Empire. Bethesda.

Abraham K. / Sokoloff M. 2011: Aramaic Loanwords in Akkadian. A Reassessment of the Proposals, AfO 52, 22–76.

Abusch T. / Schwemer D. 2009: The Chicago Maqlû fragment (A 7876), Iraq 71, 53–87.

Adamthwaite M. R. 2001: Late Hittite Emar: the chronology, synchronisms, and socio-political aspects of a Late Bronze Age fortress town (= ANES Suppl. 8). Louvain.

Ahmed K. M. 2012: The Beginnings of Ancient Kurdistan (c. 2500-1500 BC). A Historical and Cultural Synthesis. Diss. Leiden.

Al-Rawi F. N. H. / Dalley S. 2000: Old Babylonian Texts from Private Houses at Abu Habbah, Ancient Sippir (= Edubba 7). London.

Anbar M. 1978: Review of OBTR, BiOr 25, 208–215.

Anbar M. / Stol M. 1991: Textes de l'époque babylonienne ancienne III, RA 85, 13–48.

Archi A. 1973: L'Organizzazione Amministrativa Ittita e il Regime delle Offerte Cultuali, OrAnt 12, 209–226.

Arkhipov I. 2012: Le vocabulaire de la métallurgie et la nomenclature des objets en métal dans les textes de Mari (= ARM 32). Paris.

Arnaud D. 1991: Textes Syriens de l'Âge du Bronze Récent (= AulaOr Suppl. 1).

Arnaud D. 1996: Études sur Alalah et Ougarit à l'Âge du Bronze Récent, SMEA 37, 47–65.

Arnaud D. 2007: Corpus des textes de bibliothèque de Ras Shamra-Ougarit (1936–2000) en sumérien, babylonien et assyrien (= AulaOr. Suppl. 23).

Bagg A. 2000: Assyrische Wasserbauten (= BagF 24). Mainz.

Baker H. D. 2004: The Archive of the Nappāḫu Family (= AfO Bh. 30). Wien.

Baker H. D. 2010: The meaning of *ṬUPPI*, RA 104, 131–162.

Balkan K. 1954: Kassitenstudien. I. Die Sprache der Kassiten. (= AOS 37).

Balkan K. 1992: The Conception of Trinity in the Tablets of Kültepe, in: Fs. Alp, 15–44.

Barjamovic G. 2011: A Historical Geography of Anatolia in the Old Assyrian Colony Period (= CNIP 38). Copenhagen.

Barjamovic G. / Larsen M. T. 2008: An Old Assyrian Incantation against the Evil Eye, AoF 35, 144–55.

Bartelmus A. 2007: *talīmu* and the Relationship between Assurbanipal and Šamaš-šumu-ukīn, SAAB 16, 287–302.

Bayram S. / Veenhof K. R. 1991/2: Unpublished Kültepe Texts on Real Estate, JEOL 32, 87–100.

Beaulieu P.-A. 1992: New Light on Secret Knowledge in Late Babylonian Culture, ZA 82, 98–111.

Beaulieu P.-A. 1999: Un Inventaire de Joaillerie Sacrée de l'Eanna d'Uruk, RA 93, 141–155.

Beaulieu P.-A. 2003: The Pantheon of Uruk during the Neo-Babylonian Period (= CunMon. 23). Leiden / Boston.

Beaulieu P.-A. 2005: Eanna's contribution to the construction of the North Palace at Babylon, in: H. D. Baker / M. Jursa (eds.), Approaching the Babylonian Economy (= AOAT 330), Münster, 46–73.

Beckman G. 1996: Texts from the Vicinity of Emar in the Collection of Jonathan Rosen (= HANEM 2). Padua.

Beckman G. 1999: Hittite Diplomatic Texts (= WAW 7, 2nd ed.). Atlanta.

Beckman G. 2007: A Hittite Ritual for Depression (CTH 432), in: D. Groddeck / M. Zorman (eds.), Tabula Hethaeorum. Hethitologische Beiträge Silvin Košak zum 65. Geburtstag (DBH 25). Wiesbaden, 69–81.

Besnier M.-F. / Boutrolle P. / Chanut C. / Hawley R. 2015: On the junipers of Ugarit. Part 2, The word diprānu and the genus Juniperus, in: C. Roche-Hawley / R. Hawley (eds.), Devins et lettrés dans l'orbite de Babylone. Travaux réalisés dans le cadre du projet ANR Mespériph 2007-2011 (= Orient & Méditerranée 16), 81–158. Paris.

Bezold C. 1926: Babylonisch-assyrisches Glossar. Heidelberg.

Biggs R. D. 1993: Descent of Ištar, line 104, NABU 1993/74.

Bilgiç E. 1945–1951: Die Ortsnamen der "kappadokischen" Urkunden im Rahmen der alten Sprachen Anatoliens, AfO 15, 1–37.

Bilgiç E. 1954: Die einheimischen Appellativa der kappadokischen Texte und ihre Bedeutung für die Anatolischen Sprachen. Ankara.

Bilgiç E. 1992: Ebla in Cappadocian Inscriptions, in: Fs. S. Alp, 61–66.

Black J. A. / Al-Rawi F. N. H. 1987: A Contribution to the Study of Akkadian Bird Names, ZA 77, 117–126.

Bloch Y. 2008: The Order of Eponyms in the Reign of Shalmaneser I, UF 40, 143–178.

Bonechi M. 1997: Lexique et idéologie royale à l'époque proto-syrienne, MARI 8, 477–535.

Bongenaar A. C. V. M. 1997: The Neo-Babylonian Ebabbar Temple at Sippar: its Administration and ist Prosopography (= PIHANS 80). Leiden.

Borger R. 1962: Review of CAD D, I/J, BiOr 19, 252–254.

Borger R. 1970: Vier Grenzsteinurkunden Merodachbaladans I. von Babylon. Der Teheran-Kudurru, SB 33, SB 169 und SB 26, AfO 23, 1–26.

Borger R. 1984: Altorientalische Lexikographie. Geschichte und Probleme (= Nachrichten der Akademie der Wissenschaften in Göttingen. I. Philologisch-Historische Klasse, 1984/2). Göttingen.

Borger R. 1988: König Sanheribs Eheglück, ARRIM 6, 5–11.

Borger R. 2010a: Review of CAD T, Ṭ, BiOr 67, 344–348.

Borger R. 2010b: Mesopotamisches Zeichenlexikon (= AOAT 305). Münster.

Bottéro J. 1962: Review of CAD D, E, I/J and AHw Lieferung 2–3, Or. 31, 451–459.

Bottéro J. 1995: Textes culinaires mésopotamiens (= MesCiv. 6). Winona Lake.

Brinkman J. A. 1996: Kassite *timiraš* and *sirpi* as Cattle Designations, NABU 1996/40.

Brinkman J. A. 2004: Administration and Society in Kassite Babylonia (Review of Sassmannshausen 2001), JAOS 124, 283–304.

Brown D. / Fermor J. / Walker C. 1999/2000: The Water Clock in Mesopotamia, AfO 46/7, 130–148.

Cancik-Kirschbaum E. C. 1996: Die Mittelassyrischen Briefe aus Tall Šēẖ Ḥamad (= BATSH 4/1). Berlin.

Cancik-Kirschbaum E. C. 1999: LÚ*sāpi'u/sēpû*. Eine akkadische Berufsbezeichnung aus dem Bereich der Textilherstellung, in: Fs Renger (= AOAT 267, Münster), 79–93.

Cavigneaux A. 2007: Les oiseaux de l'arche, AuOr. 25, 319f.

Çeçen S. / Gökçek L. G. 2017: Uṣur-ša-Ištar Ailesinden fŠimat-Su'en'e Ait Dört Mektup, Cappadocia Journal of History and Social Sciences 9, 463–82.

Charpin D. 1980: Archives familiales et propriéte privée en Babylonie ancienne: étude des documemts de "Tell Sifr". Genève.

Charpin D. 1989-90: Compte rendu du CAD volume Q (1982), AfO 36/37, 92–106.

Charpin D. 1990: *dirru(m)* « (mois) bis », NABU 1990/64.

Charpin D. 2005: Données nouvelles sur la vie économique et sociale de l'époque paléobabylonienne (Review of Sigrist 2003: Old Babylonian Account Texts in the Horn Archaeological Museum), Or. 74, 409–421.

Cherry Z. 2017: Aramaic Loanwords in Neo-Assyrian, 900–600 B.C. Uppsala.

Civil M. 1973: Notes on Sumerian Lexicography, II, JCS 25, 171–177,

Civil M. 1987: The Early History of HAR-ra: The Ebla Link, in: Cagni L. (ed), Ebla 1975-1985 (= IUO SSA 27), 131–158.

Civil M. 1998: "Adamdun," the Hippopotamus, and the Crocodile, JCS 50, 11–14.

Cohen Y. 2004: Kidin-Gula – The Foreign Teacher at the Emar Scribal School, RA 98, 81–100.

Cohen Y. 2010: The “Second Glosses” in the Lexical Lists from Emar: West Semitic or Akkadian?, in: Babel und Bibel 4, 813–839.

Cohen Y. 2013: Wisdom from the Late Bronze Age (= WAW 34). Atlanta.

Cohen Y. 2018: An Old Babylonian List of Sheep Body Parts (BM 29663), Fs. Geller 131–148.

Cole W. 1996: Nippur IV: The early Neo-Babylonian governor’s archive from Nippur (= OIP 114). Chicago.

Conti G. / Bonechi M. 1992: *tīšānum* éblaite = akkadien de Mari *tīšānum*, NABU 1992/11.

Da Riva R. 1999: Recogiendo leña en los jardines de Šamaš, Isimu 2, 81–94.

Da Riva R. 2002: Der Ebabbar-Tempel von Sippar in frühneubabylonischer Zeit (640–580 v. Chr.) (= AOAT 291). Münster.

Da Riva R. 2012: The twin inscriptions of Nebuchadnezzar at Brisa, Wadi Esh-Sharbin, Lebanon: a historical and philological study (= AfO Bh. 32).

Dalley S. 2000: Hebrew *taḥaš*, Akkadian *duhšu*, Faience and Beadwork, JSS 45, 1–19.

Dalley S. 2009: Babylonian Tablets from the First Sealand Dynasty in the Schøyen Collection (= CUSAS 9). Bethesda.

Dalley S. / Walker S. B. F. / Hawkins J. D. 1976: The Old Babylonian Tablets from Tell al Rimah. London.

de Boer R. 2016: From the Yaḫrūrum Šaplûm Archives. Three Unpublished Administrative Texts in Leiden, BiOr 73, 590–612.

Deller K. 1992: Götterstreitwagen und Götterstandarten: Götter auf dem Feldzug und ihr Kult im Feldlager. Einleitung, BaM 23, 291–298.

Deller K. / Mayer W. R. / Sommerfeld W. 1987: Akkadische Lexikographie: CAD N, Or. 56, 177–218.

Dercksen J. G. 1991: Review of Donbaz, Keilschrifttexte in den Antikenmuseen zu Stambul II (= FAOS Beih. 2), BiOr 48, 179–183.

Dercksen J. G. 1996: The Old Assyrian Copper Trade in Anatolia (= PIHANS 75). Leiden.

Dercksen J. G. 1997/1998: Review of TPAK, AfO 44/45, 333–339.

Dercksen J. G. 2005a: Metals according to documents from Kültepe-Kanish, in: Ü. Yalçin (ed.), Anatolian Metal III (= Der Anschnitt Beiheft 18, Bochum) 17–34.

Dercksen J. G. 2005b: Adad is King! The Sargon Text from Kültepe (with an appendix on MARV 4, 138 and 140), JEOL 39, 107–129.

Dercksen J. G. 2007: On Anatolian Loanwords in Akkadian Texts from Kültepe, ZA 97, 26–46.

Dercksen J. G. 2007a: Die altassyrischen Handelsabgaben in Nordmesopotamien und Anatolien im 19.–18. Jh. v. Chr. in Verträgen und Praxis, in: H. Klinkott / S. Kubisch / R. Müller-Wollermann (eds.), Geschenke und Steuern, Zölle und Tribute. Antike Abgabenformen in Anspruch und Wirklichkeit (= CHANE 29), 187–211.

Dietrich M. 1989: Das Einsetzungsritual der Entu von Emar (Emar 6/3, 369), UF 21, 47–100.

Dietrich M. 2001a: Babylonische Sklaven auf der Schreiberschule, in: Fs. Veenhof, 67–81.

Dietrich M. 2001b: Zu den Urkunden aus dem Lande Ḫana. Bemerkungen zu A.H. Podanys Buch über die Geschichte und Kultur eines mitteleuphratischen Regionalkönigtums im 2. Jt. v. Chr., UF 33, 641–656.

Dietrich M. 2003: The Babylonian Correspondence of Sargon and Sennacherib (= SAA 17). Helsinki.

Di Vito R. A. 1993: Studies in Third Millennium Sumerian and Akkadian Personal Names (= SPSM 16). Rome.

Dombradi E. 1996: Die Darstellung des Rechtsaustrags in den altbabylonischen Prozeß-urkunden (= FAOS 20). Stuttgart.

Dombradi E. 2000: Studien zu *mitḫārum*/*mitḫāriš* und die Frage des Duplums: I. Zum semantischen Feld von *mitḫārum* in juristischem Kontext, ZA 90, 40–69.

Donbaz V. 1999: Cuneiform Texts in the Sadberk Hanim Museum. Istanbul.

Donbaz V. 2001: Some Recently Discovered Kārum 1-b Tablets and Related Observations, in: StBoT 45, 106–114.

Donbaz V. 2004: Some Old Assyrian Texts with Rare Terminology, in: Fs. Larsen, 179–189.

Dornauer A. 2014: Das Archiv des assyrischen Statthalters Mannu-kī-Aššūr von Gūzāna/ Tall Ḥalaf (= VFMOS 3,III). Wiesbaden.

Dosch G. 1993: Zur Struktur der Gesellschaft des Königreichs Arrapḫe (= HSAO 5). Heidelberg.

Driver G. R. 1960: Review of CAD D, E, JSS 5, 156-158.

Durand J.-M. 1983a: Textes administratifs des salles 134 et 160 du Palais de Mari: transcrits, traduits et commentés (= ARM 21). Paris.

Durand J.-M. 1983b: Relectures d'ARMT XIII. II: La correspondance de Numušda-nahrârî, MARI 2, 151–163.

Durand J.-M. 1983c: A propos des noms de parenté à Mari, MARI 2, 215–217.

Durand J.-M. 1987a: Villes Fantômes de Syrie et Autres Lieux, MARI 5, 199–234.

Durand J.-M. 1987b: La défaite de Zûzû, roi d'Apum, MARI 5, 621–622.

Durand J.-M. 1987c: Documents pour l'histoire du royaume de haute-Mésopotamie, I, MARI 5, 155–198.

Durand J.-M. 1988: Archives Epistolaires de Mari I/1 (= ARM 26/1). Paris.

Durand J.-M. 1989: L'assemblée en Syrie à l'époque pré-amorite, QuSem 16, 27–44.

Durand J.-M. 1990a: Documents pour l'histoire du royaume de haute-mesopotamie II, MARI 6, 271–301.

Durand J.-M. 1990b: ARM III, ARM VI, ARMT XIII, ARMT XXII, in: Fs. Kupper, 149–177.

Durand J.-M. 1990c: La culture matérielle à Mari (I): Le bijou *HÚB.TIL.LÁ, MARI 6, 125–158.

Durand J.-M. 1992: Unité et Diversités au Proche-Orient à L'Époque Amorrite, CRRAI 38, 97–128.

Durand J.-M. 1997: Documents épistolaires du palais de Mari I (= LAPO 16). Paris.

Durand J.-M. 1998: Documents épistolaires du palais de Mari II (= LAPO 17). Paris.

Durand J.-M. 2000: Documents épistolaires du palais de Mari III (= LAPO 18). Paris.

Durand J.-M. 2001: Une alliance matrimoniale entre un marchand assyrien de Kanesh et un marchand Mariote, in: Fs. Veenhof, 119–132.

Durand J.-M. 2005: *diānum* D, NABU 2005/85.

Durand J.-M. 2009: La nomenclature des habits et des textiles dans les textes de Mari (= ARM 30). Paris.

Durand J.-M. / Marti L. 2004: Chroniques du Moyen-Euphrate 3. Les documents du Tell Bi'a, RA 98, 121–150.

Edzard D. O. 1961: Review of CAD D, E, I/J, ZA 54, 249–255.

Edzard D. O. 1982: Qīšum, Ensi von Kazallu, in: Fs. Kraus, 26–33.

Eidem J. 1992: The Shemshara Archives. Vol. 2: The Administrative Texts. Copenhagen.

Eidem J. 2011: The Royal Archives from Tell Leilan. Old Babylonian Letters and Treaties from the Lower Town Palace East (= PIHANS 117). Leiden.

Eidem J. / Læssøe J. 2001: The Shemshara Archives. Vol. 1: The Letters. Copenhagen.

Erol H. 2015: *ina maqāt ubrī lu kaspam lu hurāṣam ašāmma*… "Yabancılar Geldiğinde ya gümüş ya da altın satın alacağım…", in: Fs. Günbattı, 87–98.

Fadhil A. 1990: Die in Nimrud/Kalhu aufgefundene Grabinschrift der Jabâ, BagM 21, 461–470.

Fales F. M. 2003: *tuanu*: an Aramaic Loanword in Neo-Assyrian, NABU 2003/103.

Fales F. M. 2005: Assyrian-Aramaic cultural interrelation: older and newer results, in: HANE/M 6/2, 596–615.

Fales F. M. / Jakob-Rost L. 1991: Neo-Assyrian Texts from Assur. Private Archives in the Vorderasiatisches Museum of Berlin. Part 1 (= SAAB 5). Padova.

Farber W. 1977: Beschwörungsrituale an Ištar und Dumuzi. *attī Ištar ša ḫarmaša Dumuzi* (= Veröffentlichungen der Orientalischen Kommission, Akademie der Wissenschaften und der Literatur 30). Wiesbaden.

Farber W. 1990: *Mannam lušpur ana Enkidu*: Some New Thoughts about an Old Motif, JNES 49, 299–321.

Farber W. 2001: "… but she refuses to take the silver!" The Strange Case of the *aššat rabi sisi'e*, in: Fs. Veenhof, 137–43.

Farber W. 2004: *Ana šinīšu TaBBuqātu* = Doppelt so viele Töpfe und Probleme!, NABU 2004/2.

Farber W. 2014: Lamaštu: An Edition of the Canonical Series of Lamaštu Incantations and Rituals and Related Texts from the Second and First Millennia B. C. (= MesCiv. 17). Winona Lake.

Fincke J. 1993: Die Orts- und Gewässernamen der Nuzi-Texte (= RGTC 10). Wiesbaden.

Fincke J. 1995: Beiträge zum Lexikon des Hurritischen von Nuzi, in: SCCNH 7, 5–21.

Fincke J. 1998: Beiträge zum Lexikon des Hurritischen von Nuzi. Teil 2, in: SCCNH 9, 41–48.

Fincke J. 2000: Augenleiden nach keilschriftlichen Quellen. Untersuchungen zur altorientalischen Medizin. Würzburg.

Fincke J. 2015: SIG7.ALAN = Nabnitu Tablet B Source B (K. 4165+) Joined to K. 14889, NABU 2015/104.

Finet A. 1956: L'Accadien des lettres de Mari. Bruxelles.

Finkel I. L. 1999: The Lament of Nabû-šuma-ukîn, in: Renger (ed.), Babylon: Focus mesopotamischer Geschichte, Wiege früher Gelehrsamkeit, Mythos in der Moderne (= CDOG 2), 323–342.

Finkel I. L. 2000: Old Babylonian Medical Training, in: Fs. Lambert, 137–223.

Finkel I. L. 2007: On the Rules for the Royal Game of Ur, in: id. (ed.), Ancient Board Games in perspective. Papers from the 1990 British Museum colloquium, with additional contributions, 16–32.

Finkel I. 2014: The Ark before Noah. London.

Fleming D. E. 2000: Time at Emar: The Cultic Calendar and the Rituals from the Diviner's Archive (= MesCiv. 11). Winona Lake.

Ford J. N. 2001: The Verb tqnn in RS 1992.2014, UF 33, 201–212.

Foster B. R. 2005: Before the Muses. An Anthology of Akkadian Literature. Third Edition.

Frahm E. 1997: Einleitung in die Sanherib-Inschriften (= AfO Bh. 26). Wien.

Frame G. 1999: The Inscription of Sargon II at Tang-i Var, Or. 68, 31–57.

Frankena R. 1960: Review of E. Reiner, Šurpu. A Collection of Sumerian and Akkadian Incantations (= AfO Beih. 11), BiOr 17, 172–174.

Frankena R. 1966: Briefe aus dem British Museum: LIH und CT 2-33 (= AbB 2). Leiden.

Frankena R. 1974: Briefe aus dem Berliner Museum (= AbB 6). Leiden.

Frankena R. 1978: Kommentar zu den Altbabylonischen Briefen aus Lagaba und anderen Orten (= SLB 4). Leiden.

Freydank H. 1974: Zwei Verpflegungstexte aus Kār-Tukultī-Ninurta, AoF 1, 55–89.

Freydank H. 2007: *ṭuppu* in anderer Sicht, AoF 34, 225–236.

Freydank H. 2010: Betrachtungen zur Weidewirtschaft in Dūr-Katlimmu, in: H. Kühne (ed.) Dūr-Katlimmu 2008 and Beyond (= StCh 1), 87–99.

Friberg J. 1987–1990: Mathematik, in: RlA 7, 531–588.

Friberg J. 2001: Bricks and Mud in Metro-Mathematical Cuneiform Texts, in: BBVO 19, 61–154.

Friberg J. / Hunger H. / al-Rawi F. 1990: 'Seed and Reeds'. A Metro-Mathematical Topic Text from Late Babylonian Uruk, BagM 21, 483–557.

Fuchs A. 1994: Die Inschriften Sargons II. aus Khorsabad. Göttingen.

Gabbay U. 2011: Laments in Garšana, in: Garšana Studies (= CUSAS 6), 67–74.

Garelli P. / Charpin D. / Durand J.-M. 1982: Rôle des prisonniers et des déportés à l'époque médio-assyrienne, in: H. Klengel (ed.) Gesellschaft und Kultur im alten Vorderasien (= SGKAO 15), 69–75.

Gaspa S. 2007: Vessels in Neo-Assyrian Documents: Capacity Measure and Listing Conventions, SAAB 16, 145–184.

Gaspa S. 2012: Alimenti e pratiche alimentari in Assiria: Le materie alimentari nel culto ufficiale dell'Assiria del primo millennio A.C. (= HANE/M 13). Padova.

Gehlken E. 1995: Grüße aus Uruk und Larsa, in: Fs. Boehmer, 167–174.

Geller M. 1984: Review of Köcher, Die babylonisch-assyrische Medizin in Texten und Untersuchungen, Bd. V und VI (1980), ZA 74/2, 292–297.

Geller M. 1992: A Vocabulary of Rare Words, Or. 61, 205–207.

Geller M. 2000: Incipits and Rubrics, in: Fs. Lambert, 225–258.

George A. R. 1990: The Day the Earth Divided: a Geological Aetiology in the Babylonian Gilgameš Epic, ZA 80, 214–219.

George A. R. 1992: Babylonian topographical texts (= OLA 40). Louvain.

George A. R. 1994: *tazzīqum*, « vexation », NABU 1994/27.

George A. R. 1995: The bricks of E-sagil, Iraq 57, 173–197.

George A. R. 1997: Sumerian tiru = «eunuch», NABU 1997/97.

George A. R. 2000: Four Temple Rituals from Babylon, in: Fs. Lambert, 259–299.

George A. R. 2003: The Babylonian Gilgamesh-Epic. Oxford.

George A. R. 2008: Akkadian *turru* (*ṭurru* B) "corner angle", and the walls of Babylon, ZA 98, 221–229.

George A. R. 2010: The Dogs of Ninkilim, Part Two: Babylonian Rituals to Counter Field Pests, Iraq 72, 79–148.

George A. R. 2013: Babylonian Divinatory Texts Chiefly in the Schøyen Collection (= CUSAS 18). Bethesda.

George A. R. 2018: Enkidu and the Harlot: Another Fragment of Old Babylonian Gilgameš, ZA 108, 10–21.

George A. R. / al-Rawi F. N. H. 1998: Tablets from the Sippar Library. VII. Three Wisdom Texts, Iraq 60, 187–206.

Glassner J.-J. 2002: *takāltu*, NABU 2002/8.

Goddeeris A. 2002: Economy and Society in Northern Babylonia in the Early Old Babylonian Period (ca. 2000-1800 BC) (= OLA 109). Louvain.

Goetze A. 1958: Letters from Harmal, Sumer 14, 3–78.

Gong Y. 2000: Die Namen der Keilschriftzeichen (= AOAT 268). Münster.

Green A. 1998: Nadel, in: RlA 9, 69–73.

Guichard M 2005: La vaisselle de luxe des rois de Mari. Matériaux pour le Dictionnaire de Babylonien de Paris, tome II (= ARM 31). Paris.

Guichard M. 2015: Une prière bilingue inédite de Mari l'art d'amadouer son dieu et seigneur de la littérature à la pratique, in: Durand / Marti / Römer (eds.), Colères et repentirs divins (= OBO 278), 343–376.

Günbattı C. 1996: Two New Tablets Throwing Light on the Relations Between Anatolian Kings and Assyrian Merchants in the Period of the Assyrian Colonies, ArAn 2, 25–35.

Günbattı C. 1997: Kültepe'den Akadlı Sargon'a âit bir tablet, ArAn 3, 131–55.

Günbattı C. 1999: Ankara Etnografya Müzesi'nde Buluna Bir Kapadokya Tablet, Belleten 63/237, 391–93.

Günbattı C. 2004: Two Treaty texts found at Kültepe, in: Fs. Larsen, 249–68.

Günbattı C. 2014: The Letter Sent to Hurmeli King of Harsamna and the Kings of Kaniš. Türk Tarih Kurumu Yayınları, V. Dizi – Sayı 3. Ankara.

Gurney O. R. 1983: The Middle Babylonian Legal and Economic Texts from Ur. Oxford.

Haas V. / Wilhelm G. 1974: Zum hurritischen Lexikon II, Or. 43, 87–93

Hackl J. 2013: Materialien zur Urkundenlehre und Archivkunde der spätzeitlichen Texte aus Nordbabylonien. Diss. Vienna.

Hackl J. 2016: An Old Iranian Loanword for a Subdivision of the Shekel from Late Achaemenid Uruk, NABU 2016/53.

Hämeen-Anttila J. 2000: A Sketch of Neo-Assyrian Grammar (= SAAS 13). Helsinki.

Hecker K. 1997: Über den Euphrat… Ortsbezogene Restriktionen in aA Kaufurkunden, in: Gs. Bilgiç (= Archivum Anatolicum 3), 157–172.

Hecker K. / Kryszat G. / Matouš L. 1998: Kappadokische Keilschrifttafeln aus den Sammlungen der Karlsuniversität Prag (= Prag). Prague.

Heeßel N. P. 2000: Babylonisch-assyrische Diagnostik (= AOAT 43). Münster.

Heeßel N. P. 2007: Divinatorische Texte I. Terrestrische, teratologische, physiognomische und oneiromantische Omina (= KAL 1, WVDOG 116). Wiesbaden.

Heeßel N. P. 2012: Divinatorische Texte II. Opferschau-Omina (= KAL 5, WVDOG 139). Wiesbaden.

Heimpel W. 1996a: Šutāwûm und šutaptûm, ZA 86, 163–169.

Heimpel W. 1996b: More light on the dark fate of Qarni-Lim, NABU 1996/47.

Heimpel W. 1997: Crack of dawn, NABU 1997/4.

Heimpel W. 2003: Letters to the King of Mari (= MesCiv. 12). Winona Lake.

Heimpel W. 2009: Workers and Construction Work at Garšana (= CUSAS 5). Bethesda.

Heltzer M. 1978: Goods, Prices and the Organization of Trade in Ugarit. Wiesbaden.

Hinz W. 1969: Altiranische Funde und Forschungen.

Hölscher M. 1996: Die Personennamen der kassitenzeitlichen Texte aus Nippur (= IMGULA 1). Münster.

Horowitz W. 2011: Mesopotamian Cosmic Geography (= MesCiv. 8), 2nd printing. Winona Lake.

Høyrup J. 1993: On Subtractive Operations, Subtractive Numbers, and Purportedly Negative Numbers in Old Babylonian Mathematics, ZA 83, 42–60.

Høyrup J. 2002: Lengths, Widths, Surfaces: A Portrait of Old Babylonian Algebra and Its Kin. New York/Berlin/Heidelberg.

Huehnergard J. 1987: Ugaritic Vocabulary in Syllabic Transcription (= HSS 32). Winona Lake.

Hunger H. / Sachs A. 1988: Astronomical Diaries and Related Texts from Babylon, I, Diaries from 625 BC. to 262 B.C. Wien.

Ikeda J. 2003: A New Contribution to Northwest Semitic Lexicography (Review of Pentiuc 2001), BiOr 60, 263–279.

Jacquet A. 2011: Documents relatifs aux dépenses pour le culte (= FM 12, Mémoires de NABU 13). Paris.

Jakob S. 2009: Die mittelassyrischen Texte aus Tell Chuēra in Nordost-Syrien. Mit einem Beitrag von D. I. Janisch-Jakob (= VFMOS 2/3). Wiesbaden.

Jakob S. 2003: Mittelassyrische Verwaltung und Sozialstruktur (= CunMon. 29). Groningen.

Jakob S. 2009: Die mittelassyrischen Texte aus Tell Chuēra in Nordost-Syrien. Wiesbaden.

Janssen T. 2007: Tuppišu in der AKL - Berechnung, Konzept, Bedeutung, Akkadica 128, 99–108.

Jas R. 1996: Neo-Assyrian Judicial Procedures (= SAAS 5). Helsinki.

Jeyes U. 1989: Old Babylonian Extispicy (= PIHANS 64). Leiden.

Jeyes U. 2000: A Compendium of Gall-Bladder Omens Extant in Middle Babylonian, Nineveh, and Seleucid Versions, in: Fs. Lambert, 345–373.

Jiménez E. 2017: The Babylonian Disputation Poems (= CHANE 87). Leiden.

Joannès F. 1989: Archives de Borsippa. La famille Ea-ilûta-bâni. Geneve.

Joannès F. 1993: La culture matérielle à Mari (V), MARI 7, 251–270.

Joannès F. 1997: La mention des enfants dans les textes néo-babyloniens, Ktèma 22, 119–133.

Joannes F. 2006: Haradum II: Les textes de la période paléo-babylonienne (Samsu-iluna – Ammi-ṣaduqa). Paris.

Jursa M. 1995: Die Landwirtschaft in Sippar in neubabylonischer Zeit (= AfO Beih. 25). Wien.

Jursa M. 1995/1996: Review of Wunsch, Die Urkunden des babylonischen Geschäftsmannes Iddin-Marduk. Zum Handel mit Naturalien im 6. Jahrhundert v. Chr. (= CunMon. 3a–b), AfO 42/43, 255–262.

Jursa M. 1997/1998: Review of OIP 114, AfO 44/45, 419–424.

Jursa M. 1999: Das Archiv des Bēl-rēmanni (= PIHANS 86). Leiden.

Jursa M. 2001: *ša taturru*, nochmals, NABU 2001/103.

Jursa M. 2001/2002: Review of CTMMA 3, AfO 48/49, 223–225.

Jursa M. 2003: Betten, Kopfpölster und 'Kühlschränke', in: Fs. Kienast, 229–238.

Jursa M. 2006: Agricultural Management, Tax Farming and Banking: Aspects of Entrepreneurial Activity in Babylonia in the Late Achaemenid and Hellenistic Periods, in: Briant, P. / Joannès, F. (eds.), La transition entre l'empire achéménide et les royaumes hellénistiques (vers 350-300 av. J.-C.) (= Persika 9), 137–222.

Jursa M. 2009: Die Kralle des Meers und andere Aromata, in: Gs. Sima, 147–180.

Jursa M. 2010: Aspects of the Economic History of Babylonia in the First Millennium BC. Economic Geography, Economic Mentalities, Agriculture, the Use of Money, and the Problem of Economic Growth (= AOAT 377). Münster.

Kellenberger E. 2000: *tēbibtum* in den Archiven von Mari und Chagar Bazar, UF 32, 243–260.

Kessler K. 1991: Uruk. Urkunden aus Privathäusern. Die Wohnhäuser westlich des Eanna-Tempelbereichs. Teil I: Die Archive der Söhne des Bēl-ušallim, des Nabû-ušallim und des Bēl-supê-muḫur (= AUWE 8). Mainz.

Kinnier Wilson J. V. 1972: The Nimrud wine lists: a study of men and administration at the Assyrian capital in the eighth century B.C. (= CTN 1). Hertford-London.

Kinnier Wilson J. 2005: On the Cryptogams in the lexical and related texts, JMC 6, 1–21.

Kleber K. 2016: On the ghost word *tasniqtu* "verification" and the stone called "beginning" in Hh. XVI, 189, NABU 2016/89.

Klein H. 1983: *Tudittum*, ZA 73, 255–284.

Kleinerman A. / Owen D. I. 2009: Analytical Concordance to the Garšana Archives (= CUSAS 4). Bethesda.

Köcher F. 1980: Die babylonisch-assyrische Medizin in Texten und Untersuchungen (= BAM) 5 and 6. Berlin.

Koch U. S. 2005: Secrets of Extispicy. The Chapter Multābiltu of the Babylonian Extispicy Series and Niṣirti bārûti Texts mainly from Aššurbanipal's Library (= AOAT 326). Münster.

Koch-Westenholz U. 2000: Babylonian Liver Omens. The Chapters Manzāzu, Padānu and Pān tākalti of the Babylonian Extispicy Series mainly from Aššurbanipal's Library (= CNIP 25). Kopenhagen.

Kogan L. 2003: Popular Etymology in the Semitic Languages, in: Fs. Militarev, 120–140.

Kogan L. 2012: Les noms de plantes akkadiens dans leur context sémitique, in: Fs. Huehnergard (= SAOC 67), 229–268.

Koliński R. 2001: Mesopotamian *dimātu* of the Second Millennium BC (= BAR IS 1004). Oxford.

Kouwenberg N. J. C. 1997: Gemination in the Akkadian Verb. Assen.

Kouwenberg N. J. C. 2010: The Akkadian Verb and Its Semitic Background (= LANE 2). Winona Lake.

Kouwenberg N. J. C. 2015: Sargon's *tūdittum*, or how to make fools of your enemies, in: Fs. Günbattı, 165–70.

Kouwenberg N. J. C. 2017: A Grammar of Old Assyrian (= HdO 118; = GOA). Leiden.

Kouwenberg N J. C. forthc.: Introduction to Old Assyrian. Münster.

Kouwenberg N. J. C. / Fincke J. 2012/13: A "New" Old Assyrian Incantation, JEOL 44, 141–146.

Kraus F. R. 1970: Akkadische Wörter und Ausdrücke, I-III, RA 64, 53–61.

Kraus F. R. 1976: Akkadische Wörter und Ausdrücke, X-XI, RA 70, 165–179.

Kraus F. R. 1987: Sonderformen akkadischer Parataxe: Die Koppelungen. Amsterdam.

Kraus N. 2018: The Weapon of Blood: Politics and Intrigue at the Decline of Akkad, ZA 108, 1–9.

Krebernik M. 1984: Die Beschwörungen aus Fara und Ebla. Untersuchungen zur ältesten keilschriftlichen Beschwörungsliteratur (= TSO 2). Hildesheim/Zürich/New York.

Krebernik M. 1991: Review of Gelb/Kienast 1990, ZA 81, 133–143.

Krebernik M. 2004: Wörter und Sprichwörter: der zweisprachige Schultext HS 1461, ZA 94, 226–248.

Krebernik M. 2014–2016: Ṭirid, RlA 14, 60.

Kronasser H. 1959: Zu heth. ešḫar iya- = akkad. dāmi epēšu, in von Kienle et al. (eds.), Festschrift Johannes Friedrich zum 65. Geburtstag, 273–289.

Kühne C. 1974: Mit Glossenkeilen markierte fremde Wörter in akkadischen Ugarittexten, UF 6, 157–167.

Kupper J.-R. 1997: Bélier et tours de siège, RA 91, 121–133.

Lackenbacher S. 2002: Textes Akkadiens d'Ugarit: Textes provenant des vingt-cinq premières campagnes. Paris.

Lambert W. G. 1979: Review of AHw Lieferung 12–14, JSS 24, 268–273.

Lambert W. G. 1987: A Vocabulary of an unknown language, MARI 5, 409–413.

Lambert W. G. 1987–1990: Lulal/Lātarāk, in: RlA 7, 163–164.

Lambert W. G. 1989: A Babylonian Prayer to Anuna, in: Fs. A. W. Sjöberg, 321–336.

Lambert W. G. 1990: A New Babylonian Descent to the Netherworld, in: Fs. Moran (= HSS 37), 289–300.

Lambert W. G. 1995: Review of di Vito 1993, Or. 64, 131–136.

Landsberger B. 1934: Die Fauna des Alten Mesopotamien nach der 14. Tafel der Serie HAR-RA-hubullu, unter Mitwirkung von I. Krumbiegel. Leipzig.

Landsberger B. 1967: Über Farben im Sumerisch-Akkadischen, JCS 21, 139–173.

Langlois A.-I. 2017: Les archives de la princesse Iltani découvertes à Tell al-Rimah (XVIIIe siècle av.J.-C.) et l'histoire du royaume de Karana/Qaṭṭara, Tome 2 (= Mém. NABU 18, Archibab 2). Paris.

Larsen M. T. 1976: The Old Assyrian City-State and its Colonies (= Mesopotamia 4). Copenhagen.

Larsen M. T. / Møller E. 1991: Five Old Assyrian Texts, in: Fs. Garelli, 227–252.

Leiderer R. 1990: Anatomie der Schafsleber im babylonischen Leberorakel. Eine makroskopisch-analytische Studie. Zuckschwerdt.

Lenzi A. 2006: Tašnintu II, "Repetition, Teaching"?, NABU 2006/31.

Levavi Y. 2018: Administrative Epistolography in the Formative Phase of the Neo-Babylonian Empire (Spätbabylonische Briefe. Herausgegeben von Michael Jursa. Band 2, = dubsar 3). Münster.

Linssen M. J. H. 2004: The Cults of Uruk and Babylon. The Temple Ritual Texts as Evidence for Hellenistic Cult Practices (= CunMon. 25). Groningen.

Lion B. 1991: Bêtes rares, NABU 1991/60.

Lion B. 1992: La circulation des animaux exotiques au Proche-Orient antique, in: CRRAI 38, 357–365.

Liverani M. 1999-2001: The Sargon Geography and the Late Assyrian Mensuration of the Earth, SAAB 13, 57–85.

Livingstone A. 2000: On the Organized Release of Doves to Secure Compliance of a Higher Authority, in: Fs. Lambert, 375–387.

Llop J. 2011: The Food of the Gods. MARV 3, 16. A Middle Assyrian Offerings List to the Great Gods of the City of Aššur, SAAB 18, 1–46.

Luukko M. / van Buylaere G. 1987: The Political Correspondence of Esarhaddon (= SAA 16). Helsinki.

MacGinnis J. 1995: Letter Orders from Sippar and the Administration of the Ebabbara in the Late-Babylonian Period. Bonami.

MacGinnis J. 2008: Review of CAD T, Ṭ, JRAS 2008, 83–85.

Magen U. 1986: Assyrische Königsdarstellungen - Aspekte der Herrschaft. Eine Typologie (= BagF 9). Mainz.

Malbran-Labat F. 2010: Pratiques marchandes dans le commerce ougaritain, in: W. H. van Soldt (ed.), Society and Administration in Ancient Ugarit (= PIHANS 114), 84–93.

Malul M 1993: Eating and drinking (one's) refuse, NABU 1993/99.

Marcus D. 1980: Some Antiphrastic Euphemisms for a Blind Person in Akkadian and Other Semitic Languages, JAOS 100, 307–310.

Márquez Rowe I. 2001: The Akkadian Word for aristoi?, in: Montero Fenollós J.-L. et al. (eds.), De la Estepa al Mediterráneo (= Monografies Eridu 1), 457–460.

Marti L. 2001: Notes lexicologiques, NABU 2001/81.

Manassa C. 2012: From Wool to Baketry, Lingua Aegyptia 20, 99–110.

Matouš L. 1964: Einige Bemerkungen zur akkadischen Lexikographie (Review of CAD E, D, I/J, Z, Ṣ; AHw Lief. 2–4), ArOr. 32, 127–138.

Matsushima E. 1995: Quelques problèmes supplémentaires de l'elippu ša kusīti, Orient 30-3, 171–181.

Maul S. M. 1988: 'Herzberuhigungsklagen'. Die sumerisch-akkadischen Eršaḫunga-Gebete. Wiesbaden.

Maul S. M. 1994: Zukunftsbewältigung: eine Untersuchung altorientalischen Denkens anhand der babylonisch-assyrischen Löserituale (Namburbi) (= BagF 18). Mainz.

Maul S. M. 2000: Die Frühjahrsfeierlichkeiten in Aššur, in: Fs. Lambert, 389–420.

Mayer W. 1998: Der Weg auf den Thron Assurs. Sukzession und Usurpation im assyrischen Königshaus, in: Fs. Loretz (= AOAT 250), 533–555.

Mayer W. 2001: Tall Munbāqa – Ekalte II: Die Texte (= WVDOG 102). Saarbrücken.

Mayer W. R. 1976: Untersuchungen zur Formensprache der babylonischen „Gebetsbeschwörungen“ (= StPohl series minor 5). Rom.

Mayer W. R. 1985: Eine spätbabylonische Verwaltungsurkunde, Or. 54, 483–486.

Mayer W. R. 1989: Die Verwendung der Negation im Akkadischen zur Bildung von Indefinit- bzw. Totalitätsausdrücken, Or. 58, 145–170.

Mayer W. R. 1990: Sechs Šu-ila-Gebete, Or. 59, 449–490.

Mayer W. R. 1992: Ein Hymnus auf Ninurta als Helfer in der Not, Or. 61, 17–59.

Mayer W. R. 2003: Waffen und Stricke in einer altbabylonischen Urkunde, Or. 72, 368–389.

Mayer W. R. 2009: Akkadische Lexikographie: CAD T und Ṭ, Or. 78, 423–438.

Mayer W. R. 2010: Die Tätigkeiten und Regungen, Haltungen und Zustände des Menschen im Spiegel der Sprache: zur akkadischen Idiomatik, Or. 79, 304–341.

Mayer W. R. 2016: Zum akkadischen Wörterbuch A–L, Or. 85, 181–235.

Mayer W. R. 2017a: Zum akkadischen Wörterbuch M–S, Or. 86, 1–40.

Mayer W. R. 2017b: Zum akkadischen Wörterbuch Ṣ–Z, Or. 86, 202–252

McEwan G. J. P. 1980: A Seleucid Augural Request, ZA 70, 58–69.

McEwan G. J. P. 1981a: Priest and Temple in Hellenistic Babylonia (= FAOS 4). Stuttgart.

McEwan G. J. P. 1981b: Arsacid Temple Records, Iraq 43, 131–143.

McEwan G. J. P. 1988: Babylonia in the Hellenistic Period, Klio 70, 412–421.

Michel C. 1991a: *tânîstum* dans les textes paléo-assyriens, NABU 1991/25.

Michel C. 1991b: Innāya dans les tablettes paléo-assyriennes I. Paris.

Michel C. 1991c: Innāya dans les tablettes paléo-assyriennes II. Paris.

Michel C. 1995: Validité et durée de vie des contrats et reconnaissances de dettes paléo-assyriens, RA 89, 15–27.

Michel C. 2001a: Le lapis-lazuli des assyriens au début du IIe millénaire av. J.-C., in: Fs. Veenhof, 341–359.

Michel C. 2001b: Correspondance des marchands de Kaniš au début du IIe millénaire avant J.-C. (= LAPO 19). Paris.

Michel C. 2004: Deux incantations paléo-assyriennes. Une nouvelle incantation pour accompagner la naissance, in: Fs. Larsen, 395–420.

Michel C. 2008: Nouvelles données de géography historique Anatolienne d'après des archives récentes de Kültepe, in: K. Strobel (ed.), New Perspectives on the Historical Geography and Topography of Anatolia in the II and I Mill. B.C. (= Eothen 16), 235–52.

Michel C. / Nosch M.-L. 2010: Textile Terminologies in the Ancient Near East and Mediterranean From the Third to the First Millennia BC (= Ancient Textiles 8).

Michel C. / Veenhof K. R. 2010: The Textiles Traded by the Assyrians in Anatolia (19th–18th centuries BC), in: Michel /Nosch 2010, 210–271.

Milano L. 1994: Drinking in ancient societies: history and culture of drinks in the ancient Near East (= HANE/S 6). Padova.

Militarev A. / Kogan L. 2000: Semitic Etymological Dictionary, Vol. 1: Anatomy of Man and Animals (= AOAT 278/1). Münster.

Militarev A. / Kogan L. 2005: Semitic Etymological Dictionary, Vol. 2: Animal Names (= AOAT 278/2). Münster.

Mirelman S. 2008: *Tuḫru* "Achilles' Tendon"?, NABU 2008/65.

Mirelman S. / Krispijn T. J. H. 2009: The Babylonian Tuning Text UET VI/3 899, Iraq 71, 43–52.

Moran W. L. 1981: *duppuru* (*dubburu*) - *ṭuppuru* too?, JCS 33, 44–47.

Moran W. L. 1992: The Amarna Letters. Baltimore / London.

Müller G. G.W. 1994: Studien zur Siedlungsgeographie und Bevölkerung des mittleren Osttigrisgebietes (= HSAO 7). Heidelberg.

Müller M. / Marzahn J. 2000: Fünf altassyrische Texte aus dem Vorderasiatischen Museum zu Berlin, in: Fs. Oelsner, 285–309.

Muss-Arnolt W. 1894–1905: A Concise Dictionary of the Assyrian Language. Berlin / New York.

Na'aman N. 1973: The Political Disposition and Historical Development of Eretz-Israel according to the Amarna Letters. Diss. Tel Aviv.

Nasrabadi B. M. 1999: Untersuchungen zu den Bestattungssitten in Mesopotamien in der ersten Hälfte des ersten Jahrtausends v. Chr. (= BagF 23). Mainz.

Naumkin V. / Kogan L. / Cherkashin D. / ʿĪsā ad-Daʿrhī A. / Gumʿān ad-Daʿrhī I. 2016: Soqotri Lexical Archive: the 2012 Fieldwork Season, ZDMG 166, 57–80.

Neugebauer P. / Weidner E. 1915: Ein astronomischer Beobachtungstext aus dem 37. Jahre Nebukadnezars II (= BSGW 67).

Niedorf 2008: Die mittelbabylonischen Rechtsurkunden aus Alalaḫ (Schicht IV) (= AOAT 352). Münster.

Olmo Lete G. del / Sanmartín J. 2004: A Dictionary of the Ugaritic Language in the Alphabetic Tradition (= HdO 112; = DUL). Leiden.

Oshima T. 2011: Babylonian Prayers to Marduk (= ORA 7). Tübingen.

Oshima T. 2014: Babylonian Poems of Pious Sufferers (= ORA 14). Tübingen.

Owen D. I. 1981: Of Bird, Eggs and Turtles, ZA 71, 21–47.

Parpola S. 1983: Letters from Assyrian Scholars to the Kings Esarhaddon and Assurbanipal. Part II: Commentary and Appendices (= AOAT 5/2). Kevelaer/Neukirchen-Vluyn.

Parpola S. 1993: Letters from Assyrian and Babylonian scholars (= SAA 10). Helsinki.

Paulus S. 2014: Die babylonischen Kudurru-Inschriften von der kassitischen bis zur frühneubabylonischen Zeit: Untersuchung unter besonderer Berücksichtigung gesellschafts- und rechtshistorischer Fragestellungen (= AOAT 51). Münster.

Pearce L. 1993: Statements of Purpose: Why the Scribes Wrote, in : Fs. Hallo, 185–193.

Peled I. 2016: Masculinities and Third Gender: The Origins and Nature of an Institutionalized Gender Otherness in the Ancient Near East (= AOAT 435). Münster.

Pentiuc E. J. 2001: West Semitic Vocabulary in the Akkadian Texts from Emar (= HSS 49). Winona Lake.

Pettinato G. 1981: Testi Lessicai Monolingui della Biblioteca L. 2769 (= MEE 3).

Pongratz-Leisten B. 1994: ina šulmi īrub. Die kulttopographische und ideologische Programmatik der *akītu*-Prozession in Babylonien und Assyrien im 1. Jahrtausend v. Chr. (= BagF 16). Mainz.

Popova O. V. 2018: Une attestation du mot *taqtītu* « la fin d'une période de temps » à la période néo-babylonienne sous la forme *taqdītu*, NABU 2018/108.

Postgate J. N. 1994: Gleanings from ADD, SAAB 7, 5–7.

Postgate J. N. 2000: Assyrian Felt, in: Fs. Saporetti, 213–217.

Postgate J. N. 2003–2005: Pfeil und Bogen. A. I, RlA 10, 456–458.

Postgate J. N. 2005: Platane, RlA 10, 591–592.

Powell M. A. 1978: Ancient Mesopotamian Weight Metrology, Technikatörténetí Szemle 10, 109-112.

Powell M. A. 1988: Agriculture and waterworks in Babylonian mathematical texts, BSA 4, 161–172.

Prechel D. 1996: Die Göttin Išḫara. Ein Beitrag zur altorientalischen Religionsgeschichte (= ALASPM 11). Münster.

Radner K. 1997: Die neuassyrischen Privatrechtsurkunden als Quelle für Mensch und Umwelt (= SAAS 6). Helsinki.

Radner K. 2002: Die neuassyrischen Texte aus Tall Šēḫ Ḥamad (= BATSH 6. Texte 2). Berlin.

Radner K. 2003: Review of Freydank 2001, ZA 93, 120–123.

Radner K. 2004: Das mittelassyrische Tontafelarchiv von Giricano/Dunnu-Sha-Uzibi (= Subartu 14). Turnhout.

Reiner E. 1958: *Šurpu*. A Collection of Sumerian and Akkadian Incantations (= AfO Beih. 11). Graz.

Reiner E. 1990: Nocturnal Talk, in: Fs. Moran (= HSS 37), 421–424.

Reiner E. 1999: One Potato, Two Potato, in: Fs. Renger (= AOAT 267), 381–384.

Reiner E. 2007: Supplement to Chicago Assyrian Dictionary T (Volume 18), JNES 66, 47–61.

Reiter K. 1997: Die Metalle im Alten Orient unter besonderer Berücksichtigung altbabylonischer Quellen (= AOAT 249). Münster.

Richter T. 1991: Akkadisch *têb/pum*, NABU 1991/46.

Richter T. 2012: Bibliographisches Glossar des Hurritischen. Wiesbaden.

Richter T. / Lange S. 2012: Das Archiv des Idadda (= Qaṭna Studien 3). Wiesbaden.

Robson E. 2008: Mathematics in Ancient Iraq. A Social History. Princeton/Oxford.

Röllig W. 1996: Akkadisch *tuʾum*, *diʾum*, phönizisch *tw*, aramäisch *twn*: Versuch einer Klärung, in: Fs Moscati Vol. 3, 1203–1207.

Roth M. T. 1989: Babylonian Marriage Agreements 7th-3rd Centuries B.C. (= AOAT 222). Münster.

Roth M. T. 1989/1990: The Material Composition of the Neo-Babylonian Dowry, AfO 36/37, 1–55.

Sachs A. J. / Hunger H. (eds.) 1988–1996: Astronomical Diaries and Related Texts from Babylonia, 1–6.

Sallaberger W. 1996: Der babylonische Töpfer und seine Gefäße nach Urkunden altsumerischer bis altbabylonischer Zeit sowie lexikalischen und literarischen Zeugnissen (= MHEM 3). Ghent.

Sallaberger W. 2011: Sumerian Language Use at Garšana. On Orthography, Grammar, and Akkado-Sumerian Bilingualism, in: D. I. Owen (ed.), Garšana Studies (= CUSAS 6, Bethesda) 335–372.

Salonen A. 1959–1960: Review of AHw Lieferung 1–2, AfO 19, 156–159.

Salonen A. 1965: Die Hausgeräte der alten Mesopotamier. Helsinki.

Saporetti C. 1979: Assur 14446: la Famiglia A. Ascesa e declino di persone e famiglie all'inizio del medio-regno assiro, I. Malibu.

Sassmannshausen L. 2001: Beiträge zur Verwaltung und Gesellschaft Babyloniens in der Kassitenzeit (= BagF 21). Mainz am Rhein.

Sasson J. M. 1966: Canaanite Maritime Involvement in the Second Millenium B. C., JAOS 86, 126–138.

Schaudig H. 2001: Die Inschriften Nabonids von Babylon und Kyros' des Großen samt den in ihrem Umfeld entstandenen Tendenzschriften. Textausgabe und Grammatik (= AOAT 256). Münster.

Schaudig H. 2003: Nabonid, der "Archäologe auf dem Königsthron". Zum Geschichtsbild des ausgehenden neubabylonischen Reiches, in: Fs. Kienast (= AOAT 274), 447–497.

Schneider-Ludorff H. 1998: Filz in Nuzi?, in: Owen / Wilhelm (eds.), General Studies and Excavations at Nuzi 10/2 (= SCCNH 9), 163–168.

Schneider-Ludorff H. 2002: Das Mobiliar nach den Texten von Nuzi, SCCNH 12, 115–149.

Schneider-Ludorff H: 2005: *takulatḫu* 'Lampenständer, Kandelaber', SCCNH 15, 161–168.

Schneider-Ludorff H. 2009: Metallgefäße aus Nuzi nach den schriftlichen Quellen, in: G. Wilhelm (ed.), General Studies and Excavations at Nuzi 11/2: in honor of David I. Owen on the occasion of his 65th birthday, October 28, 2005 (= SCCNH 18), 491–529.

Schwemer D. 2001: Die Wettergottgestalten Mesopotamiens und Nordsyriens im Zeitalter der Keilschriftkulturen. Materialien und Studien nach den schriftlichen Quellen. Wiesbaden.

Scurlock J. A. 1991: *Taklimtu*: A Display of Grave Goods?, NABU 1999/3.

Scurlock J. A. 2003: Review of Heeßel 2000, JAOS 123, 399–402.

Scurlock J. A. / Andersen B. R. 2005: Diagnoses in Assyrian an Babylonian Medicine. Urbana.

Segert S. 1962: Zur Etymologie von Lappīd "Fackel", ZAW 74, 323–324.

Sever H. 1998: Asur Ticaret Kolonileri Çağında Anadolu'da Madenler ve Yeni Maden Çeşitleri, in: Alp / Süel (eds.): III. Uluslararası Hititoloji Kongresi Bildirileri Çorum 16-22 Eylül 1996, 525–533.

Sigrist M. 2004: Fabrication d'images, in: Fs. Pettinato, 251–256.

Sigrist M. / Zadok R. / Walker C. B. F. 2006: Catalogue of the Babylonian Tablets in the British Museum III. Londion.

Simmons S. D. 1961: Early Old Babylonian Tablets from Ḫarmal and Elsewhere (Continued), JCS 15, 49–58; 81–3.

Simons F. 2017: Burn Your Way to Success – Studies in the Mesopotamian Ritual and Incantation Series Šurpu. Diss. Birmingham.

Sivan D. 1984: Grammatical Analysis and Glossary of the Northwest Semitic Vocables in Akkadian Texts of the 15th–13th C.B.C. from Canaan and Syria (= AOAT 214). Kevelaer/Neukirchen-Vluyn.

Sjöberg Å. W. 1996: UET 7 no. 93. A Lexical Text or a Commentary?, ZA 86, 220–237.

Sjöberg Å. W. 1998: Studies in the Emar Sa Vocabulary, ZA 88, 240–283.

Sjöberg Å. W. 2003: Notes on Selected Entries from the Ebla Vocabulary eš2-bar-kin5 (IV), in: Fs. Wilcke, 251–266.

Sommerfeld W. 1985: Der Kurigalzu Text MAH 15922, AfO 32, 1–32.

Stadhouders H. 2018: The unfortunate Frog: On Animal and Human Bondage in K 2581 and related Fragments with Excurses on BM 64526 and YOS XI, 3, RA 112, 159–176.

Stadhouders H. / Panayotov S. V. 2018: From Awe to Audacity. Stratagems for Approaching Authorities Successfully: The Istanbul Egalkura Tablet A 373, in: Fs. Geller, 623–697.

Starke F. 1993: Zur Herkunft von akkadisch *ta/urgumannu(m)* "Dolmetscher", WdO 24, 20–38.

Starr I. 1983: The Rituals of the Diviner (= BiMes. 12). Malibu.

Stockhusen M. 2018: Studien zum Transfer astralwissenschaftlicher Konzepte zwischen Ägypten und Mesopotamien in spätpharaonischer Zeit. Diss. Leipzig.

Stol M. 1993: Milk, Butter, and Cheese, BSA 7, 99–113.

Stol M. 1994: Beer in Neo-Babylonian Times, in: Milano 1994, 155–183.

Stol M. 1995a: Old Babylonian Corvée (*tupšikkum*), in: Fs. Houwink ten Cate, 293–309.

Stol M. 1995b: Old Babylonian Cattle, BSA 8, 173–213.

Stol M. 2000: Birth in Babylonia and the Bible. Its Mediterranean Setting (= CunMon. 14). Leiden.

Stol M. 2004: Wirtschaft und Gesellschaft in Altbabylonischer Zeit, OBO 160/4, 641– 975.

Stol M. 2006: The Digestion of Food according to Babylonian Sources, in: L. Battini / P. Villard (eds.), Médecine et médecins au Proche-Orient ancien (= BAR IS 1528), 103–119.

Stol M. 2007: Remarks on Some Sumerograms and Akkadian Words, in: Fs. Biggs, 233–242.

Stol M. 2007a: Fevers in Babylonia, in: I. L. Finkel / M. J. Geller (eds.), Disease in Babylonia (= CunMon. 36), 1–39.

Stol M. 2010: Review of CAD T, Ṭ, OLZ 105, 170–179.

Stol M. 2016: Würfel, RlA 15/1–2, 132–134.

Stolper M. W. 1988: The šaknu of Nippur, JCS 40, 127–155.

Stolper M. W. 2006: Iranica in post-Achaemenid Babylonian Texts, in: P. Briant/F. Joannès (eds.), La transition entre l'empire achéménide et les royaumes hellénistiques (= Persika 9), 231–257.

Streck M. P. 1995: *ittasab ibakki* „weinend setzte er sich": *iparras* für die Vergangenheit in der akkadischen Epik, Or. 64, 33–91.

Streck M. P. 1997: Review of AbB 13, BiOr 54, 143–148.

Streck M. P. 1997a: Review of BATSH 4, ZA 87, 271–276.

Streck M. P. 2000: Das amurritische Onomastikon der altbabylonischen Zeit (= AOAT 273/1). Münster.

Streck M. P. 2003: Die akkadischen Verbalstämme mit *ta*-Infix (= AOAT 303). Münster.

Streck M. P. 2004: Dattelpalme und Tamariske in Mesopotamien nach dem akkadischen Streitgespräch, ZA 94, 250–29.

Streck M. P. 2007: Review of George 2003, Or. 76, 404–423.

Streck M. P. 2009: Altorientalistik, in: U. von Hehl / U. John / M. Rudersdorf (eds.), Geschichte der Universität Leipzig 1409–2009, Band 4: Fakultäten, Institute, Zentrale Einrichtungen (Leipzig), 345–366.

Streck M. P. 2009a: Review of CAD T and CAD Ṭ, ZA 99, 135–140.

Streck M. P. 2009–2011: Schimpfwort, RlA 12, 189–191.

Streck M. P. 2011: Akkadian and Aramaic Language Contact, in: S. Weninger (ed.), The Semitic Languages. An International Handbook (Berlin/Boston) 416–424.

Streck M. P. 2012: *tartāmū* "mutual love", the noun pattern *taPtaRS* in Akkadian and the classification of Eblaite, in: C. Mittermayer/S. Ecklin (ed.), Altorientalische Studien zu Ehren von Pascal Attinger (= Orbis Biblicus et Orientalis 256, 2012) 353–357.

Streck M. P. 2016: Wurm, RlA 15, 134.

Streck M. P. 2017: The Terminology for Times of the Day in Akkadian, in: Y. Heffron / A. Stone / M. Worthington (eds.), At the Dawn of History. Ancient Near Eastern Studies in Honour of J. N. Postgate (Winona Lake) 583–609.

Streck M. P. / Wasserman N. 2008: The Old Babylonian Hymns to Papulegara, Or. 77, 335–358.

Streck M. P. / Wasserman N. 2018: The Man is Like a Woman, the Maiden is a Young Man: A new edition of Ištar-Louvre, Or. 87, 1–38, pl. II–III.

Streck M. P. / Wasserman N. 2018a: On Wolves and Kings. Two Tablets with Akkadian Wisdom Texts from the Second Millennium B.C., Iraq 78, 241–252.

Such-Gutiérrez M. 2018: Die Sprachsituation in Adab während der altakkadischen Periode, in: S. Fink / M. Lang / M. Schretter (eds.), Mehrsprachigkeit. Vom Alten Orient bis zum Esperanto (= dubsar 2), 131–150.

Tadmor H. 1958: Historical Implications of the Correct Rendering of Akkadian *dâku*, JNES 17, 129–141.

Tarasewicz R. 2018: The Neo-Babylonian Records from Ur from the Hall Collection of the British Museum (= dubsar 7). Münster.

Thavapalan S. 2018: Purple Fabrics and Garments in Akkadian Documents, JANEH 3, 1–28.

Tsukimoto A. 1999: "By the Hand of Madi-Dagan, the Scribe and *Apkallu*-Priest". A Medical Text from the Middle Euphrates Region, in: K. Watanabe (ed.), Priests and Officials in the Ancient Near East (Heidelberg), 187–200.

Tsukimoto A. forthc.: Manuscript transliteration of fifteen omen tablets from Tigunānum.

Turner G. 1970: Tell Nebi Yūnus: The Ekal Māšarti of Nineveh, Iraq 32, 68–85.

van der Spek R. J. 1995: Land Ownership in Babylonian Cuneiform Documents, in: M. J. Geller / H. Maehler / A. D. E. Lewis (eds.), Legal Documents of the Hellenistic

World. Papers from a Seminar arranged by the Institute of Classical Studies, the Institute of Jewish Studies and the Warburg Institute, University of London, February to May 1986. London, 173–245.

van der Spek R. J. 2000: Review of G. F. del Monte, Testi dalla Babilonia Ellenistica, Vol. I (1997), Or. 69, 433–438.

van der Spek R. J. 2001: The Theatre of Babylon in Cuneiform, in: Fs. Veenhof, 445–456.

van der Toorn K. 1985: Sin and Sanction in Israel and Mesopotamia. A Comparative Study. Assen/Maastricht.

van Driel G. 1990: Neo-Babylonian Agriculture. III. Cultivation, BSA 5, 219–266.

van Driel G. 1992: Wood, Reeds and Rushes. A note on Neo-Babylonian practical texts, BSA 6, 171–176.

van Driel G.1995: Cattle in the Neo-Babylonian period, BSA 8, 215–240.

van Driel G. 2002: Elusive Silver. In Search of a Role for a Market in an Agrarian Environment (= PIHANS 95). Leiden.

van Soldt W. H. 1990: Fabrics and Dyes at Ugarit, UF 22, 321–357.

Veenhof K. R. 1972: Aspects of Old Assyrian Trade and Its Terminology. Leiden.

Veenhof K. R. 1987: 'Dying tablets' and 'hungry silver'. Elements of figurative language in Akkadian commercial terminology, in: M. J. Geller et al. (eds.), Figurative Language in the Ancient Near East (London) 41–75.

Veenhof K. R. 1989: Status and Offices of an Anatolian Gentleman. Two Unpublished Letters of Ḫuḫarimataku from Kārum/Kanish, in: K. Emre / B. Hrouda / M. Mellink/ N. Özgüç (eds), Anatolia and the Ancient Near East. Studies in Honor of Tahsin Özgüç. Ankara. 515–525.

Veenhof K. R. 1996: An Old Assyrian Incantation Against a Black Dog (kt a/k 611), WZKM 86 (= Fs. Hirsch), 425–433.

Veenhof K. R. 2001: The Old Assyrian Period, in: R. Westbrook / R. Jasnow (eds.), Security for Debt in Ancient Near Eastern Law (= CHANE 9), 93–159.

Veenhof K. R. 2003: The Old Assyrian List of Year Eponyms from Karum Kanish and its Chronological Implications. Publications of the Turkish Historical Society, VI/64. Ankara.

Veenhof K. R. 2005: Letters in the Louvre. Transliterated and Translated (= AbB 14). Leiden.

Veenhof K. R. 2008/9: A New Volume of Old Assyrian Texts from kārum Kanesh, JEOL 41, 179–202.

Veenhof K. R. 2010: Kültepe Tabletleri V. The Archive of Kuliya, son of Ali-abum (Kt. 92/k 188-263). Türk Tarih Kurumu Yayınları VI/33c (= AKT 5). Ankara.

Veenhof K. R. 2015a: Some Contributions to the Old Assyrian Lexicon, Or. 84, 217–275.

Veenhof K. R. 2015b: *Ba'ārum*, "to start a fight", in Old Assyrian, NABU 2015/11.

Veenhof K. R. 2015c: Nuhšatum, the Wife of an Old Assyrian Trader. Her Status, Responsibilities and Worries (With Two New Letters), in: Fs. Günbattı, 2712–2788.

Veldhuis N. 2004: Religion, Literature, and Scholarship. The Sumerian Composition "Nanše and the Birds" (= CunMon. 22). Groningen.

Villard P. 1990: Review of Nashef, Rekonstruktion und Reiserouten zur Zeit der altassyrischen Handelsniederlassungen (= TAVO Bh. B 83), BiOr 47, 675–684.

Villard P. 2006: Les guérisseurs à la cour néo-assyrienne, in: Battini / Villard (eds.), Médicine et médecins au Proche-Orient ancient (= BAR S1528), 139–160.

Vincente C. A. 1992: The 1987 Tell Leilan tablets dated by the Limmu of Habil-kinu. Ann Arbor.

Vita J.-P. 2010: The Power of a Pair of War Chariots in the Late Bronze Age. On Letters RS 20.33 (Ugarit), BE 17 33a (Nippur), and EA 197 (Damascus Region), in: Vidal J. (ed.), Studies on War in the Ancient Near East (= AOAT 372), 87–93.

Volk K. 1999: Imkerei im alten Mesopotamien?, in: CRRAI 41 (= BBVO 18), 279–290.

von Soden W. 1957: Grundsätzliches zum Akkadischen Wörterbuch, OLZ 52, 485–492.

von Soden W. 1958–1981: Akkadisches Handwörterbuch. Unter Benutzung des lexikalischen Nachlasses von Bruno Meissner (1868–1947). Wiesbaden.

von Soden W. 1960: Review of CAD D, E, OLZ 55, 485–489.

von Soden W. 1981: Review of McEwan 1981, ZA 71, 292–296.

von Soden W. 1984: Untersuchungen zur babylonischen Metrik, Teil II, ZA 74/2, 213–234.

von Soden W. 1986: Review of AbB 9, BiOr 43, 732–736.

von Soden W. 1987: Kleine Bemerkungen zu Urkunden und Ritualen aus Emar, NABU 1987/46.

von Soden W. 1990: Review of Westenholz, Old Sumerian and Old Akkadian Texts in Philadelphia (= CNIP 3), ZA 80, 135–136.

von Soden W. 1991: Review of SAA 3, WO 22, 189–195.

von Soden W. 1992: Eine altbabylonische Rationenliste von ungewohnter Art, NABU 1992/52.

Waerzeggers C. 2002: Endogamy in Mesopotamia in the Neo-Babylonian Period, in: C. Wunsch (ed.), Mining the archives. Festschrift for Christopher Walker on the occasion of his 60th birthday 4 October 2002 (= BabA 1), 319–342.

Waerzeggers C. 2010: The Ezida Temple of Borsippa. Priesthood, Cult, Archives (= Achaemenid History 15). Leiden.

Waetzoldt H. 2006–2008: Rad. A. Philologisch, RlA 11, 214–217.

Waetzoldt H. 2010: 11. The Colours of Textiles and Variety of Fabrics from Mesopotamia, in: Michel / Nosch 2010, 201–209.

Wasserman N. 2011: Adzes, not Skirts in CUSAS 10, No. 7, NABU 2011/53.

Wasserman N. 2012: Most Probably. Epistemic Modality in Old Babylonian (= LANE 39). Winona Lake.

Wasserman N. 2018: Labor Pains, Difficult Birth, Sick Child: Three Old Babylonian Incantations from a Private Collection, BiOr. 75, 14–25.

Watson W. G. E. 2008: Some Akkadian and Hittite Equivalences, NABU 2008/68.

Watson W. G. E. 2009: More Akkadian and Hittite Equivalences, NABU 2009/21.

Wee J. Z.-E. 2012: The Practice of Diagnosis in Mesopotamian Medicine: With Editions of Commentaries on the Diagnostic Series Sa-gig. Diss. New Haven.

Wehr H. 1985: Arabisches Wörterbuch für die Schriftsprache der Gegenwart. 5. ed. Wiesbaden.

Weidner E. 1959–1960: Review of CAD D, E, G, Ḫ, AfO 19, 155–156.

Weißbach F. H. 1938: Bezold, RlA 2, 23–24.

Westbrook R. 2003: The Case of Elusive Debtors: CT 4 6a and CT 6 34b, ZA 93, 199–207.

Westenholz A. 1970: *berūtum*, *damtum*, and Old Akkadian KI.GAL: Burial of dead enemies in Ancient Mesopotamia, AfO 23, 27–31.

Westenholz A. 2000: Assyriologists, Ancient and Modern, on Naramsin and Sharkalisharri, AOAT 252, 545–556.

Westenholz A. / Westenholz J. G. 1977: Help for Rejected Suitors – The Old Akkadian Love Incantation MAD V 8, Or. 46, 198–219.

Westenholz J. G. 1997: Legends of the Kings of Akkade (= MesCiv. 7). Winona Lake.

Westenholz J. G. 2010: The Tale of Two Little Organs: the Spleen and the Pancreas, JMC 15, 2–24.

Westenholz J. G. / Ikeda J. 2000: Cuneiform inscriptions in the collection of the Bible Lands Museum Jerusalem: the Emar tablets. Vol. 1. (= CunMon. 13). Groningen.

Westenholz J. G. / Westenholz A. 2006: Cuneiform Inscriptions in the Collection of the Bible Lands Museum Jerusalem: The Old Babylonian Inscriptions (= CunMon. 33). Groningen.

Wiggermann F. A. M. 2000: Agriculture in the Northern Balikh Valley. The Case of Middle Assyrian Tell Sabi Abyad, in: Jas, R. M. (ed.), Rainfall and Agriculture in Northern Mesopotamia (= PIHANS 88), 171–231.

Wilcke C. 1971: Review of TLB 4, OLZ 66, 544–555.

Wilcke C. 1978: Zur Deutung der SI.BI-Klausel in den spätaltbabylonischen Kaufverträgen aus Nordbabylonien, WdO 9, 206–212.

Wilcke C. 1987: A Riding Tooth: Metaphor, Metonymy and Synecdoche, Quick and Frozen in Everyday Language, in: Figurative Language in the Ancient Near East, 77–102.

Wilhelm G. 1985: Das Archiv des Šilwa-Teššup, 3: Rationenlisten II. Wiesbaden.

Wilhelm G. 1998: Hurr. *šinussi* "Scheuklappe"?, in: D. I. Owen / G. Wilhelm (eds.), General Studies and Excavations at Nuzi 10/2 (= SCCNH 9, Winona Lake) 173–176.

Wilhelm G. 1999: *turoni* "Unterseite, Grundplatte, Basis" im Hurritischen von Qatna, in: D. I. Owen / G. Wilhelm (eds.), Nuzi at Seventy-Five (= SCCNH 10). 415–421.

Worthington M. 2012: Principles of Akkadian Textual Criticism (= SANER 1). Berlin.

Yamada K. 2005: "From the Upper Sea to the Lower Sea" – The Development of the Names of Seas in the Assyrian Royal Inscriptions, Orient 40, 31–55.

Zaccagnini C. 1990: Review of Wilhelm 1985, OLZ 85, 40-43.

Zaccagnini C. 1995: War and Famine in Emar, Or. 64, 92–109.

Zaccagnini C. 1997: On the Juridical Terminology of Neo-Assyrian and Aramaic Contracts, in: CRRAI 39 (= HSAO 6), 203–208.

Zadok R. 1976: Three Iranian Words in Late Babylonian Documents, BiOr 33, 5–6.

Zadok R. 1984: Assyro-Babylonian Lexical and Onomastic Notes, BiOr 41, 33–46.

Zawadzki S. 2006: Garments of the Gods, Vol. 1: Studies on the textile industry and the Pantheon of Sippar according to the texts from the Ebabbar Archive (= OBO 218). Fribourg – Göttingen.

Zawadzki S. 2013: Garments of the Gods, Vol. 2: Texts (= OBO 260). Fribourg/Göttingen.

Zeeb F. 1995: Das teqnītu in den Immobilienkaufurkunden aus Alalaḫ VII, in Fs. von Soden (= AOAT 240), 541–549.

Ziegler N. 1999: Zwei Söhne Samsi-Addus, in CRRAI 42 (= OLA 96), 493–505.

Ziegler N. 2005: Les vaisseaux sanguins et Enûma eliš VI: 5, JMC 5, 4–5.

Ziegler N. 2007: Les Musiciens et la musique d'après les archives de Mari (= FM 9). Paris.

Zimmern H. 1917: Akkadische Fremdwörter als Beweis für babylonischen Kultureinfluss. Leipzig.

Zomer E. 2018: Review of Farber 2014, JAOS 138, 181–183.

Bibliographical Abbreviations

AAA	Annals of Archaeology and Anthropology 1–28 (Liverpool 1908–1948).
AbB	Altbabylonische Briefe in Umschrift und Übersetzung.
ABL	R. F. Harper, Assyrian and Babylonian letters belonging to the Kouyounjik collection of the British Museum.
AdŠ	G. Wilhelm / D. L. Stein, Das Archiv des Šilwa-Teššup, 1–9.
AfO (Beih.)	Archiv für Orientforschung (Beihefte).
AHw.	W. von Soden, Akkadisches Handwörterbuch.
Akkadica	Akkadica. Revue semestrielle de la Fondation Assyriologique Georges Dossin.
AKT	Ankara Kültepe Tabletleri (Ankaraner Kültepe-Tafeln).
ALL	N. Wasserman, Akkadian Love Literature of the Third and Second Millennium BCE (= LAOS 4).
AlT	D. J. Wiseman, The Alalakh Tablets.
AMD	(Studies in) Ancient Magic and Divination.
AMT	R. C. Thompson, Assyrian medical texts from the originals in the British Museum (London 1923).
Amurru	Amurru (Paris 1996ff.).
ANES	Ancient Near Eastern Studies. An annual (publ.) by the School of Fine Arts, Classical Studies and Archaeology University of Melbourne.
AnSt.	Anatolian Studies. Journal of the British Institute of Archaeology at Ankara.
AO	Tablets in the collections of the Musée du Louvre.
AOAT	Alter Orient und Altes Testament.
AoF	Altorientalische Forschungen.
AOS	American Oriental Series.
API	E. Herzfeld, Altpersische Inschriften.
ArAn	Archivum Anatolicum.

ARM	Archives Royales de Mari.
ArOr.	Archív Orientální.
ARRIM	Annual Review of the Royal Inscriptions of Mesopotamia Project.
AS	Assyriological Studies (Chicago).
ASJ	Acta Sumerologica.
Ass.	Field number of tablets excavated at Assur.
Astronomical Diaries	A. J. Sachs / H. Hunger, Astronomical Diaries and Related Texts from Babylonia.
Atra-ḫasīs	W. G. Lambert / A. R. Millard, Atra-ḫasīs. The Babylonian story of the flood.
AUCT	Andrews University Cuneiform Texts.
AulaOr.	Aula Orientalis. Revista de estudios del Próximo Oriente Antiguo.
AUWE	Ausgrabungen in Uruk-Warka. Endberichte, DAI Baghdad (Mainz 1987–).
BagF	Baghdader Forschungen.
BagM	Baghdader Mitteilungen.
Ballad of Early Rulers	Line numbering after Y. Cohen, Wisdom from the Late Bronze Age (Atlanta 2013) 132–139.
BAM	F. Köcher et al., Die babylonisch-assyrische Medizin in Texten und Untersuchungen.
BATSH	Berichte der Ausgrabung Tall Šēḫ Ḥamad / Dūr-Katlimmu.
BE	The Babylonian Expedition of the University of Pennsylvania.
Bēl rēmanni	M. Jursa, Das Archiv des Bēl-rēmanni (= PIHANS 86).
BiMes.	Bibliotheca Mesopotamica.
BIN	Babylonian Inscriptions in the Collection of James B. Nies, Yale University
BiOr.	Bibliotheca Orientalis.
BIWA	R. Borger, Beiträge zum Inschriftenwerk Assurbanipals.
BM	Tablets in the collections of the British Museum.

BMS	L. W. King, Babylonian magic and sorcery.
Bo.	Field number of tablets excavated at Boghazköy.
BRM	J. P. Morgan, Babylonian records in the library of J. Pierpont Morgan.
BSA	Bulletin on Sumerian Agriculture.
BWL	W. G. Lambert, Babylonian wisdom literature.
CAD	The Assyrian Dictionary of the University of Chicago.
CBS	Tablets in the collections of the University Museum of the University of Pennsylvania, Philadelphia).
CCT	Cuneiform Texts from Cappadocian Tablets in the British Museum.
CH	Codex Hammurapi.
CHANE	Culture and History of the Ancient Near East.
Chuera	S. Jakob, Die mittelassyrischen Texte aus Tell Chuēra in Nordost-Syrien.
CNIP	Carsten Niebuhr Institute Publications.
CRRAI	Compte rendu, Rencontre Assyriologique Internationale.
CT	Cuneiform Texts from Babylonian Tablets in the British Museum.
CTMMA	Cuneiform Texts in the Metropolitan Museum of Art.
CTN	Cuneiform Texts from Nimrud.
CunMon.	Cuneiform Monographs.
CUSAS	Cornell University Studies in Assyriology and Sumerology.
DamM	Damaszener Mitteilungen.
DCCLT	N. Veldhuis (ed.), Digital Corpus of Cuneiform Lexical Texts. http://oracc.museum.upenn.edu/dcclt/.
DCS	D. Charpin/J.-M. Durand, Documents cunéiformes de Strasbourg conservés à la Bibliothèque nationale et universitaire (= RGC Cah. 4).
EA	J. A. Knudtzon, Die El-Amarna-Tafeln. Cf. W. L. Moran, The Amarna letters.

Edubba 7	F. N. H. Al-Rawi / S. Dalley, Old Babylonian Texts from Private Houses at Abu Habbah, Ancient Sippir.
Emar	D. Arnaud, Recherches au Pays d'Aštata. Emar 6/1–4. Textes sumériens et accadiens.
FAOS (Beih.)	Freiburger Altorientalische Studien (Beihefte).
FLP	Tablets in the collections of the Free Library of Philadelphia.
FM	Florilegium Marianum (= Mémoires de NABU).
Fs. Alp	H. Otten / E. Akurgal / H. Ertem / A. Süel (eds.), Hittite and other Anatolian and Near Eastern Studies in honour of Sedat Alp (= Anadolu Medeniyetleri Araştırma ve Tanıtma Vakfı Yayınları 1, Ankara 1992).
Fs. Donbaz	Ş. Dönmez (ed.), *DUB.SAR É.DUB.BA.A* Studies Presented in Honour of Veysel Donbaz (Istanbul 2010).
Fs. Garelli	D. Charpin / F. Joannès (eds.), Marchands, diplomates et empereurs. Études sur la civilisation mésopotamienne offertes à Paul Garelli (Paris 1991).
Fs. Geller	S. V. Panayotov / L. Vacín (eds.), Mesopotamian Medicine and Magic. Studies in Honor of Markham J. Geller (Leiden/Boston 2018).
Fs. Günbattı	İ. Albayrak / H. Erol / M. Çayır (eds.), Studies in Honour of Cahit Günbattı (Ankara 2015).
Fs. Kraus	G. van Driel / Th. J. H. Krispijn / M. Stol / K. R. Veenhof (eds.), Zikir šumim: Assyriological studies presented to F. R. Kraus on the occasion of his seventieth birthday (= Studia Francisci Scholten memoriae dicata 5, Leiden 1982).
Fs. Lambert	A. R. George / I. L. Finkel (eds.), Wisdom, gods and literature: Studies in Assyriology in Honour of W. G. Lambert (Winona Lake 2000).
Fs. Larsen	J. G. Dercksen (ed.), Assyria and beyond: studies presented to Mogens Trolle Larsen (= PIHANS 100).
Fs. Reiner	F. Rochberg-Halton (ed.), Language, Literature and History. Philological and Historical Studies Presented to Erica Reiner (= AOS 67, 1987).
Fs. Röllig	B. Pongratz-Leisten / H. Kühne / P. Xella (eds.), *Ana šadî Labnāni lū allik*: Beiträge zu altorientalischen und mittelmeerischen Kulturen: Festschrift für Wolfgang Röllig (= AOAT 247).

Fs. Sjöberg	H. Behrens / D. Loding / M. T. Roth (eds.), DUMU-E_2-DUB-BA-A. Studies in honor of Åke W. Sjöberg (= OccPubl. S. N. Kramer Fund 11, 1989).
Fs. Steve	L. De Meyer / H. Gasche / F. Vallat (eds.), Fragmenta historiae elamicae: mélanges offerts à M.-J. Steve.
Fs. Stol	R. J. van der Spek (ed.), with G. Haayer, F. A. M. Wiggermann, M. Prins, J. Bilbija, Studies in Ancient Near Eastern World View and Society, Presented to Marten Stol on the Occasion of His 65th Birtday, 10 November 2005, and His Retirement from the Vrije Universiteit Amsterdam.
Fs. Veenhof	J. G. Dercksen et al. (eds.), Veenhof Anniversary Volume. Studies presented to Klaas R. Veenhof on the occasion of his sixty-fifth birthday (= PIHANS 52, 2001).
Fs. Wilcke	W. Sallaberger / K. Volk / A. Zgoll (eds.), Literatur, Politik und Recht in Mesopotamien. Festschrift für Claus Wilcke (= Orientalia Biblica et Christiana 14, 2003).
GAG	W. von Soden, Grundriß der akkadischen Grammatik.
GAO	N. J. C. Kouwenberg, A Grammar of Old Assyrian.
Gilg.	A. R. George, The Babylonian Gilgamesh-Epic (Oxford 2003), and recent publications.
HANEM 2	G. Beckman, Texts from the Vicinity of Emar in the Collection of Jonathan Rosen (History of the Ancient Near East 2).
HEG	J. Tischler/G. Neumann, Hethitisches etymologisches Glossar.
Ḫḫ	Lexical series ḪAR-ra = *ḫubullu*, published MSL 5–11.
HSAO	Heidelberger Studien zum Alten Orient.
HSS	Harvard Semitic Series.
ICK	Inscriptions cunéiformes du Kultépé.
IM	Tablets in the collections of the Iraq-Museum.
Iraq	Iraq. Journal of the British Archaeological Institute.
Ištar Louvre	M. P. Streck / N. Wasserman, The Man is Like a Woman, the Maiden is a Young Man. A new edition of Ištar-Louvre.
ITT	Inventaire des tablettes de Tello.
JAOS	Journal of the American Oriental Society.

JCS	Journal of Cuneiform Studies.
JEOL	Jaarbericht van het Vooraziatisch-Egyptisch Genootschap “Ex Oriente Lux”.
JRAS	Journal of the Royal Asiatic Society.
JSS	Journal of Semitic Studies.
KAJ	E. Ebeling, Keilschrifttexte aus Assur juristischen Inhalts (= WVDOG 50).
KAL	Keilschrifttexte aus Assur literarischen Inhalts.
KAR	E. Ebeling, Keilschrifttexte aus Assur religiösen Inhalts.
KTT	M. Krebernik, Keilschrifttexte aus Tuttul.
KUB	Keilschrifturkunden aus Boghazköi 1–60 (Berlin 1921–1990).
Lamaštu	W. Farber, Lamaštu. An Edition of the Canonical Series of Lamaštu Incantations and Rituals and Related Texts from the Second and First Millennia B.C.
LANE	Languages of the Ancient Near East (Winona Lake 2008ff.).
LAOS	Leipziger Altorientalistische Studien.
LAPO	Littératures Anciennes du Proche-Orient (Paris 1967ff.).
LKA	E. Ebeling, Literarische Keilschrifttexte aus Assur.
M.	Field number of tablets excavated at Mari.
MAD	I. J. Gelb, Materials for the Assyrian Dictionary.
Malku	Lexical series *malku* = *šarru*, published AOAT 50.
MARI	MARI. Annales de recherches interdisciplinaires.
MARV	H. Freydank et al., Mittelassyrische Rechtsurkunden und Verwaltungstexte.
MBLET	O. R. Gurney, The Middle Babylonian legal and economic texts from Ur.
MCS	Manchester Cuneiform Studies.
MDP	Mémoires de la Délégation en Perse.
MEE	Materiali Epigrafici di Ebla (Neapel 1979–).
MesCiv.	Mesopotamian Civilizations (Winona Lake 1989ff.).

MesZL	R. Borger, Mesopotamisches Zeichenlexikon (= AOAT 305).
MHEM/T/O	Mesopotamian History and Environment. Memoirs / Texts / Occasional Publications.
MSL	Materialien zum sumerischen Lexikon / Materials for the Sumerian lexicon.
NABU	Nouvelles Assyriologiques Brèves et Utilitaires (Paris/Rouen 1987–).
NATN	D. I. Owen, Neo-Sumerian archival texts primarily from Nippur in the University Museum, the Oriental Institute and the Iraq Museum.
NBC	Tablets in the collections of the Nies Babylonian Collection (Yale University, New Haven).
ND	Field number of tablets excavated at Nimrud (Kalḫu).
OAA	Old Assyrian Archives (Leiden 2002ff.; in PIHANS).
OBO	Orbis Biblicus et Orientalis.
OBTR	S. Dalley / C. B. F. Walker / J. D. Hawkins, Old Babylonian Tablets from Tell al Rimah.
OECT	Oxford Editions of Cuneiform Texts.
OIP	Oriental Institute Publications (Chicago 1924ff.).
OLA	Orientalia Lovaniensia Analecta.
Or.	Orientalia.
ORA	Orientalische Religionen in der Antike (Tübingen 2009ff.).
PBS	The Museum Publications of the Babylonian Section, University of Pennsylvania.
Persika	Persika (Paris 2001ff.).
PIHANS	Publications de l'Institut Historique-Archéologique Néerlandais de Stamboul.
POAT	W. C. Gwaltney, The Pennsylvania Old Assyrian texts (= HUCA Suppl. 3).
Prag	K. Hecker / G. Kryszat / L. Matouš, Kappadokische Keil-schrifttafeln aus den Sammlungen der Karlsuniversität Prag.
PRAK	H. de Genouillac, Premières recherches archéologiques à Kich: mission d'Henri de Genouillac 1911–1912.

PRU	C. F.-A. Schaeffer (ed.), Le Palais Royal d'Ugarit.
PSBA	Proceedings of the Society of Biblical Archaeology.
PSD	Å.W. Sjöberg et al. (eds.), The Sumerian dictionary of the University Museum of the University of Pennsylvania.
QS 3	T. Richter / S. Lange, Das Archiv des Idadda (Qaṭna Studien 3).
RA	Revue d'Assyriologie et d'Archéologie Orientale.
RATL	J. Eidem, The Royal Archives from Tell Leilan (= PIHANS 117).
RGTC	W. Röllig et al. (eds.), Répertoire géographique des textes cunéiformes.
RIMA/E	The Royal Inscriptions of Mesopotamia. Assyrian Periods / Early Periods.
RINAP	The Royal Inscriptions of the Neo-Assyrian Period.
RlA	Reallexikon der Assyriologie und Vorderasiatischen Archäologie.
RSO	Ras Shamra – Ougarit
SAA	State Archives of Assyria.
SAAB	State Archives of Assyria. Bulletin.
SAAS	State Archives of Assyria Suppl.
Sadberk	V. Donbaz, Cuneiform Texts in the Sadberk Hanım Museum (Istanbul 1999).
SANER	Studies in Ancient Near Eastern Records.
SCCNH	Studies on the Civilization and Culture of Nuzi and the Hurrians.
SEAL	M. P. Streck / N. Wasserman, Sources of Early Akkadian Literature. http://www.seal.uni-leipzig.de.
Shemshara 1	J. Eidem / J. Læssøe, The Shemshara Archives. Vol. 1: The Letters (Copenhagen 2001).
SpTU	Spätbabylonische Texte aus Uruk.
StAT	Studien zu den Assur-Texten.
StBoT	Studien zu den Boğazköy-Texten.
StPohl SM	Studia Pohl. Dissertationes scientificae de rebus Orientis antiqui, Series Maior.

STT	O. R. Gurney / J. J. Finkelstein / P. Hulin, The Sultantepe tablets.
Subartu	Subartu, edited by the European Centre for Upper Mesopotamian Studies (Turnhout 1995ff.).
Sumer	Sumer. A Journal of Archaeology and History in Arab World.
Šūpê-amēli	Line numbering after Y. Cohen, Wisdom from the Late Bronze Age (Atlanta 2013) 84–101.
TBER	J.-M. Durand, Textes babyloniens d'époque récente.
TCL	Textes Cunéiformes. Musée du Louvre.
TCS	A. L. Oppenheim et al. (eds.), Texts from cuneiform sources.
TIM	Texts in the Iraq Museum.
TLT	C. A. Vincente, The 1987 Tell Leilan tablets dated by the Limmu Habil-kinu, 1–2.
TMH	Texte und Materialien der Frau Professor Hilprecht Collection of Babylonian Antiquities im Eigentum der Universität Jena.
TPAK	C. Michel / P. Garelli, Tablettes paléo-assyriennes de Kültepe.
UCP	University of California Publications (Berkeley 1907–).
UET	Ur Excavations. Texts.
UF	Ugarit-Forschungen. Internationales Jahrbuch für die Altertumskunde Syrien-Palästinas.
UFBG	W. R. Mayer, Untersuchungen zur Formensprache der babylonischen „Gebetsbeschwörungen“.
VAT	Tablets in the collections of the Vorderasiatische Abteilung (Staatliche Museen zu Berlin).
VS	Vorderasiatische Schriftdenkmäler.
WVDOG	Wissenschaftliche Veröffentlichungen der Deutschen Orientgesellschaft.
WZKM	Wiener Zeitschrift für die Kunde des Morgenlandes.
YBC	Tablets in the Babylonian Collection, Yale University.
YOS	Yale Oriental Series.
ZA	Zeitschrift für Assyriologie und Vorderasiatische Archäologie.

Other Abbreviations

acc.	accusative
adj.	adjective
Amor.	Amorite
Arab.	Arabic
Aram.	Aramaic
Assyr.	Assyrian
astron.	astronomical
Bab.	Babylonian
Bogh.	Boghazkoy
cf.	confer
coll.	collation, collated
comm.	commentary
corr.	correction
det.	determinative
dict.	dictionary
diff.	different(ly)
disc. (sect.)	discussion (section)
DN	divine name
ed.	edition / edited
Eg.	Egyptian
etym.	etymology
f.	following
fem.	feminine
ff.	following pages
Gilg.	Gilgameš
Gk.	Greek
GN	geographical name
gramm.	grammatical
Hebr.	Hebrew
Hell.	Hellenistic
Hitt.	Hittite
Hurr.	Hurrian
i.e.	id est
ib.	ibidem
incant.	incantation
inf. constr.	infinitive construction
inscr.	inscription
interpret.	interpretation
intrans.	intransitive
LB	Late-Babylonian
lex. (sect.)	lexical (section)
lit.	literature / literary / literally
logogr.	logogram / logographical(ly)
lw.	loanword
MA	Middle-Assyrian
masc.	masculine
MB	Middle-Babylonian
med.	medical
mng.	meaning
n	unknown number of items
n.	note
NA	Neo-Assyrian
NB	Neo-Babylonian
NN	nomen nominandum
no.	number
NWSem	Northwest-Semitic
OA	Old-Assyrian
OAkk	Old-Akkadian
OB	Old-Babylonian
Old Pers.	Old-Persian

p.	page
pl.	plural / plate
PN(N)	personal name(s)
PNf	personal name feminine
pret.	preterite
prev.	previous(ly)
prob.	probably
quot.	quoted (in)
r.	reverse
ref.	reference(s)
s.v.	sub verbo / sub voce
s.	see
Sab.	Sabean
SB	Standard Babylonian
sg.	singular
stat. cstr.	status constructus
Sum.	Sumerian
trans.	transitive
Ugar.	Ugaritic
uncert.	uncertain
unkn.	unknown
unpubl.	unpublished
WSem	West-Semitic

D

daʾāmu I, + *dâmu* "to become dark, dull"

G Var. *dâmu*: SB *i-da-mu* SpTU 1, 36: 2, s. D 2, below.

D 1. SB *du-um ṣuḫḫum* ALL no. 11 r. 11 "laughter is darkened(?)".
2. SB *du-ʾ-um i-da-mu* : MUD : *da-a-mu* SpTU 1, 36: 2 (comm.) "it becomes very dark : MUD: to become dark".
3. SB *liptīya ú-da-i-mu ḫasīsīya iṣbatū diglīya umaṭṭû* KAL 2, 8 (= KAR 80) r. 32 "(the demons) dulled my sense of touch, seized my hearing, and reduced my vision", after Landsberger 1967, 148 (pace AHw 146 "meine Male machten sie noch dunkler").

JW (D), MPS (G, D)

daʾāmu II "to stagger, wander around"; + OAkk., OB

1. OAkk. (concerning the sheep of some city elder) *[l]ā a-dú-mu-ni* FAOS 19 Di 2 = MVN 3, 101: 15 "I am certainly not going to run around".

2. OB *kīma* DN *ta-⌜du⌝-um-mi ta-su-úr-ri* CUSAS 10, 10: 47f. "like DN you stagger, you dance around".

JW (1), MPS (2)

daʾāpu, + *deʾēpu* "to push (away), struggle"; + OB, + NB

G 1. SB *šumma immeru i-de$_4$-e-ip* Emar 6/4, 698: 3 "if the sheep struggles".
2. NB DN *[d]a?-ip ḫīṭ[āti]* SAA 17, 87: 6 "DN, who pushes back cri[mes]".
3. NA *i-de-i-pi* SAA 13, 27 r. 19 "he pushed (the case)(?)" (perf.).
4. NA *issu libbi* GN *di-ʾ-[p]a kattemā-šunu* SAA 19, 183: 14 "push (the troops) away from GN (and) overwhelm them!"

D OB *aššum ana* GN *alākiša iltu ú-da-ap-ši* ARM 26/1, 222 no. 83: 13 "the goddess puts pressure on her because she went to GN", s. Durand ib. p. 223 n. c.

N "to be knocked over": NA *ina muḫḫi akkussi ša šurinni ša šarru bēlī iqbûni mā asseme ramānša ta-ad-dip*(// *ta-ad-di-ip*) *šulmu adanniš* SAA 13, 28 r. 12; 29 r. 4 "concerning the pole of the divine emblem about which the king, my lord, said: 'I have heard: 'It was knocked over on its own accord'', it is in excellent condition" (*taddîp* < *taddiʾip*).

JW (D), MPS (G, N)

dabābu I "speech, complaint"

1. OB *da-ba-bi panam irtašī* AbB 9, 156: 2 "a complaint against me has become apparent".

2. OB *d. purruku* "to make a complaint" (Wilcke 1978, 209 n. 8): *šumma da-ba-ba-am uparrak* AbB 7, 86: 38 "if he raises any objections", also AbB 11, 78: 17.

3. OB *d. nussuqu* "to look for trouble": *da-ba-ba-am lā tunassaqma* AbB 13, 71: 12 "do not look for trouble", s. van Soldt ib. n. b. JW

dabābu II "to speak, talk"

G 1. OA *ēkallum yâti i-da-ba-ba-ni* VS 26, 56: 28 "the palace is arguing with me(?)", cf. GOA § 6.4.1.1 on *atawwu*.
2. OB *āmur kīma* PN *libbam gamram ittīya i-dá-bu-bu* FM 1, 61 A.2995+ M.14337: 14 "I see that PN speaks

honestly with me", cf. ARM 26/2, 64f. no. 307: 10; 308: 27.

3. OB pret. *a-du-ub-bu-šum* ARM 26/2, 254 no. 402: 28, cf. Joannès ib. p. 255 e.

4. MB *ana pan* PN *dayyāni id-bu-bu-ma* MBLET 9: 5 "they argued their case before PN, the judge".

****Gt** s. Streck 2003, 80.

Gtn 1. OB also with *a* instead of *u* in the last syllable:

a) OB lit. *ti-da-ab-ba-a*[*b*?] ZA 75, 202: 70 "talk repeatedly!"

b) OB *ammīni atwâša lā tagmurma i-da-na-ba-ab* AbB 7, 20: 11 "why haven't you settled her matter? She complains all the time!"

2. OB *ṭapāltīya ta-ad-da-na-bu-bi* AbB 5, 138: 5 "you (f.) constantly speak scornfully of me".

D 1. OA "to harrass, call to account": *ana bēt kārim ušēribūni ú-dá-bi-bu-ni umma šunūma* VS 26, 56: 5 "they made me enter the *bēt kārim* (and) called me to account, saying (…)".

2. OB *kayyān ú-da-ab-ba-ba-ni* Shemshara 1, 38: 7 "permanently he importunes me".

3. OB *kīma du-ub-bu-ba-at īdēma* Sumer 14, 51 no. 26: 5 "I know that the suit has been brought", s. Goetze 1958, 51f.

4. OB *du-bu-ub-šu la tamaṭṭī* AbB 13, 114: 31 "do not desist concerning the complaint (against) him!", s. Streck 1997, 144.

5. For general disc. s. Kouwenberg 1997, 100.

Š On *sinništam šudbubu* "to make a woman talk (in her sleep?)" s. Reiner 1990; Durand 2001, 128.

+ N LB *perku itti* PN *ina panī bēliya id-da-bu-u*[*b*] *mamma perku ina panī bēliya ittīšu lā i-dab-bu-ub* CT 22, 210: 8 "Slander is spoken against PN before my lord. Nobody shall speak slander against him before my lord!"

EZ (D), JW (Gtn, D, Š), MPS (G, Gtn, D, N), NJCK (G, D)

d/tab/padu s. *dappātu*

dabāqu "to join together"; NWSem. lw.

SB Ugar. *uparriranni u ú-dáb-bi-qa-an-ni it-bu-ka-an-ni u īsipanni* Oshima 2011, 210: 37 "he smashed me and joined me, he poured me out and collected me". Cf. AHw 1549 "zusammenfügen" with lit. The emendation of Arnaud, AuOr. Suppl. 23, 111 and 114, to *ú-tab-bi-la*!*-an-ni* is unnecessary. Y. Cohen 2013, 168 and 171, prefers a reading *utabbikanni* "rendered me limp". However, the text carefully distinguishes *qa* (also l. 39) and *ka* (besides *it-bu-ka-an-ni* in the next line also in ll. 1, 17, 20, 21, 44); moreover, ll. 37–41 all contain antithetical statements.

dabaru s. *tabarru*

****dabāru** s. *ṭapāru*

+ dabdabu "a creeping(?) animal"; OB

Lex. *ur-me* = *da-ab-da-bu-um* UET 7, 93: 39 (after insects and before *asqūdu* "hamster(?)" or a snake). Sjöberg 1996, 228 connects the word with arab. *dabba* "to walk slowly, creep".

dabdû, *dawdû*, *dubdû* "defeat; bloodshed"

1. OB *da-aw-du-um damqiš* [*ša*! G]N *dīk* ARM 26/2, 132 no. 357 r. 28 "[G]N was well defeated."

2. SB *miqittašunu dub-da-šú-nu u kamāršunu lā išakkanū* MesCiv. 13, 1:

73 "they will not bring about their collapse, defeat and annihilation".

JW (2), EZ/MPS (1)

\+ **dābibānu** "gossipy person, plotter"; NA

[*ša*] ⌜*da*⌝-*bi-ba-nu-ti le-p*[*u-šú*] SAA 10, 240 r. 25 "(these) plotters should be afflicted!", s. Parpola 1983, 179. JW

\+ **dabriš** "aggressively"; OB

Lit. *da-ab-ri-iš tazzazz*[*ī…*] Ištar Louvre vi 9 "you stand aggressively". JW

\+ **dabru II**? "plague"; EA, NWSem. lw.

ina mūtān ina ⌜*dáb*⌝!?-*ri* EA 244: 32 (Moran 1992, 298f. with n. 5) "(consumed) by pestilence, by plague".

MPS/NR

\+ **dabru III** "plants, pasture"; OB, Amor. lw.

Lex. [*d*]*a-ab-rum* = *ša-am-m*[*u*] MARI 5, 412 BM 38590: 17 "pasture = grass" (synonym list of rare words (?)), cf. Aram. *dabrā* (Geller 1992, 206f.).

JW/MPS

dabû "bear"

Already Salonen 1959–60, 158 connected Akk. *dabû* with Egyptian *db*(*j*) "hippopotamus". This interpretation is elaborated by Militarev/Kogan 2005, 95 who think that Sem. *dabû*/*dabbu* is related to Egyptian *db*(*j*) "hippopotamus", the Afrasian etymon having the basic mng. "large animal". Civil 1998, 11f., not quoting Salonen, assumed that the Sum. column of the equation *dam*/*dím-šaḫ* = *da-bu-ú* in Ḫḫ XIV 156f. (MSL 8/2) shows an Egypt. lw. for the crocodile (cf. Arab. *timsāh*), equated by the scribe with another river animal, the hippopotamus; therefore, according to him, we should distinguish two homophones in Akk., *dabû* "bear" and *dabû* "hippopotamus".
However, the position of the entry in Ḫḫ, between hare and pig, makes the identification of *dam*/*dím-šaḫ* as "crocodile" doutbtful. Moreover, it would be surprising if the scribe translated a foreign animal by another word foreign to Akk. The right column of Ḫḫ XIV either contains the normal Akk. correspondances of the Sum. words in the left column (including loans from Sum., akkadianized by attaching the case ending), or literal translations of the Sum. phrases like *pīl šadî* "elephant of the mountain/east" Ḫḫ XIV 54 for Sum. *am-si kur-ra*. Finally, besides living in the water, crocodile and hippopotamus do not resemble each other. Therefore, the most likely interpretation is still that of Landsberger 1934, 13 and 82: *dam*/*dím-šaḫ* means "similar to a pig" (cf. *muš-dam*/*dím-* "similar to a snake" for the "gecko" Ḫḫ XIV 372), found in this position of the list because the *šaḫ* "pig" section follows. According to Landsberger, nose and skin of bear and pig look similar. This interpretation is also favored by the Practical Vocabulary from Assur (vgl. MSL 8/2, 68), in which *az* "bear" in l. 372 is followed by *dam-šaḫ* in l. 373. This means that there is only a single word *dabû* "bear" in the Akk. lexicon.

dadānu, + *tatānu* "neck muscles"

1. Ur III? lex. ⌜*sa*⌝ *gú-ĝu*$_{10}$ = *ta-ta-a-nu* CUSAS 12 p. 156 vi 14 (Ugumu).

2. For the plant *d.* s. Simons 2017, 111f.: "Green-barked acacia (Vachellia Oerfota (syn. Nubica)(?))".

3. Since UM 5, 137: 6 has the spelling *di-a-da-a-nu-ú-a*, AHw 148 analyzes the word as *diadānu* > *dâdānu*. The new ref. above, from a text which never contracts /ia/ > /â/ (s. *ra-bi-a-tum* CUSAS 12 p. 155 v 18; *e-pi-pi-a-tu-*⸢*ú-a*⸣ ib. iii 12), does not favor this analysis. Therefore, the first syllable is analyzed here with a short /a/. *di-a-da-* might a mistake.

daddaru "an ill-smelling plant, stinkweed"

1. OB lit. (you filled the mouth with bitterness) [x]-*tu-šu īwī da-da-ar-šu* Fs. Reiner 190: 29 "its […] became stinkweed" (for the suff. -*šū*(*m*) cf. GAG § 67g).

2. OB lit. *da-da-ru-um* BiOr. 75, 21: 3.

3. For etym. s. Kogan 2012, 234f.

JW (1, 3), MPS (2)

daddu "sole"

Matouš 1964, 137: del. *da-da-tum* UCP 10, 141: 12 (AHw 149a), read *id-da-tum* (pl. fem. of *iddu*, coll. in CAD I 9a), s. AHw 364b. EZ

daddu s. *dadmu*

dadmu, + *daddu*, pl. *dadmū*, + *dadnū* "villages, settlements, land, the inhabited world"; Amorite lw.(?) (Streck 2001, 87f.)

1. Lex. *da-ad-mu* // *da-ad-du* // [*d*]*a-ad-dum* = *mātu* AOAT 50, 315: 191 (malku). There is no need to postulate, with Hrůša ib. p. 315 and 478, another new var. *dattu*.

2. In OB Mari, *d.* is always used in the sg. (but not exclusively: sg. also in ref. 1 above). According to Durand 1989, 29–31; 1990a, 274f., *d.* refers to the area of Yamḫad (Aleppo), but the PN under 2, below, prob. shows that this is not always the case:

a) *da-ad-mu-um* [*ka*]*lûšu u* GN [*ul*] *kûmma u mātkama* FM 7, 21 no. 7: 25 (Durand 1989, 30) "the whole 'land' and GN, are they not yours and your country?", cf. ib. 20.

b) *ištū da-ad-*[*m*]*i-im ana* GN *illikūnim* FM 7, 18 no. 6: 9 "they will come from 'the land' to GN", s. Durand 1989, 31.

c) *ḫa-al-la-tum ša ina da-ad-mi-im u* GN *sadrat illakam* A.2237: 27 "the goats that are regularly in 'the land' and GN are coming here" (s. Durand 1987c, 171).

3. OB in PNN: *Da-ad-mi-tum* ARM 9, 291 iii 50, *Da-ad-mi-im* ib. iv 49 "Inhabitant of 'The land'(?)" (Durand 1990a, 274: "Yamḫadean", but actually a man from the clan of Niḫad, s. Streck 2000, 87f.).

4. OB lit. x-DA *da-ad-ni im-mātātu uddû binītaš* Ištar Louvre v 36 "… the settlements have made known her stature in the lands"; for the var. *dadnū* cf. OECT 11, 1: 5, 9, 36 (Streck/Wasserman 2018, 34).

5. MB DN *bēl da-ad-mi* Emar 6/3, 373: 91; 380: 20; 381: 14; 382: 11 "DN, lord of the inhabited world".

JW (2–4), MPS (1–5)

dādu I "darling, favorite; uncle"

1. Mayer 2016, 198: OB lit. *š*[*um*]*ma qašdat limqut* ⸢*da*⸣*-du-ša-a* YOS 11, 87 (= ALL 26): 8 "if she is a *qadištu*, her lover shall fall"

2. OB lit. of babies in birth incantations:

a) Mayer 2016, 198: *kīma da-di-*[*im*] *šūṣī ramānka* YOS 11, 86: 26 "like a darling, make yourself come out (from the womb)".

b) *da-du-um-mi da-du-um ukkupamma* BiOr. 75, 22: 1 "o, beloved one! The beloved one (the child) has drawn near".

c) *kīma da-di-im šulup ramānka* CUSAS 32, 28: 17 "unsheath yourself like a darling". For interpret. s. George ib. (*d.* as euphemism for penis), diff. Stol 2000, 11 (the *d.*-fish (*dādu* II) is meant, metaphorically emerging from water).

3. On *d.* in Gilg. in the context of love-making s. George 2003, 797.

4. Rarely "uncle" (Durand 1983c). Is this use a loan from Amorite (for *d.* in Amorite PNN s. Streck 2000, 407)?

a) OB *ana* PN *da-di-šu waššur* ARM 21, 560 no. 414: 4 "he has been released to PN, his uncle".

b) *maḫar* PN *mār* PN_2 *da-di-šu*! ARM 8, 1: 41 "in the presence of PN, son of PN_2, his uncle".

c) Lambert 1995, 136: The mng. of *d.* in OAkk. (and perhaps also in younger) PNN (s. di Vito 1993, 199) is unclear: "uncle" or "beloved one".

5. Del. CT 37, 3: 63 and read *it-ti* (RIME 4, 377: 70) (Mayer 2016, 198, but read OB instead of OAkk.).

JW (1, 4–5), MPS (2–4)

dādu II "a fish"

OB *šumma šulmum kīma da-di-im* ARM 26/1, 66 no. 3: 21 "if the cleft is like a *d.* fish".

dādu s. also *dīdu.*

dadurru, *dudurru* s. *tutturru*

dagālu "to see, look"

G 1. OA "to watch, look at":

a) (I have quarrelled with him) *ṣuḫārū-ka i-da-gu₅-lu* AKT 6B, 350: 16 "(while) your servants were watching".

b) *ṣīt ṣubātē u kaspim du-gu₅-ul* CCT 3, 2b: 25 (= OAA 1, 16) "observe the departure of the textiles and the silver".

c) *maḫīram lā ta-dá-ga-al* kt 92/k 428: 19 "you are not keeping an eye on the market" (s. Erol 2015, 92).

d) *u kuʾāti šunātim i-da-gu₅-lu-ni-ku-um* kt n/k 650: 20 "and as to you, people are seeing dreams about(?) you", i.e. are seeing you in their dreams (s. Çeçen/Gökçek 2017, 466).

2. OA "to watch, look at" with sentential object: "to see that", with *-ma* and more rarely *kīma*:

a) *šumma ta-da-ga-lá-ma ana ṣubātē kaspam ina* GN *ibaššī* KTH 13, 41 "if you see that in GN there is silver (to be obtained) for textiles".

b) *lā ta-da-ga-al kīma kaspum mādum-ma ina ēkallim ḫalqīni* Sadberk no. 10: 20 "do you not see that I have lost a lot of silver in the palace?" (Donbaz 1999, 21).

3. OA with *kīma* "to regard as": *kīma aḫi*[*m u ebrim*] *a-da-ga-al-*[*kà*] AKT 4, 36: 9 "I regard you as a partner and colleague".

4. OA "to look at s.o. with indifference": *mīššu ša aḫūkunu ištū* 2 *šanat marṣūma u ta-dá-ga-lá-*[*š*]*u-ni* CCT 3, 3b: 7 (= OAA 1, 33) "how is it possible that your (pl.) brother has been ill for 2 years and that you are (just) looking at him?" (sim. TC 3, 94: 35 = OAA 1, 15).

5. OA "to pay attention to, to count on":

a) *ibissāʾēʾa lā ta-dá-ga-al* TC 3, 39: 13 "do not consider my losses" (sim. AKT 6A, 75: 62).

b) *tappāʾēka lā ta-da-gal* CTMMA 1, 94 no. 72: 33 "do not count on your partners".

c) *ana aklim u šikrim lā i-da-gal* CCT 4, 28a: 33 "let him not be intent on bread and beer!". S. also Prag 607: 13 (*ta-<<ag>>-da-ga-lá-ni*).

6. OA "to look to s.o. for support" (+ *ana*, but some or all of these instances may belong to *takālu* + dative "to trust"): *amannim šanīʾem a-da-gal* Prag 468: 3 "to whom else can I look?" (and *pass.*).

7. OA "to wait for, to expect" (+ *ana* or acc.):

a) a person: *annākam du-ug-lam* TPAK 1, 57: 32 "wait here for me!" S. also CCT 3, 35b: 23; AKT 3, 88: 53.

b) an asset or a commodity: *awīlum ana erbim i-da-gal* kt n/k 388: 24 (Günbattı 1996, 31) "the man is expecting a present (or: bribe)". S. also CCT 2, 1: 8; CCT 4, 10a: 23 (= OAA 1, 44); CCT 3, 7a: 11 (= OAA 1, 50); CUSAS 34, 10: 24f.; VS 26, 56: 16.

8. OA "to claim as a surety, to lay a claim on, to hold liable, to call to account" (s. Bayram/Veenhof 1991/2, 94; Veenhof 2001, 129):

a) "to claim as a surity, to lay a claim on": *ana kaspim annīʾem bētam ṣuḫārtam u amtam i-da-gal* BIN 4, 190: 8 "for that silver he will have a claim on the house, the young woman and the slave-girl". S. also AKT 10, 23A: 19; AKT 10, 24A: 14; Prag 837: 23, 30.

b) "to hold s.o. liable, to call to account": *ilū annīʾūtum ... i-da-gu*$_5$*-lu-kà* Fs. Larsen, p. 253 kt 00/k 6: 89 "these gods … will call you to account".

c) "to own" (?): (why do you (sg.) keep storing straw and wood in [my?] house?) *bētātēkunu lā ta-da-ga-la* BIN 6, 119: 21 "do you (pl.) not have houses of your own?" (but perhaps rather: "will you not consider your own houses?").

9. OA *ana panē ... d.*: *tamkārum ana panīya i-da-gal* AKT 6B, 322: 24 "the merchant is relying on me" (tr. M. T. Larsen, or: "waiting for me"?).

10. OB *ina* ⸢*da*⸣*-gal tuppikunu* AbB 5, 239: 28 "while looking at your tablets".

11. MB "to own": *ina libbi ša ta-da-ga-lu … 2 puḫādē šūbila* CUSAS 30, 23: 18 "send me 2 lambs from whatever you own". Cf. van Soldt, ib. p. 66.

12. For PNN of the type *Panī*-DN-*adaggal* s. Mayer 1985, 485f. n. 5.

13. SB *ana Ezida uzammī sippī lalê dag-ga-li* SAA 3, 12: 7 "I have longed for Ezida, to behold the door-jambs of delight" (inf. *dagāli*).

14. SB *Adapa ... da-gil-ki* (var. *[da-g]i-il-*, *da-gil-*) *ina Eridu inaṭṭalki kâši* Lamaštu II 23 (Farber 2014, 99) "Adapa … who can see you, in Eridu will have a close look at you".

15. SB *i-dag-gal* Gilg. SB II 46 replaces *inaṭṭal u ippallas* Gilg. OB II 88.

16. NA perf. *ina muḫḫi šēpī it-ta-gal* SAA 16, 20 r. 4 "he looked at the feet"; for *ittagal* instead of *iddagal* cf. the comm. of Luukko/van Buylaere ib. p. 14.

17. LB *adi muḫḫi suluppē panīya du-gu-ul panīka kī a-di-gu-ul mimma ina qatīka ul āmur* OECT 12, A 135: 11f. "'wait for me until the dates (come)!' After I had waited for you, I did not see anything from your hands".

Gt intensive to G, s. ref. cit. AHw s.v. and CAD D s.v. *dagālu* 2c 2'. S. Streck 2003, 65 for disc.

NJCK (G), JW (G, Gt), MPS (G)

+ dāgiltu "look-out"; SB

ēbiltu u da-gi-il-tum MesCiv. 13, 1: 107 "the bird-catchers and the lookouts (who leave this city daily)". For fem. collective nouns of this type s. Lambert ib. p. 144. JW

dāgilu "sighted, observer"

1. MB *da-gi-il-ia nakru ileqqē* KAL 5, 2 r. 5 (omen apod.) "the enemy will take my observers away", cf. ib. 10 and 63 r. 3.

2. MA in personell lists:
a) 3 LÚ^{meš} *da-gi-lu*, KAJ 180: 1 "3 'seeing' men".
b) PN ^{lú}*lā da-gi-lu* BATSH 18, 3: 13 "PN, the 'blind man'", s. ib. p. 77. Usually written logogr. (IGI.NU.DU$_8$, s. BATSH 18 p. 336 for ref.).
c) The terms *d.* and *lā d.* are used to differentiate between skilled and unskilled workers (Garelli/Charpin/Durand 1982).

3. NA ^{lú}*da-gíl iṣṣūr*[*ē*] SAA 9, 2 iii 2 "observer of birds" (in broken context), s. McEwan 1980, 63 + n. 31 for ref. and disc. (Hittite origins, imported in MA period). JW (1–2), MPS (3)

+ dagnātu? "grain, cereal"; Emar, NW-Sem. lw.

[*ū*]*mi da-ag-*⌜*na*⌝-[*ti*?] Emar 6/3, 455: 9 "day of the grain(?)", s. Pentiuc 2001, 43. MPS/NR

daḫru "fierce"

SB 12 *nēšū erî namri zīmē da-aḫ-ru-ti* RINAP 3/1, 121 vi 75 (Senn.) "12 striding lions of shining copper (and) fierce demeanor", s. Frahm 1997, 85. JW/MPS

daḫtu s. *diʾ*(*a*)*tu*

daḫû I "pressed (in)"; + NA

A.ŠÀ NUMUN *da-ḫi-i* BATSH 6, 107: 3 "field with pushed in seeds (?)", otherwise A.ŠÀ (ŠE).NUMUN. JW

daḫû II "to beat, press down", + NA/SB

mātu ana māte lid-ḫu-šú-nu(*-ti*) SAA 2, 2 r. v 11 "may one country beat them (PN and his soldiers) into (another) country".

dāʾiku "murderer"; + OA

1. OA *šumma dāmu ina mātika ittabšī dá-i-kē lū taddunūniʾātima lū nidukku* Bilgiç 1992, 65 kt n/k 794: 9 "if there is bloodshed in your land, do give the murderers to us and we shall kill them".

2. SB *rašbu da-i-ku lemn*[*ūtī*] KAL 2, 12: 14 "fearsome one, killer of the evil ones". JW

daʾīmu "spear, lance"

SB *uštīb šaptīya kī da-ʾi-i-mi ašṭā* Ludlul I 117 "I sweetened my lips but they were hard as a lance", s. Oshima 2014, 219 pace George/al-Rawi 1998, 201 who take the word to be derived from *daʾāmu*. JW

****dāʾišu** "arrogant"

Von Soden 1960, 489 ad CAD D 27: read *da-wu-ú*!*-um*, from *dāwû* "Taumelnder" (AHw 166). EZ

****daʾiš** "toward" (CAD D 27)

In the OAkk. ref. (Rīmuš) and RA 46, 94: 9 (OB Anzu III) read DA-*iš* for *idiš*, s. RIME 2, 68: 17. In Agušaya read with AHw 1340 *tāʾiš* from *tāʾu* "inner room".

dāʾišu "thresher"

1. Lex. *lú-še-bad-da* = *da-i-šu* Emar 6/4, 542: 247 (Ḫḫ). Cf. *lú-še-bad*(*-da*) = *pētû* MSL 5, 77: 338.

2. OB ÁB.GUD$^{ḫi.a}$ *da-i-i*[*š*]*-ti* AbB 7, 170: 6 "threshing cow", sg.; ÁB.GUD$^{ḫi.a}$ *da-i-iš-tam* ib. 10; cf. GUD$^{ḫi.a}$ *da-i-šu-ti* AbB 7, 3: 28; cf. AbB 11, 86: 24; JCS

24, 61 no. 53 r. 5; cf. GUD$^{ḫi.a}$ *mu-di-ša*!*-tim* YOS 12, 421: 2, s. Stol 1995b, 184f. JW (2), MPS (1)

dakāku I "to crush", D "to wear out"; + OB

D OB (I brought the drum safely to GN) *alûm ṣābam kalâšu ud-da-ak-ki-ik* ARM 26/1, 132 no. 20: 15 "(carrying) the drum wore out my entire troop". Less likely Heimpel 2003, 187: "kept hopping", deriving the form from *dakāku* II "to gambol", for which no D stem is attested so far.

dakāku II "to gambol, scamper; to make (a joyous) noise"

G 1. Mayer 2016, 198: Lex. *gù-dé-a* = *da-ka-ka* Or. 74, 160: 29.
2. Mayer 2016, 199: SB *šumma gušūru issīma* ^{giš}[…]*-nu issû i-da-ak-ku-ku* Or. 40, 133 no. 44: 3 "if a beam creaks and the wooden […] creak (and) make noise, (you gather dirt from the beams)", s. Caplice ib. p. 134 ("to make a joyous noise").
3. Del. **a)** Antagal F 241 (read ⌜*ra*⌝*-qà-*⌜*du*⌝ after MSL 17, 219; s. Mayer 2016, 198).
b) RA 36, 112: 11 (cit. CAD D 34a), read *I-da-ma-*<*ra*>*-aṣ* (coll. ARM 26/1, 133). JW

dakāšu, +*dakāsu* "to pierce, become severed, bulge"

G 1. Lex. *da-ka-šu* = *kanāšu* AOAT 50, 387: 128B (malku) "to press in = to bow down". Cf. Hrůša ib. 245.
2. SB *šumma martu ana imitti*/*šumēli da-ki-is-ma u di-ki-sà kami* Emar 6/4, 669: 23f. "if the gall bladder is severed to the right/left and its severed part is attached". Cf. *da-ki-is* ib. 21f.
3. On *d.* in math. texts "to extend forward everywhere (by a given fraction)" s. Friberg/Hunger/al-Rawi 1990, 488ff.
4. NA *martu … dak-šat* SAA 4, 320 r. 5 "the gall bladder is swollen".

Gt s. Jeyes 2000, 365, 367; Streck 2003, 73.

D 1. OB lit. *du-uk-ku-šu* CUSAS 18, 31: 12 "(if the intestines) are bulged".
2. OB lit. *šumma rēš rēʾîm du-uk-ku-ša* CUSAS 18 p. 296: 15 "if the head of the shepherd bulges in several places". JW (G, Gt), MPS (G, D)

dakkannu, *dukkannu* "dais, platform; bedroom, private quarters"

1. The ref. cit. CAD T 74 s.v. *takkannu* B belongs here: *kī širku ana muḫḫi dak-kan-ni-šú ittalku u liginnī ultaqab-bû ḫīṭu ša šarri išaddad* YOS 19, 110: 7 "if a temple slave goes to his (PN's) bedroom, and he lets him recite the excerpt tablets, he (PN) will bear the punishment of the king", s. Beaulieu 1992, 101–103; George 2003, 303 n. 22; AOAT 414/1 p. 134.

2. Cf. Hebr./Aram. *dukkān*(*/ā*), s. Dietrich 2001a, 77.

3. For Gilg. MB Ur 22 (CAD T 74 *takkannu* A a) cf. *dinnû*(*tu*). JW (1–2), MPS (3)

dakkassu s. *takkassu*

****dakkukum** (AHw 152) read *Tá-ku-ma-tum* (MAD 3, 138). JW

dakšiu s. *takšiʾu*

dâku "to kill, beat"

G 1. OA *awāta d.* "to clear up an affair": *šumma ištē* PN *awātam i-du-uk ṣuḫāram ištēn lā tabeʾʾel uznī pitē*(*ma*) AKT 1, 16: 18 "if he has cleared up the

affair with PN, do not economize on just one servant and inform me!"
2. OA *ina idīnim i-du-ku-šu* (s. CAD D 40 2b 1') s. AKT 10 p. 46 with further ref. and disc.
3. OA *tuppam d.* "to break (a tablet)" (also figuratively) s. Veenhof 1987, 46ff.; Michel 1995, 19f.
4. OB *ʿayra dâku* instead of *ʿayra qa-tālu*: *ḫa-a-ri* [*i*]*ttī Ḫurrāyī i-du-uk* ARM 28, 66: 7 "he killed donkey foals with the Ḫurraeans".
5. OB *ina qanîm i-du-ku-šu* ARM 26/2, 292 no. 413: 22 "they killed him with a reed".
6. OB *akalam ina berîkunu napištam a-da-ak* ARM 26/2, 193 no. 380 r. 16 "I will let you hunger for bread and let (you) die".
7. OB PN *akalam u šikaram imšuʾ u* 1 *warad ēkallim adī napištim i-du-uk* ARM 27, 56: 22 "PN took away bread and beer and he killed (lit. killed until (the end of) life) 1 slave of the palace".
8. OB PN *ana niqim ṣuḫārī wardīka ana da-ki-im ušēṣûšuma* FM 8, 110 no. 32: 7 "they brought him out to kill (him) to avenge the boys, your servants".
9. OB lit. "to beat": *i-du-ka-an-ni-ma ana bābim uštāṣânni* CUSAS 10, 17: 29 "he beat me and drove me out through the gate"; *i-du-ka-an-ni šalam-tī iddī* ib. 35 "he beat me and threw away 'my corpse'".
10. OB in transferred mng. "to harass, disrupt, to beat up(?)" (s. CAD D 39):
a) *ana palgīya petêm alikma u yâtini i-du-ka-ni* AbB 9, 227: 25 "I went to open my canals, but then he 'killed' me", cf. further ref. AbB 9, 259: 18; 255: 10 (*ana da-ak-ki-šu*), ib. 15.
b) *awīlū annûtum i-du-ku-ni-i*[*n-ni*] FM 2, 112 no. 71 r. 3 "those men 'killed' me".
c) PN *maṣṣarī i-du-kam* AbB 13, 4: 2' "he 'killed' PN, my guard".
d) *epēšum annûm damiqkum ša tušāḫi-zuma nukarippam i-du-ku* AbB 12, 166: 8 "does this behavior seem right to you, that you gave instructions to 'kill' my gardener?"
11. OB *sarabu*[*m*] *panīya i-da-ak* ARM 26/1, 432 no. 203: 8 "cold is beating my face".
12. SB *šumma immeru uzun imittišu ana šumēlišu i-dá-ak* Emar 6/4, 698: 16 "if a sheep – its right ear beats in the direction of its left (ear)". Cf. *i-da-ak* ib. 18.
13. NB *lā di-ka-nu-ma mārūna ana maškanūtu ṣabtū* SAA 17, 152 r. 18 "we have not been killed, but our sons are being held as hostages".
14. LB "to cut down (trees, dates)":
a) (carpenters enter the forest) *ana da-ku ša ḫuṣābu kuburru u ūrē* JCS 28 no. 7: 20 "in order to cut trees, saplings, and branches", s. van Driel 1992, 172.
b) *raṭbu ... ul i-da-ka-a* TMH 2/3, 135: 21 "he(!) will not strike off the fresh (date palms)".

Gt "to fight" (CAD D 42, 7; CAD T 396 s.v. *tidūku* A and **B), s. Streck 2003, 23:
1. OB *eqlam amkurma ti-du-ku* AbB 7, 55: 5 "I irrigated the field, but they are fighting"; *ṣuḫārum ti-du-ku-um-ma ul illikam* ib. 12 "the lad is quarrelling (with me) and did not come".
2. OB *anāku ittī* PN *ti-du-ku-ú ad-da-ak* OBTR 121: 13 "must I fight with PN?"

+ **Gtn** SB (*šumma ṣēru*) *nammašti bīt amēli* ⌜*id*⌝*-da-na-ak* KAL 1, 9 iii 9 "if a snake keeps killing the animals in a man's house".

JW (G, Gt, Gtn), MPS (G), NJCK (G)

dalāḫu "to disturb, stir up"

G 1. OB lit. *ta-*⌜*ad*⌝*-lu-uḫ māmī* RB 59 = Fs. Reiner 190: 30 "you stirred up water".
2. OB DN *aššum enētišuma [da]liḫtam annītam id-lu-uḫ* ARM 10, 123: 12 "DN stirred up this trouble because of his priestesses".
3. OB PN *ša ana da-la-aḫ māt bēliya izzīzu* ARM 13, 146: 5 "PN, who was ready to disturb my lord's land".
4. SB Ugar. *dal-ḫat-e-re-tum* (sandhi) ORA 7, 208: 5 "the omens are confused".
5. SB *qerbīya id-lu-ḫu* ORA 14, 88: 65 "they stirred up my belly".
6. SB in med. texts (said of eyes) s. Scurlock/Andersen 2005, 186, 712 n. 7.
7. NB *mannu ina libbišunu ša lumnu ana* PNf *ippušma i-dal-làḫ-šú* dubsar 7, 2: 17 "anyone among them who does evil against PNf and troubles her", cf. ib. p. 117.
8. NA in koppelung "to hurry": *ad-da-làḫ addiris* SAA 10, 235 r. 14 "I quickly erased(?)" (s. *darāsu*). This mng. is otherwise attested for *dalāḫu* D (s. CAD D 45 *d.* 3b).
9. NA PNf *mītat u aḫū-ku da-li-iḫ* SAA 19, 144: 15 "PNf is dead and your brother is troubled".

D 1. OA PN *bētī ú-da-lu-ḫu* AKT 5, 31: 4 "(I hear that) PN is troubling my household", cf. CCT 2, 33: 10.
2. OB *appiš māt* GN *da-al-ḫu lu-da-[a]l-li-iḫ-šu-nu-ti-ma* ARM 13, 146: 22 "since the country of GN is in confusion, I want to (further) confuse them (and return them to my lord)".
3. SB *ú-dal!-liḫ-ši-na-ti* KAL 1, 11: 33 "([if a snake] falls on top of [weavers]) and disturbs them", cf. *ú-dal-li-iḫ-ši-na-tì* KAL 1, 14 ii 15.

N 1. OB *inanna mātum it-ta-ad-la-aḫ* ARM 28, 61: 6 "now the country has been thrown into confusion".
2. OB lit. *it-ta-ad-la-aḫ ṭēmī* PBS 1/1, 2 iii 117 "my reason has been disturbed".

Ntn 1. OB GN *u* GN_2 … *ina bīrišunu it-ta-ad-la-ḫu-ú-ma* ARM 26/2, 79 no. 315: 81 "GN and GN_2 were in constant confusion amongst themselves".
2. OB lit. *šumma it-ta-na-ad-la-aḫ* YOS 11, 15: 21 "if he is constantly troubled".

JW (G, D, N, Ntn), MPS (G, N, Ntn), NJCK (D)

dalālu I "to be small"

D "to oppress": Lex. *dul-lu-lu* = *ḫabālu* AOAT 50, 387: 134 (malku) "to oppress = to do wrong".

dalālu II "to praise, proclaim"

G 1. OB *šarram ayyêm id-lu-lu u suqat mātim ayyītim ilputū* ARM 26/2, 317 no. 423: 46 "which king have they praised, which countries' chin have they touched (i.e. to whom have they shown solidarity)?" For further Mari ref. s. Joannès ib. p. 318 n. h.
2. SB Ugar. *ša da-la-li Marduk* ORA 7, 208: 25' "Marduk is to be praised".

+ D Mayer 2016, 199: SB *dannūtki lu-da-lil* LKA 18: 7 "I shall praise your strength"; cf. [*ú*?]*-da-lil* K.2025+: 18.

JW (G, D), MPS (G)

dalāpu I "to stir up, keep sleepless, be restless"

G 1. OB *aššum ina šūlîm lā i-da-al-li-pu* ARM 14, 28: 15 "so that they will not get tired while lifting", s. Durand 2000, 147 and FM 8, 76 no. 20.
2. OB *ina šitappur[-im/-ša] i-da-al-pa-an-n[i* …] AbB 5, 195: 14 "[she?] kept me sleepless through [her] persistent writing".

3. OB *ummānum lā* ⌜*da-al*⌝*-pa-at* CUSAS 36, 64: 29 "the work force shall not be harassed".
4. OB lit. *ta-ad-da-li-ip mušēniqtam* OECT 11, 2: 10 "you have kept the wet-nurse awake".
5. OB lit. *adī birkāšuma zībiš i-da-li-p[a]* Iraq 78, 243: 5 "until his knees become restless like a vulture/jackal".
6. NA *bēt mardīʾāti ša sisêka di-lip alka* SAA 19, 194: 8 "travel ceaselessly along the road stations with your horses!"
7. LB *lū mādu ana muḫḫi di-*⌜*il*⌝*-pu* AOAT 414/1, 221: 19 "take care of the matter without rest!", cf. *di-lip-ma* ib. 201: 14.
8. On the mng. "to keep sleepless, exhausted" s. MSL 9 p. 85f. In the context of watching over the sick, s. Villard 2006, 147 with ref.

Š 1. SB Ugar. *šu-ud-lu-pa-k[u]* ORA 7, 208: 23 "I was made worried".
2. NA *anḫākuma šá-ad-da-lu-pu-ka lāniya* SAA 9, 9: 15 "I am worn out and my body is exhausted for your sake". JW (G), MPS (G, Š)

****dalāpu II**

Von Soden 1960, 489: del. *dalāpu* B (CAD D 49), *ta-da-lip* AMT 18, 9: 4 is to be emended to *ta-ša*!*-paḫ*. NR

dalbānu, *dulbānu* "intervening space, corridor"

1. Weidner 1959–1960, 155: SB *ana dul-ba-an-ni kī ērubu* JCS 42, 95 no. 9: 7 "when I entered the corridor".

2. NA *du-lu-ba-ni* SAA 15, 283: 7.
MPS (2), EZ (1)

dalḫu "troubled, disturbed"; + OB

1. OB [*da*]*-li-iḫ-tam* ARM 10, 123: 12, cf. *dalāḫu* G 2, above.

2. OB *awâtim da-al-ḫa-tim lā immarū* ARM 14, 103 r. 16 "they shall not see confused things".

3. OB *ur lù-lù* (var. *lu-lu*, *ì/al-lu-lu*) = *kalbum da-al-ḫu-um* Fs. Wilcke p. 142 (BT 9) 11 "disturbed dog" (list of insults), s. Klein ib. p. 146. JW

dalīlu, *dilīlu* "praise; propaganda"

1. OB *di-li-li-ki ludlul* AbB 13, 164: 18 "I will sing your praises". This var. is otherwise only attested in M/NA; but cf. *da-li-li* ib. 15.

2. NA *ša* 80 *ṣābi ina libbišunu kappīšunu sapsapīšunu aššīma ana da-li-li undešširšunūti* BagM 21 p. 344 no. 2 ii 9 "I took the hands and lips from 80 of their men and then released them to (spread our) reputation." S. disc. Cavigneaux/Ismail ib. p. 353f. with further ref.; s. also Mayer 2016, 199f. JW

dallālu "frog(?)"

On *dal-la-li* in Gilg. VI 76 s. disc. George 2003, 838: "dwarf(?)". JW

+ **dallāwu** "water drawer"; OB

400 *ṣābum* [*d*]*a-al-la-wu ša ālānī* MARI 6, 288 A.2796: 13 "400 men, water drawers from the towns"; cf. *dālû.* JW

dallu "small, stunted"

OB *ṣābašu damqam iklāma ṣābam da-al-la-am*!(text: *i*) *ana ṣērini iṭrudamma* MARI 6, 338: 70 "he has held back his good troops and sent the mediocre troops towards us" (coll. Durand 1998, 149 n. 340). For the opposition *dallu* : *damqu* cf. Durand ib. p. 153 ad AbB 14, 21: 9–11. JW/MPS

daltu "door"

1. Lex. MIN (= *gi*)-*ig-izi-lá* = *da-la-at gizillê* Emar 6/4, 546: 11 (Ḫḫ) "door with(?) torch".

2. OB lit. *siparra retītān da-al-ta-an* MesCiv. 7, 198: 49 "the fixed double doors were made of bronze".

3. OB lit. *da-la-at šīrim* CUSAS 18, 12: 27; *da-al-tum ša šīrim* ib. 82 "door of flesh".

4. SB *epušma* gišIG *ša* 6 NINDAN *mēlûša* 2 NINDAN *rupussa* 1 KÙŠ *upûša šukûša sāḫirša u šagammaša ša ištēnma* Gilg. SB V 295 "make a door the height of which is 6 rods (30m), the breadth of which is 2 rods (12m), the thickness of which is 1 cubit (50cm), the pole, lower pivot and upper pivot of which are of a single (piece)!"

5. Borger 1970, 11: in MDP 10, 91 iv 2 (AHw 154 *d.* 4, CAD D 55 *d.* 2) read *ri-ta*; del. the mng. sluice gate".

6. NA "single 'leaf' of hinged writing-board", cf. SAA 7, 49–50, s. Stol 1998, 343f.

7. LB gišIG *šamê* Nbn. 1121: 12 (cf. Cam. 415: 9) "(curtain for) the 'door of heaven'", i.e. a special chapel or chamber in Babylonian temples (Zawadzki 2006, 135f.). JW (5–7), MPS (1–5)

dâlu I "to move, roam around, circle"; + EA, + MA

G 1. OB *panīšu āmurma kīma da-lu-um-ma i-da-al awātam kīʾam aqbīšum-ma anākuma mīnam ta-da-al* ARM 26/2, 221 no. 391: 50–52 "I saw his face, and when he was indeed changing (his mind), I spoke to him as follows: 'Why do you change (your mind)?'". Cf. *da-lu-um-ma a-da-al* MARI 6, 272 M.6669: 12.

2. MA 2 *Sūtī*[*ʾū*] ... *ina ḫuribte ina libēte* GN *i-du-*⌜*lu*⌝ BATSH 4, 13: 22 "2 Suteans … were roaming the desert in the vicinity of GN".

3. NA *kī libbika du-ú-lu* SAA 1, 1: 53 "move around as you please!"

4. NA *issīya i-du-la* SAA 1, 171: 26 "he moves around with me".

5. NA *ina qabsi* GN *i-du-u-lu* SAA 1, 154 r. 4 "they roamed about in GN".

6. In transferred mng. "to walk around s.o." = "to beg for s.th.": NA *mušarki-sānī idātūʾa i-du-lu tibnu ana aṣappī laššu* SAA 5, 119: 7 "the recruitment officers are now 'running around me' (because) there is no straw for the pack animals."

D 1. OB *ištū kaspam ilqīʾam du-ul-ma adī inanna ṣibûssu ul īpuš* AbB 8, 102: 12 "since he received the silver, he has been restless and he has not executed his plan until now"; *du-ul-la-a-ku* ib. 37 "(the palace has moved my home and) I am unsettled".

2. EA *ti-da-lu-na*, s. Moran 1992, 184 n. 11:

a) [*u*] *annû mārū* PN [*ti*]-*da*!-*lu-na amīlī* GN [*kīma kal*]*bī* EA 109: 48 "[but] now the sons of PN make men from GN prowl about [like do]gs".

b) *u ti-da-lu-na ḫazanna ša yurraduka ina kītti* EA 114: 65 "they make a mayor who serves you with loyalty prowl about"; pace CAD D 59b an emendation to *ti-da-*<*ga*>-*lu-na* is not necessary.

Š 1. NA/SB *narkabātīkunu ana qinniš lu-šá-di-*(*il-*)*lu* SAA 2, 6: 575 "may they make your chariots run backwards".

2. NA/SB *kī allutti ana qinniš lu-šá-di-lu-ku-nu* SAA 2, 6: 620 "may they make you run backwards like a crab".

NR (G, D), MPS (G, D, Š), JW (G, D)

****dâlu II** "to watch carefully"

Von Soden 1960, 489: del. *dâlu* B (CAD B 59b). ABL 248: 14 read with SAA 10, 329 [*ma*!]-*a di-il-*⌜*pa*⌝! *is-si-šú*. ABL 724 r. 8 read with SAA 13, 18 *me-di-li* "pickled meat". EZ/MPS

dalû I, *dālu* "bucket"

1. NA [*bīt*] *da-la-a-ni* CTN 2, 64: 9 "field irrigated (by drawing water) with buckets", s. disc. Bagg 2000, 107ff. Cf. *bīt dālu* in LB (CAD D 57).

2. LB *ina da-a-lu idall*[*u*] CunMon. 20B, 23: 4 "he will water (the field) with a bucket".

3. LB pl. ^{dug}*da-la-né-e* dubsar 7, 40: 9.

4. S. Gaspa 2007, 163 for general disc.

JW

dalû II "to draw water, hoist"; + MA

G LB *i-da-l*[*u*] CunMon. 20B, 23: 4, s. *dalû* I.

+ **N** MA said of barley: *ana elîš id-da-al-lu* BATSH 9, 87: 14 "will be hoisted up", s. Freydank 2010, 99. JW

+ **dalû III** (mng. unkn.)

SB *lā id-li-ʾ* (var.: *id-lu-ʾ*, *id-li-ʾ-ú*) *kalbu ṣalmu* Farber 1990, 315: 10 "(may they draw water where no unclean woman has washed her hands, no tabooed woman has washed her clothes, no cave bird has flapped its wings,) no black dog has ...-ed", s. Farber ib. p. 316 n. 60. S. Arab. *ṭalaʿa* "aufsteigen, hinaufklettern" Wehr 1985, 780? JW/MPS

dālû "water drawer"

In MB ration lists s. Sassmannshausen 2001, 107f. JW

dalūtu s. *daluwātu*

dalūwātu, + *dalīwātu*, pl. tant. "field irrigated by means of drawing water"; OB

1. Early OB (sesame) *šu da-li-wa-tìm* ARM 19, 393: 3 "from a field irrigated by drawing water".

2. OB *ugār mēreštim u da-lu-wa-tum ša* GN *rapšā* ARM 26/1, 349 no. 171: 16 "the planted field and the field watered by drawing water of GN are wide". JW (1), MPS (2)

damāmu "to wail, to moan, to sob"

G 1. OA *ašša kaspum lā imḫurinnima ana ālim lā attalku iṣṣēr luqūtiya a-dá-mu-um* CCT 6, 14: 47 "shall I moan over my goods, because no silver has reached me and I have (therefore) not (yet) left for the City?".

2. OB lit. [*d*]*u-um-ma-šu-ma* ⌜*bitkī*⌝ UET 6/2, 395: 2 "lament for him, sob", cf. *du-ma-šu-um-ma* ib. 4 (Lambert 1990). Further ref. s. PBS 1/1, 2 iii 99f. (Lambert 1989).

3. SB *anenna summātu da-me-me-tum* Šūpê-amēli 122 "where are the wailing doves?"

4. SB [*nīšī āšibūt*? *B*]⌜*abili*⌝ *i-*⌜*da*⌝*-mu-mu summiš* KAL 3, 74 b 8 "[the inhabitants(?) of] Babylon were wailing like doves".

5. SB *ana amēlūti da-ma-ma īzib* Lamaštu I 169 (Farber 2014, 88) "for mankind she has left behind mourning".

6. Said of a pig: SB *šumma šaḫû ina tarbaṣišu i-dam-mu-um* SpTU 3, 94: 109 "if a pig moans in its pen".

+ **D** SB *kīma summ*(*at*)*i* ⌜*ú*⌝*-dá-am-m*[*i-im*] Gilg. Megiddo r. 14 "he sobbed like a dove"; cf. George 2003, 347.

Š OB lit. *iṣarraḫ* ⌜*la-al*⌝*-la-ra-ma ú-ša-*[*a*]*d-ma-am rēma* PBS 1/1, 2 ii 91 "he laments as a mourner, he institutes mourning for mercy", s. Lambert 1989, 326, 335.

+ **R** OB lit. *tarṣā kappāya da-ma-am-ma-a-ma* CunMon. 8, 112: 79 "my two palms are stretched out, wailing".

JW (G, Š, R), NJCK (G), MPS (G, D)

damāqu "to be(come) good"

G OA stat. also "to be financially sound": *šumma tadaggalāma* PN *da-mì-iq* ... *ṣabtāšuma kaspam šašqilāšu-(ma)* TPAK 1, 29: 10 "if you see that PN is financially sound, seize him ... and make him pay the silver!"

D 1. OAkk. *immeram liṭbuḫma paššū-ram li-da-mì-iq-ma* CUSAS 27, 63: 7 "he shall slaughter a sheep and prepare a joyful meal".
2. Matouš 1964, 132 (with disc. and further ref.): OA *dammuqu* "to refine silver".
3. OB *kaspam ana immerim nu-da-ma-qá-am ana kâšim u* PN *addinma* CT 6, 34b: 8 "I have given you and PN silver for one ram – (with the remark) 'we will make good'(?)", s. Kraus 1987, 35; Dombradi 2000, 43–45, 47; Westbrook 2003, 200f.
4. S. further Dalley/Walker/Hawkins 1976, 50 (mng. "to repair"); Kraus 1987, 34f. (for use in koppelung).

JW (D), NJCK (G)

damāṣu "to humble o.s."

Gt *ad-da-mu-ṣu* in ZA 43, 66 = BWL 86 = SAACT 9: 251 is Gt rather than Gtn (AHw 156b, *pace* CAD D 64, s. Streck 2003, 58). JW

+ **damdammatu?** "molly"; SB

[*ša* A]NŠE.NUN.NA-*tum anenna mā-rūšu* (sic) Šūpê-amēli 124 "[of the m]olly – where are its sons?" The spelling may also stand for a fem. of *parû* (s. SAD B/P, 72 *parūtu* IV) or of *kūdanu*.

damdammu "mule"

Lex. [MIN (= *anše*)-*nun*-]*na* = *dá-am-dá-mi* Emar 6/4, 550: 224 (Ḫḫ).

damiqtu "favor"

OB Susa PN *Sîn-da-mi-iq-tum* MDP 24, 380: 18 "Sîn is favor".

+ **dammāmu** "mourner"; OB

Lit. *akalšu ittī da-ma-mi ikkal* CUSAS 18 p. 296: 5 "he will eat his bread with mourners".

damqiš "well, benevolently"

OB *mamman ša šumī lā damqiš iqabbû lā tešemmē* ARM 10, 49 r. 6 "you shall listen to no-one who says my name without kindness". JW

damqu "good"

1. OA for *damqu watru* "very fine quality" as a qualification of textiles, s. Michel/Veenhof 2010, 246.

2. OB in opposition to *masku*: *dam-qá u maska malā imhurakka ṭēmka ul tašpur* AbB 9, 154: 9 "you did not write your report about anything that happened to you, good or bad".

3. OB *kutalli* PN *kīl aššum lemnim ū lā dam-qí* FM 7, 38 no. 13: 21 "have the reserve of PN ready, for bad or unfavorable (conditions)".

4. SB *amīlu* ⌜*dam*⌝-*qá īni ša īnāšu* ... SpTU 4, 144: 16 (comm.) "man 'good of eye': whose eyes are ...". On *damqa īni* as euphemism for "blind", s. Marcus 1980; Fincke 2000, 194. Cf. *dam-qam*(-)*īnam* (AHw 157a s.v. *da*[*m*]*ga-minam*) "an eye disease, hydrophthalmus", s. Fincke 2000, 193–195.

5. On the mng. "of good family, well to do" (cf. CAD D 70f.) s. Frankena 1978 with further ref.

6. On *damqūtu māt* GN "elders; foremost of the land" in the MB treaty AlT 3 s. Márquez Rowe 2001.

JW (1–6), MPS (4)

damtu "destruction(?), burial mound(?)"

On a possible mng. "burial mound(?)" s. A. Westenholz 1970, 28. JW

dāmu "blood"

1. Lex. *da-mu* = *māru* AOAT 50, 437: 179B (exp. malku) "blood = son". Cf. Hrůša ib. p. 285.

2. OAkk. *lū agammalušu kakki da-me alšu lā ašakkanu* FAOS 19 Gir 37 r. 7 "(I swear) I will spare him, I will not raise 'the weapon of blood' against him"; cf. Kraus 2018, 3: 12.

3. OAkk. lit. [*in*] *da-me-em tanīʾal* BiMes 1, 7 i 2 "you will lie in blood".

4. Ur III *esēp da-ma nakirī* PN *zikrūʾa šumšu* RIME 3/2, 135: 8 "'gathering the blood of the enemies of PN (in?) my name' is its name", cf. Krebernik 1991, 142.

5. Early OB pl. *anāku aḫūka šīrka u da-mu-kà anāku* AS 22, 11: 4 "I am your brother, I am your flesh and your blood".

6. OA *māmītkunu ninaddī da-ma-ni kīma kāsim lū tabik* kt n/k 794: 41 (Bilgiç 1992, 65) "if we violate your oath our blood shall pour as from a bowl."

7. OA *ammakam nuwāʾum da-me-a lā išattī* AKT 4, 53: 23 "the native shall not drink my blood here!"

8. OA pl. "blood money" (CAD D 79 2b) s. AKT 6C p. 31–47; VS 26, 2: 12; 26: 12.

9. OA *da-mu-um da-ma-mu-um* kt a/k 611: 1 (Veenhof 1996, 428), magic formula based on phonetical repetition of a lexeme. Similar phrases are attested in OB incantations.

10. OB *lemut*[*tam*] *ana qaqqad* PN *lušpukma ša da-mi-*⸢*im*⸣ *lūpuš* RATL 167 no. 94: 12 "I will heap evil on PN's head and I will shed blood", s. Eidem ib. p. 168.

11. OB *da-ma-am ina pursītim akṣur* FM 9, 136 no. 27: 8 "I gathered blood in the offering bowl" (in context of educating an apprentice), cf. Ziegler 2005.

12. OB 2/3 *da-mi erēni ana piššat dalāti* CUSAS 9, 143: 2–4. "2/3 (liter) of cedar blood as lubricant for doors".

13. OB in context of oath-taking and treaties (Mari, Tell Leilan) s. Eidem 2011, 315f.; s. also *dāmuttu*, below.

14. On the element *dāmu* (*damû*?) in OB Mari PNN ("kin by marriage(?)") s. Durand 1992; cf. Bonechi 1997, 477ff.

15. OB lit. *nuʾû ulāp da-me labiš* BWL 228 iii 14 "(the wise man wears a loincloth,) the fool is clad in a 'blood' cloak" (perhaps "scarlet cloak"?).

16. OB lit. *ištī erṣetum da-mi qarrādī* FM 14 i 25 "the ground has drunk the blood of the warriors".

17. SB Ugar. [*d*]*a-mi-šu-nu ramkū* ORA 7, 208: 11 "they bath in their blood"; *da-ma-am* (as a drink) ib. 18.

18. SB *nēšu ākilu da-mi* … *tābik da-mi* … *lāpit da-mi* MesCiv. 7, 46: 62–64 ("the lion, devourer of blood … (the …), spiller of blood, … (the …), smearer of blood".

19. SB *iš/ltanatti da-mi našpūti ša amēlūti* Lamaštu I 187, 190 (Farber 2014, 90) "she keeps drinking the spilt(?) blood of mankind", s. Farber ib. 219f. (transl. "blown(?) blood").

20. MB *da-am mārī* GN *kīma mê itbuk* CUSAS 17, 61: 15 "he spilt the blood of the sons of GN like water".

21. NA *da-a-mu ulabbušū* SAA 10, 354: 17 "they will be clothed with blood". Further NA/SB plene spellings: *da-a-mu/e* SAA 2, 5 iv 4; 6: 256 var.

22. For the relation between *dāma epēšu* and Heth. *esḫar iya-*, s. Kronasser 1959. JW (2–12, 14–16, 19–20), MPS (1, 13, 17–18, 21–22)

+ **dāmuttu** "blood bonds"; OB

da-mu-ut-tum ina [*b*]*īrini iššakkana* RATL 160 no. 89: 34 "(until you and I meet and swear an oath to each other) and blood bonds are established between us", s. Eidem ib. p. 315. Refers to slaughtering a donkey as a symbolic act accompaying the making of a treaty. JW/MPS

+ **dānakku** "1/8 shekel"; LB, Old Pers. lw.

3 *da-nak-ku* KÙ.BABBAR Or. 86, 60 no. 5 (BM 109972): 14f., cf. 16 "3 *d.* silver"; cf. Hackl, ib. p. 58 and Hackl 2016 (etym.: *Old Pers. *dānaka-*, cf. Old Pers. **dānā* "grain").

danānu I "power, strength, force"

ana (instead of *ina*) *danāni*:

1. NB *kasapšu a-na da-na-ni iššû* OIP 114, 80: 24 "his silver which they took by force".

2. LB *suluppī ... a-na da-na-nu in qātī*⌈*ya*⌉ *ittašû* AUWE 5, 136 r. 7 "they forcefully took the dates from me", s. Gehlken ib. p. 114; cf. LKA 64: 11. JW (2), MPS (1)

danānu II, NA *da'ānu* "to be(come) strong"

G 1. OA ref., s. Veenhof 2015a, 246f.
2. OB *midde wardūšu* [*i*]*-da-an-ni-nu-šum-ma* ARM 26/2, 220 no. 391: 16 "I fear that his servants put pressure on him" s. Charpin, ib. 222 n. f.
3. NA perf. *i-da-nu* SAA 16, 40 r. 9 (*idda'nū* or *iddānū*). Not mentioned in Hämeen-Anttila 2000, 100.

+ **Gtn** With *ittī*: OB lit. *ḫupšum ša ittī bēlišu i-id-da-na-an-ni-nu* CUSAS 18 p. 304 obv. 4 "*ḫ.* who will repeatedly become stronger than their lord".

D 1. OB *alpī du-un-ni-in-ma* AbB 3, 94: 3 "strengthen the oxen"; cf. 1 *alpam li-da-an-ni-nu-ma* ib. 6' "they shall strengthen one ox".
2. *panī d.* "to be relentless, strict, determined" (s. also *dannu* and *dunnu*):
a) OB *panīka mādiš du-ni-in-šu* AbB 7, 66: 15 "be relentless towards him!"
b) OB *panīya ú-da-an-ni-in-ma panīša ul ubil* AbB 3, 2: 8 "I was stern and showed her no leniency."
c) *ana* PNN *panīya ú-da-an-ni-in-ma* ARM 14, 64: 7 "I was stern towards PNN (and had them swear a strong oath)".
3. "to speak severely" (CAD D 86 e):
a) OB (*tuppī*) *ú-da-an-ni-na-am-ma uštābilam* AbB 12, 2: 14 "I have sent strongly worded letters"; cf. FM 7, 153 no. 45: 59.
b) OB *kunuk* PN...*lūmu*[*r šu*]*mma lā tu-da-ni-na-am meḫrīka utarrakkumma* AbB 9, 218: 24 "I want to see the sealed document of PN. If you are not insistent on my behalf, I will return your copies to you (and break the sealed documents)."

4. Without obj.: OB *ana maṣṣarti ālim u nepārātim nu-da-ni-in* ARM 26/1, 319 no. 154: 19 "we provided reinforcements for the guard of the city and the prisons".
5. NA/SB *du*ʾʾ*unu*: *masṣartušu tu-da-a-na* SAA 2, 6: 206 "you (should) strengthen his guard."
6. For use in koppelung s. Kraus 1987, 20ff.

Dt 1. EA [*u*] *yi-*⌈*da*⌉*-ni-en libbušu* EA 91: 12 (Moran 1992, 165) "his intentions were reinforced".
2. "to strengthen one another": NA *aḫēyiši nu-ti-in* SAA 5, 227 r. 15 "we want to strengthen one another" (*nuttîn* < *nudtîn* from the NA var. *da*ʾ*ānu*).

JW (G, D), MPS (G, D, Dt, Gtn), NR (Dt)

dandannu, + *dandanû* "all-powerful"; + OB

Var. *dandanû* in OB lex. ^{d}*dìm-tur-*⌈*tur*?⌉ = *dan-da-nu-ú-um* UET 7, 93 r. 19, name or epitheton of a demon, s. Sjöberg 1996, 232.

danna "hardly, with difficulty"

1. OB *ina da-an-na* 15 *awīlū ana* 1 *epinnim kašdū* ARM 27, 1: 9 "15 men are hardly enough for 1 plow".

2. OB *ina da-an-na* n *eqlam iṣṣidū* ARM 27, 102: 16 "they hardly harvest n field".

3. OB *šê awīlī ṣippatum īkul awīlū udappir u da-an-na šunu wašib*! ARM 28, 141: 37 "salt has eaten the grain of the people. The people have moved away as they could only stay with difficulty".

dannatu "strength; fortress; binding (agreement); distress"; pl. *dannātu* "strict (command), firm (order)"

1. For OA ref. s. Veenhof 2015a, 237–242; for the pl. *dannātu* s. ib. 240, 242.

2. OB "fortress":
a) *anāku ina da-na-ti-im ša bēliya kalī*ʾ*āku* AbB 8, 18: 5 "I am detained in my lord's fortress".
b) OB *āl dan-na-ti-ia u bītātīya atammarānim* ARM 26/1, 106 no. 10: 30 (cf. 23) "view, one by one, (all) my fortified cities and houses!"

3. OB *ina da-an-na-at kuṣṣi tuštamīssunūti* AbB 10, 96: 3 "you let (the cattle) die in the harshness of winter".

4. OB *dan-na-tim aškunšunūšim* ARM 14, 67 r. 3 "I put pressure on them"; cf. *dan-na-t*[*i*]*m ašakkan* ARM 14, 69: 17.

5. SB also logogr. KALAG^{mí} MDP 14 p. 50 i 7.

6. On sale contracts *ana*/*ina dan-na-ti* "in times of distress" in Emar s. Adamthwaite 2001, 155ff.

7. Borger 1961, 154: NA *ša ina pušqi* KI.KAL *ušēzibu* AAA 20, 81: 12 "who saves from distress (and) hardship".

8. NA *dannutu* documents:
a) *ana* PN_1 *adi da-na-a-su* (var.: *da-na-su*) PN_2 *ú-*⌈*bal*⌉*-a-ni … peti … da-ni-*[*t*]*e-šú* BATSH 6, 109: 4–5 "against PN_1, PN_2 brought (his claim) with his document; his document is opened".
b) Radner 1997, 56–60 with further ref. and disc.; Zaccagnini 1997; Fales 2005, 612f.

9. In building inscriptions "solid mudbrick of a decayed building" (cf. CAD D 90 mng. 3b "bottom of the foundation pit"), s. Turner 1970, 71 n. 24b.

10. For KBo. 1, 3: 9 (CAD D 89 2 a) s. *tanattu*. JW (2, 3–6, 8–10), MPS (1, 2, 5, 7)

danniš "strongly; very"

1. OAkk. add. ref. for *aṣeḫḫamme danniš danniš(me)* s. FAOS 19 Di 5: 5f.; Di 11: 4f.

2. Early OB ⌜*dan*⌝*-ni-iš-ma lemun* AS 22, 48: 20 "it is very wicked" (broken context). JW

dannišamma "very much"; OA

OA *da-ni-ša-ma lamnūšu nīnu ulammun* AKT 9A, 55: 6 "his wickedness has harmed us terribly". JW

dannu I, fem. *dannatu*, +*daʾattu* (*dâttu*?) "strong, powerful, mighty, great"

1. OA ref. s. Veenhof 2015a, 235–237.

2. Early OB *têrti bēliya dan-na-at* AS 22, 8: 5 "the omen report concerning my lord is strong".

3. Early OB *ina āliya da-na-ku* AS 22, 9: 16 "(even in wartime) I remain secure in my city"; cf. *maṣṣarti bēliya da-na-at* ib.: 7 "the garrison of my lord is 'strong'".

4. OB *gamartum da-na-tum šaknat* AbB 8, 35: 9 "strict completion is in place" (concerning livestock, s. Kraus 1976, 174f.).

5. OB *šattum dan-na-at-ma ḫurnû ul ibaššû* ARM 14, 34: 15 "the year is tough, there is no mint"; cf. *šattum da-an-na-at* AbB 8, 94: 11.

6. OB *īnāšu elī bāšītim da-an-na-ma* MARI 8, 355 no. 5: 12 "(PN is not releasing our goods.) His eyes are strong on the goods".

7. OB 10 *enzētum dan-na-tum* ARM 26/1, 132 no. 20: 9 "10 strong goats". Cf. 10 *enzētum enšētum* ib. r. 6 "10 weak goats".

8. Of a weapon: OB *šukurri siparrim dan-na-am* ARM 27, 107 r. 16 (cf. ib. r. 24) "the strong bronze lance".

9. Of time: MB Emar *mārī ṣeḫrūti ina šanāti dan-na-ti uballiṭ* Emar 6/3, 216: 7 "she has kept the small children alive during difficult years".

10. With *panu* (s. Kraus 1970, 58f.; cf. *dunnu* and *danānu*):

a) OB *ana šê panū mādiš da-an-nu* AbB 14, 87: 12 "they are strongly interested in barley (lit. 'the face is very strong')", s. Mayer 2010, 309 and 311.

b) EA KALAG.GA *ina panīšunu* EA 108: 42 (Moran 1992, 182 n. 7) "they are strong in their faces".

c) SB *da-an panī* SpTU 5, 247 v 7 "strong of face".

11. SB *dan-na-ta kappī summata umaššir* AuOr. Suppl. 23, 65: 11 "strong of wings, I released a dove"; s. Cavigneaux 2007, 319.

12. NA 1 SÌLA NINDA *dan-ni* SAA 9, 11: 8 "1 liter of strong(?) bread".

13. NA fem. *daʾattu* < *daʾantu*, cf. Hämeen-Anttila 2000, 100, wr. *da-ʾ-tú* SAA 1, 119: 11 or *da-at-ti* (= *daʾattu* or *dâttu*) ib. 150: 8.

JW (2–6, 10), MPS (1, 7–9, 10, 11–13)

dannu II "a storage container, pithos"

1. Replaces *našpaku* as standard word for "storage vessel" from OB on (Sallaberger 1996, 111); s. ib. for further lit.

2. LB as dowry, s. Roth 1989/90, 24; add. LB ref.: CT 55, 60: 1f.; 125: 4; 137: 1; 142: 7; 433: 4f.; 439: 6; CT 56, 281: 6; 294: 8. JW

dannūtu "strength"

1. OA ref. s. Veenhof 2015a, 242–245.

2. OB *awīlū dan-nu-ti šunu* ARM 26/1, 129 no. 18: 20 "they are men of strength".

****dapāru** “to be sated” (CAD D 104)

For G s. *epēru* III Gt; for D s. *dapāru*.

dapāru “to go away, leave”

+ **G** OB lit. *akkuš di-pi-ir lā teseḫḫēma* CUSAS 10, 12: 3 “I am going. Move on! Do not make trouble!”

+ **Gt** Mayer 2016, 202: OB lit. *napiḫ-tam di-[i]t-pa-ar tuqumtam* Westenholz 1997, 218 vii 7 “drive burning battle far away!”

D 1. After Moran 1981, all ref. cit. AHw 177 s.v. *duppuru*, AHw 1380 s.v. *ṭapāru* D, CAD D 104 s.v. *dapāru* D and CAD D 186–188 s.v. *duppuru* belong to a single verb *duppuru* with both intrans. and trans. mng. Valid arguments for his suggestion are: there is no spelling with ḪI = *ṭà* attested so far for the trans. verb in regions where we would expect it, and several spellings with DA and DU occur in regions where we do not expect these syllabograms for /ṭa/ and /ṭu/. However, at least three OB ref. favor a reading *ṭuppuru* for the verb with trans. mng.:
a) There is, pace Moran 1981, no reason to emend TU-*pí-ra-aš-šu-nu-ti* ARM 1, 39 r. 6 “expel them!” to *tu-*<*še-*>*-bi-ra-*; cf. Durand 1998, 48. Šamšī-Adad elsewhere uses DU for /du/, although TU = *dú* is sometimes used in other texts from Upper Mesopotamia or the Middle Euphrates area.
b) OB *eleppam šâtu li-*TA*-ap-pí-ru* Shemshara 1, 47: 17 “they shall remove that ship”. The same text writes DA for /da/ in *ú-da-ba-bu* ib. 27. DU-*pu-ur eleppim šâtu* ib. 28 “removing of that ship” is ambigious.
c) OB lit. TU-*pu-ru-tum uššabū* CUSAS 18, 29: 7 “expelled people will settle”. The same text writes DU for /du/ in *a-ša-re-du-ta* ib. 20 and *re-du-*us_4*-sú* ib. 38. Cf. already George ib. p. 206.
There is, at the moment, no way to resolve this problem.

2. trans.:
a) OB *ša kakkam annīʾam ina qāt* DN *ù-dáp-pa-ru-ma* MARI 3, 62 A.4510: 3 “he who removes this weapon from the hand of DN” (curse formula, cf. ref. cit. CAD D 183, 2b).
b) OB *šarrum* ^{túg}*lullumtam ú*!*-da-ap-*<*pa*>*-ar-ma* FM 3, 60 no. 3 iv 17 (ritual) “the king will take off the *l.*-garment (and perform a libation)”.
c) SB *ú-da-[p]a-ra kâša* Lamaštu ND 2 (Farber 2014, 266) “I will expel you!”

3. intrans.:
a) OB with ina: *u ṣuḫārūka ina panīšu ú-da-pa-ru* Shemshara 1, 35: 39 “and your servants stay away from him”; *ina zumur bēliya ú-da-ap-pa-ar-ma* ARM 26/1, 367 no. 185: 23 “he will depart from the person of my lord”; *inanna i-na [ṭ]êrtim šâti ú-da-ap-pí-ra-am* ARM 27, 108: 8 “now I have left that position”.
b) OB 1 *amtum ša bītini qadūm mārātīša ú-da-ap-pí-ir-ma* AbB 13, 18: 9 “one of the slave-girls of our household has run away with her daughters”; *[du-up-p]u-rum ú-da-ap-pí-ir* ib. 24 “(if) she has indeed run away”; cf. AbB 7, 128: 7.
c) OB *zūzam ṣāb[um in]a karāšīšu li-da-ap-pí-ir-ma* ARM 14, 104: 13 “the troops shall go half a league from their camp”, cf. ib. 16.
d) OB ^{lú}DIRI.GA^{meš} *we-du-ú-um kalûšu ša eqlī ašrānum ukallū du-up-pu-ru* FM 7, 99 no. 26: 7 “all his high-ranking functionaries who possessed fields there have been driven away”, s. Durand ib. p. 76.

e) OB *sugāgūt* GN *ul eppeš du-pu-ra-ku* ARM 14, 46: 10 "I will not act as *sugāgu*-official of GN! I am driven out!"
f) OB *du-up-pí-ir lā tazzâz ittīšu* FM 9, 270 no. 67: 19 "leave, do not stay with him!"
g) Mayer 2016, 203: OB lit. *du-up-pi-ir* YOS 11, 16: 3b; 77: 14 "be gone".

4. The reading of the verb in Gilg. MB Ur 28 is uncertain: George 2003, 298 suggests ⌜*li*⌝-*de*-⌜*ep-pi*!⌝-[*ir*] "congregate" (cf. *epēru* III?). Read perhaps *li-de-ip-k*[*i*!?] "(may the [...] of the street, your brothel, push [you] away" (*daʾāpu* D).

Dt SB (diseases) *li-id-dap-pí-ru* Fs. Lambert, p. 202: 12 "they shall be driven away", cf. Streck 2003, 111.

Dtn OB *awīlam šâtu ina bītiya li-id-da-ap-pí-ru* ARM 10, 154 r. 7 "they shall keep that man out of my house".

+ **ŠD** Mayer 2016, 203: SB *uš-dap-pa-ru* Ludlul I 26 (var. *-dab-*) "(through Marduk's incantation) they drive out (cold and fever)", cf. Oshima 2014, 183.

MPS (G, Gt, D), JW (D, Dt, Dtn, ŠD)

dāpinu, *dapīnu* "ferocious, savage"

1. OB lit. *Girra da-pí-nu* AnSt. 33, 148: 16 "Girra, the savage one".

2. OB lit. *Erra da-pí-nu-um-ma ina imnišu* FM 14 iii 38 "Erra, the savage one, (walked) on his right".

3. OB lit. in independent use: *ittī* ⌜*da*!⌝-*pi-nim* Iraq 78, 243: 3 "with the savage one" MPS (1), JW (2–3)

dapnu "aggressive"

NA *ana tāḫāzi dáp-ni* KAL 3, 61 i 13 "towards the raging battle". JW

dappānu "warlike"; + OB

1. OB lex. *giš-ma-ra-gíd-da* "wagon" = *da-pa-an* UET 7, 93 r. 7, s. Sjöberg 1996, 229.

2. Unclear var. of *tāpalu* in lex. texts from Emar, s. CAD T 117 *tāpalu* lex. sect.

dappastu s. *tappaštu*

dappātu "a garment"; + MA

(CAD *tapātu*, AHw *t*/*dap*/*batu*)

1. For further OB ref. s. Durand 2009, 32f. (^{túg}*da-ba-du*, cf. $^{\text{(túg)}}$*da-ba-tum* in Ur III). It is clear from the Mari texts that the word is not fem. and denotes a type of garment rather than a type of fabric.

2. MA 12 *dap-pa-te* ... *ilaqqiʾū* MARV 4, 138: 24, 25 "(the priests) will take 12 *d.*" (made from *tabarru*-wool) in rit. context, s. Dercksen 2005b, 123ff.

JW/MPS

dappurtu (mng. uncert.); OA

1. OA *kaspam* 10 *manā malā awīlūti-kunu lū da-pu-ur-tí bīt abīni u bīt abīni ebbubim epšāma* AKT 6A, 236: 23 "make 10 minas of silver as true gentlemen (so that it) shall be the *d.* of our father's house and (of?) our father's cleared house".

2. Etym. and mng. remain unclear. S. CAD Ṭ, 49 s.v. *ṭappurtu*. JW

daprānu, + *diprānu* "juniper"; + MB Ugar.

1. OB ^{giš}*dáp-ra-nu ana šubšul* 3 GAG SAG ARM 23, 439 no. 514: 1 "(6 1/2 minas of) juniper wood for melting down 3 best-quality nails".

2. MB Ugar. A.ŠÀ$^{\text{ḫi.a}}$: *dì-ip-ra-ni-ma* PRU 3, 64 RS 16.190: 4 "juniper fields", for disc. s. Kühne 1974.

3. LB *qaštu ša dap-⸢ra?-ni⸣* AOAT 414/1, 194: 8 "a bow made of juniper".

4. Cf. Hurr. tabra/i=ne/I, s. Haas/ Wilhelm 1974, 89; Richter 2012, 441; Besnier et. al. 2015.

JW (1, 4), MPS (3), NR (2)

daqqu "minute, fine"; + MB Emar

1. OB fem. pl. "small amounts left over": n *šiqil kaspam da-qá-ti ... muḫurma* AbB 12, 84: 6 "collect the n shekels of silver, the amount left over".

2. MB Emar *ḫi?-šu?* GUŠKIN *qadu da-qú-ti-šu* HANEM 2, 10: 12 "gold necklace together with its small pieces", s. disc. Pentiuc 2001, 44.

JW (1), MPS/NR (2)

dār s. *dāru* I

daraggu, *tarqu* "way, track"

1. For lex. *tar-qu* MSL 5, 71: 281 (Ugar.) and its possible Ugar. etym. s. Huehnergard 1987, 120; del Olmo Lete/Sanmartin 2004, 860 s.v. *tdrq*.

2. SB [...] *ip-ru-su* (x) ⸢*da-rag*(?)-*gu*(?)⸣ [(...)] Or. 68, 38: 41 "[...] blocked *the trails*", s. Frame 1999, 47.

3. SB lex. *da-rag-gu* = *kibsu* AOAT 50, 337: 93 (malku) "path = track".

MPS (1, 3), NR (1–2)

darāku "to pack"; OA

1. Imp. *du-ur-ka-ší-ma* AKT 4, 52: 16 "pack it (= the wool)!"

2. Pres. *a-beʾūlātīšu lā i-da-ra-kam lā taggarāšu* AKT 8, 275: 2 "(if) he does not do the packing for his working capital, do not hire him!" JW

****darāku III** "to thresh"

Both passages cit. s.v. in AHw 1550a can be read differently (*lu-du-ri-*[*su*] SAA 19, 53 r. 9; *ú-du-⸢bi⸣-ku* SAA 19, 109: 7). S. also *mudarriktu*. JW

darāru I "to move freely"; + MB Ekalte

G 1. OB lit. *ilū mātim id-ru-ru-ma iššiqū šēpīšu* RA 52, 90: 42 (OB Anzu II) "the gods of the land (rejoiced), they ran free (to Ningirsu) and kissed his feet, cf. ZA 68, 66: 245 (court. Olga Sek, Jena).

2. NA (in date) EGIR *da-⸢ra-ri⸣* SAA 6, 259 s. 1 "after becoming free (of debts)". Cf. *andurāru*.

N 1. OB lit. [*k*]*īma būrū id-⸢da⸣-a*[*r-ru-ú*] *ana lîʾātim id-da-ar-ru-ú lalû ana enzē*[*tim*] *namzītum mārat* DN *li-da-ri-ir ana terḫiša* CUSAS 32, 32 r. 2–4 "just as calves ran f[ree] to cows, kids ran free to nanny-goats, let the brewing jar, daughter of DN, run free to her jug".

2. MB Ekalte (silver) *ul uṣṣab ul id-da-ra-a*[*r*] WVDOG 102, 68: 4 "does not yield interest and does not diminish (lit. become free)".

+ **Ntn** OB lit. *mu-ut-ta-ad-ri-ra-at* [...] Lamaštu OB$_3$: 2 (Farber 2014, 260) "she who is constantly on the move".

JW (G, Ntn), MPS (G, N)

darāru II "to intercalate (a month)"

NA *urḫu anniʾu da-ri-ir* SAA 10, 44 r. 3 "this month is intercalary".

darāsu "to trample, push back, thresh"; + OB

G 1. OB lit. *ina emūqim da-ar-sa-an-ni-ma* CUSAS 10, 17: 52 "he had driven me out by force".

2. OB lit. *ina eqli dar*$_6$(TAR)*-sa-nu ina dīni lēʾênu* CUSAS 18, 20: 13 "in the

field, we are thrown back, in court, we are overcome". Cf. George ib. p. 125 for parallels in other OB Tigunānu tablets (*dar-sa-nu, da*!*-ar-sà-nu*): *nakram ina eqlim ummānšu a-dar*$_6$*-ri-ìs ina dīnim ni-le-i*!*-šu* Tsukimoto forthc. no. 1: 11–22 "I shall force back the enemy in the field (and) his army, we shall overcome him in court"; *i-dar-ri-ìs* CUSAS 18 p. 302: 14; *i-dar-ri-sa-an*?*-ni* ib. p. 303: 20; *ni-da-ri-ìs* ib. p. 311 iv 2; *i-da-ar-ri-sú-né-ti-*⌜*im*⌝ ib. p. 312: 6.
3. NA *ina timāli tēgirtu ina muḫḫi lā dagāli assakan ūma addalaḫ ad-di-ris* SAA 10, 235 r. 15 (cit. CAD D 110, 1c as ABL 379) "yesterday I made an excuse for not having looked (at the writing), today I hurried to erase(?) (it)" (CAD T 324 s.v. *tēgirtu*, *pace* Parpola 1993, 188 and SAA 10; s. also Cherry 2017, 98f., who argues for an Aram. origin of the word in NA).

****Gt** s. Streck 2003, 81.

D 1. OB PN *ina eqlim*? *u mê* ⌜x⌝ *ú-*⌜*da*⌝*-a*[*r*]*-r*[*i*]*-s*[*a*]*-an-ni-ma* AbB 13, 119: 9 "PN has taken the field and the water from me by intimidation."
2. OB *ṣeḫrī ana mê ṣapêšu aṭrudma ud-da-ar-ri-su-šu* AbB 13, 149: 11, 12 "I sent my servant to soak it (the field) in water, but they drove him away".
3. OB *aššat* PN *ša* PN *qadūm wildīša ú-da-ra-sú-ši* AbB 5, 249: 6 "the wife of PN, whom PN wants to drive away with her children".
4. NA "to thresh": *alpūšunu lillikūni ebūršunu lu-du-ri-*[*su*] SAA 19, 53 r. 9 "let their oxen come (and) thresh their harvest" (cf. Cherry 2017, 99f.).

N SB *Ea ša ina tulîšu Bēl i-dar-su-ma* SAA 3, 38: 9 "Ea, from whose breast Bēl was pushed back".

JW (G, D), MPS (G, D, N),

dārâtu s. *dārītu*

dargiš "couch"; Iran. lw.

1. LB 2 ^{giš}*da-ar-gi-iš* TBER 93f.: 18.

2. On etym. s. Zadok 1984; also as lw. in Aram., s. Abraham/Sokoloff 2011, 29 with further lit. JW

dārīʾātu s. *dārītu*

dārītu, pl. *dārīʾātu, dārâtu* "continuity, eternity"; + Ur III

1. Ur III *simat da-ri-a-tim* RIME 3/2, 145: 1 "befitting eternity".

2. The sg. only occurs in peripheral OB and MB (cf. CAD D 114, where it is separated from *dārâtu*). JW

darīku "(container for) pressed dates"; + NA

1. NA "basin(?)": *bibbī ša* [*kis*]*allu kupru kaprū* [...] *ša da-ri-ki šaknat* ⌜*rēḫtu*⌝ *ša bēt napṭarte raṣip* SAA 19, 60: 12 "the drainage pipes of the courtyard are covered with bitumen. The ... for the *d.* container is installed. The rest of the quarter is built". M. Luukko in SAA 19 translates "basin".

2. LB *da-ri-ku* CT 56, 235: 8; cf. CT 55, 103.

3. The doubts of Abraham/Sokoloff 2011, 29 about the Aram. etym. are unjustified, s. Streck 2011, 419: the mng. "to press" is attested in Mandaic as well as in Bibl. and Middle Hebr., the word has no Akkad. etym. and is attested only in late Akk. texts. All this favors an Aram. etym.

JW (2), MPS (1, 3)

dariʾu, *darrû* "sacrificial sheep"

1. The Susa ref. UDU *dar-ru-um* MDP 10, 68: 3, cit. CAD D 115 s.v. *darru* might belong here.

2. MA KUŠ … *ša* UDU^{meš} *da-ri-ú-tu*? StAT 5, 26: 5 "skins of sacrificial sheep".

3. NA *d. nasāḫu* "to perform a *d.*-sacrifice": *dà-ri-u ina pan* DN_1 *u* DN_2 *ittasaḫ* A.499+500: 15 (StPohl SM 10, T41) "he sacrificed a *d.* in front of DN_1 and DN_2", cf. Deller/Mayer/Sommerfeld 1987, 184 (with further ref.) and 188 (logogr. UDU.SISKUR in NA?).

JW

darku "following"

1. SB lex. *dar-ka-a-tum* = *aḫrâ*[*t ūmī*?] AOAT 50, 365: 84 (malku) "following = fut[ure]". Cf. Hrůša ib. p. 233.

2. SB lex. *de-er-ku* = *ṣeḫru* AOAT 50, 439: 237 (exp. malku) "following = child".

darru s. *dariʾu*

dāru II "lifetime, generation"; + SB

SB PN *da-a-ri* (var.: *a-da-ri*) PN_2 *mārūšu kussâ iṣbat* RlA 6, 110 § 47 "during the lifetime of PN, PN_2, his son, seized the throne"; cf. Mayer W. 1998, 539f. ("60-year period"). S. also Streck 2000, 88 (Amor. lw.).

JW/MPS

darû "to last forever"

G OB *šulum balāṭi u da-ri-i lušmē* CUSAS 9, 6: 22–24 "may I hear greetings of long life and of lasting forever", s. Dalley 2009, 24.

dārû "everlasting"

Said of goddess: SB ^{d}LAMA GN *da-ri-ti/tu*$_4$ SpTU 1, 3 r. 4, 13 "the everlasting tutelary goddess of GN".

dâru s. *dūʾāru*

****dasû** s. *takšiʾu*

dāṣtu, + *dīṣtu* "lie, deception"; + OB

1. OB *tillat* PN *asīrū ina sarrātim*[*ma u*] *di-ṣa-ti*[*m*] *ittīšu it-ta-na-šu* [*awā*]*s-su ul ileqqû* ARM 26/1, 435 no. 207: 42 "the reinforcements of PN are captives. They keep … with him through lies and deception. They do not follow his order" (after Heimpel 2003, 257; CAD S s.v. *sarrātu* emends *it-ta-na-*<*la-*>*ku*).

2. Mayer 2016, 201: OB *salīmātum ša awīl* GN *da-aṣ-tum-ma* ARM 10, 80: 12 "the peaceful overtures of the man of GN are lies".

3. Mayer 2016, 201: **a)** OB *da-ṣa-tim-ma-mi kīma šabšūtimma ītanappalāni* AbB 10, 57: 10 "they keep replying to me with lies like midwives".
b) *šunu da-ṣ*[*a*]*-tim-ma ītanappalū* ib. 15 "they (too) keep replying to me with lies".

JW

dâṣu "to treat unjustly, with disrespect; to cheat"

G 1. OB *šanîš ina awâtim i-da-aṣ-ka-ma* ARM 26/1, 82 no. 5: 15 "he deceived you with words a second time".
2. OB [*i*]*špatma nāgiram i-du-uṣ*$_4$ ARM 26/2, 90 no. 323: 12 "he acted maliciously(?) and treated the herald with disrespect", cf. Heimpel 2003, 302.
3. OB *ina awâtim i ni-da-as-sú-ma* ARM 14, 104: 16 "we shall deceive him with words".

+ **D 1.** OB *tubqam lā tu-d*[*a*]*-sí-ma* A.4471 (Durand 1990a, 291): 7 "you shall not let her be mistreated in the harem".
2. OB *awīlam tu-da-aṣ-ma iḫalliq* AbB 5, 41: 16 "(if) you treat the gentleman unjustly, he will perish".

3. OB *š[umm]an lā ú-da-aḫ-ìs-su* (*udaʾʾissu*) *ullāman ībirakkim* AbB 6, 188: 39 "if I had not mistreated him, he would not have come to you".

MPS (G), JW (G, D)

dašannu? "a piece of jewellery"; + NB

NB *da-šá-an-ni šup-ru* OIP 114, 2: 36 "send *d*.s!" Cf. CAD D 119 and Cole, OIP 114 p. 42. However, the NA ref. is analyzed as pl. of *daššu* "buck, ram" in AHw 165b *daššu* 2.

dašnu "mighty"

SB *daš-ni* KAL 9, 1 r. 2.

da(š)šiya "a functionary"; LB, Iran. lw.?

S. Zadok 1976, 5 on etym. JW

daššu "buck, ram; a metal implement"; + OB

1. Early OB ⌜*da*⌝*-šu-um bīt* DN KTT 46: 3f. "buck for the temple of DN".

2. Early OB 1 *da-šum* ARM 19, 166, 167, 168; 2 *da-šá-an* ib. 184; s. ib. p. 164 for add. ref.

3. NA 1*-te da-áš-*⌜*šú*⌝ KÙ.BABBAR SAA 16, 53 r. 3 "1 'buck' made of silver". Cf. *dašannu*.

4. A weapon:

a) Lex. *nam-gaz = dá-aš-šu = itānu ša* giš!PAN Emar 6/4, 545: 518 (Ḫḫ) "slaughter-bench(?) = buck = horn(?) of the bow". For *si = itānu* s. CAD I 293f., in AHw s.v. *itannu* "mesh".

b) Lex. *nam-gaz-níg-bù-bù-re = dá-aš-šu pallušu* Emar 6/4, 545: 519 (Ḫḫ) "perforated slaughter-bench(?) = perforated 'buck'".

c) Cf. Cohen 2010, 819, who reads *taššu* of unknown mng. and etym.

JW (2), MPS (1, 3–4)

daššuptu s. *duššuptu*

dâšu s. *dīʾāšu*

dāta s. *dātu*

dātabar(r)u "a law officer, judge"; LB, Old Pers. lw.

1. *ana šarri* lú*da-a-tu₄-bar-ra dayyāni u mamma pitnu* WZKM 97, 257 (BM 120024): 8 "(he shall not bring charges) before king, *d*., judge, or anyone powerful", s. Jursa/Stolper ib. p. 263.

2. S. Stolper 2006, 230, 243 for disc. and add. ref. JW

+ datteru "a fish"; SB

Lex. *suḫur-dàra*ku6 = [*d*]*a-at-te-ru* Emar 6/4, 555: 8 (Ḫḫ). Cf. DCCLT MB Ura 11.

dātu "law, decree"; LB, Old Pers. lw.

1. *da-a-ti ip-tu-ú-ʾ-i* [*u*]*ltu da-a-ti* n *amēluttu ina muḫḫi* PN ⌜...⌝ AfO 50, 255f. BM 25098: 15, 16 "(the judges) consulted (lit. opened) the (royal) regulation. On the basis of the (royal) regulation (the payment of) n slaves ⌜was imposed(?)⌝ upon PN", s. Jursa ib. p. 257, 259.

2. *kī ana šanû lā ittannu libbū da-*[*a*]*-tú* [*in*]*andin* CT 49, 102: 7 "if he does not repay double the amount, he shall repay according to the edict", s. Stolper 2006, 243f. with further ref. and ib., 230f. for disc.

3. *akī* [*d*]*a-at-ta* AOAT 414/1, 49 r. 8 "according to the decree".

4. *libbū da-a-ta šarri* AOAT 414/1, 63: 21 "according to the royal command".

JW (1–2), MPS (3–4)

dātu s. *ṭātu* and *diʾ(a)tu*

****datû** "family member"

The only ref. cit. AHw 166a is to be read *it-tu-ú-a-a* YOS 10, 46 v 11 "my neighbors" (s. AHw 407 *itû* B 1). Likewise, read *it-te-e ša bīt abīni* AbB 3, 52: 22 "the neighbors of our father's house" (pace Frankena, ib. and 1978, 170: *da-te-e* "Angehörige"), as already suggested by Wilcke 1971, 555. JW

daʾummatu, + *duʾummatu*, + *daʾummu*(?) "gloom, darkness"

1. OB *ana mātim šapil*[*tim*] *du-ḫu-umma-tum iš*[*šakkan*] ARM 26/1, 433 no. 205: 5 "darkness is pl[aced] over the lowland".

2. OB [*da*?-*u*]*m-mu-um ina* [*libbi*]*ya iššakinma* ARM 26/2, 104 no. 333: 6 "darkness(?) has been placed in my heart", s. Charpin ib. p. 106 n. b. JW

+ **da-wa-da-ar-ša** "a designation of persons"; foreign word(?)

OB Chogha Gavaneh 4 $^{⌜lú⌝.m[eš]}$⌜*da-wa*⌝-*da-ar-ša* JCS 59 p. 57 ChG 23: 16 (in list of persons). JW

dawû, *damû* "to jerk"

D OB lit. *aklāk du-wa-ku* CUSAS 10, 9: 15 "I am consumed, convulsed".

dāwû *s. dāʾiṣu*

dayyāltu "(hunting) foray, excursion"

1. NA *midbar* ... *ana da-a-la-t*[*ú adanniš*] *ṭābma* SAA 1, 13: 17 "the steppe is [very] good for hunting expeditions".

2. NA *da-a-la-*[*te*] SAA 10, 51: 15 (said of Venus, in broken context).

dayyālu "scout, inspector"

Also as lw. in Aram. (Abraham/Sokoloff 2011, 29. JW

dayyāntu, MB also *diyyāntu* "female judge"

1. MB PNf: ^{f}*Da-a-a-an-du* CUSAS 30, 372: 17; s. also Hölscher 1996, 58f.

2. MB PNf: ^{f}*Di-ia-an-d*/*tum* BE 15, 190 iii 18; PN ^{f}*Di-ia-an-di-i-na*-UNUG^{ki} BE 15, 188 'iv' 8 (Sommerfeld 1985, 9; s. Hölscher 1996, 58f. for further ref.).

3. SB [*d*]*i-ia-na-tu*$_4$ *lišmû amātūya* Stadhouders/Panayotov 2018, 630: 17, s. their comm. ib. 650ff. Note that the transl. proposed there ("may my arguments be heard as judges") is not reconcilable with the verbal form.

JW (2–3), MPS (1)

dayyānu, MB also *diyyānu* "judge"

1. OA (this memorandum is a copy) *tuppim ḫarmim ša kunuk da-a-né* AKT 7A, 21: 28 "of the enclosed tablet with the judges' seal".

2. OB $^{⌜lú⌝}$DI.KU$_5$ *šarrim* Haradum 2, 23: 4 "the royal judge (and the city elders)" (s. CAD D 29 d2'b'); s. also AbB 5, 250 r. 4. For further OB ref. s. Dombradi 1996, vol. 2, 5–17.

3. MB *di-ia-a-nu ša kīma* DN *iberru kīnam* AfO 32 p. 2: 12 "the judge who, like DN, chooses the righteous". JW

dekû "to raise, shift"

G 1. OAkk. *id-ké-aś-śu-nu-ma* RIME 2, 108 iii 21 "(PN) rallied them".
2. OB *iniʾātim lā te-de-ki* AbB 3, 31: 10 "don't bring out the plough-oxen (before I arrive)".
3. OB *eqlam l*[*i*]-*i*[*d*]-*ke-e* AbB 9, 251: 7 "he shall 'raise' the field" (Stol ib. translates "*weed* the field").
4. OB *ana napišti de-ka-ku* AbB 8, 82: 21 "I am brought to life" (uncert. context).

5. OB *ibaššī mummum ša de-ke-e-em lā īšû* FM 9, 114 no. 18 r. 6 "is there (such a thing as) a (performer of the) conservatory who has no commissions?"

6. OB lit. "to wake (s.o.) up":

a) *šumma aṣṣalal* ⌜*di*⌝*-ke-en-ni att*[*i*] CUSAS 10, 12: 2 "if I fall asleep, wake me up!"

b) *ina ereš nadâku di-ke-an-ni* AbB 12, 99: 14 "raise me up from the bed on which I am lying!"

c) *adī ummašu i-de-ku-ú-šu ay iggeltī* OECT 11, 2: 27 "until his mother rouses him, may he not awaken!"; cf. ZA 71, 62: 5, 6, 8.

7. Said of winds: SB DN *ana Ḫumbaba id-kaš-šum-ma meḫê rabûtu* Gilg. SB V 137 "DN roused against Ḫumbaba the great storms".

8. SB *ummānāt* DN *id-de-ki ana kullat dadmē malkī id-de-ki ša kal kibrāte* RINAP 4, 76: 10–11 "he mustered the workmen of DN for all of the settlements (and) mustered the rulers of all (four) quarters".

9. SB ^{giš}MA.NU *ta-da-ke-šú-nu-ti* KAL 2, 13 iv 9 "you move them (= figurines) around (in a pot) with an *ēru*-stick", s. Heeßel ib. p. 46; *nakra* ⌜*a-da*⌝*-*[*ki/u*] ib. 15 "I lift up the enemy", cf. *a-da-ku* KAL 2, 14 r. 10.

10. LB *majjāri i-de-ek-ke u izaqqap* BM 59590: 5 (Jursa 1995, 141) "he will plough the field and sow it", s. ib. 140f.; van Driel 1990, 238f. For further N/LB ref. s. Tarasewicz 2018, 123f.

D 1. OB PN *du-uk-ki-i-šu-ma eqlam mê lirattibū* AbB 10, 170: 14 "mobilize (fem.) PN so that they may moisten the field (in preparation for ploughing)".

2. OB *awīlam ú-de-ek-ki-ma tuppi ... ittalkam* AbB 12, 3: 5 "I notified the gentleman and (consequently) the document arrived".

Š OB *ina ṭūbātimma eqlam šuʾāti lā epēšam* PN *šu-ud-ki* AbB 3, 2: 42 "kindly keep PN from working this field" (pace AHw 708: *šu-ud-di*, s. Frankena 1978, 11f.); cf. *šu-ud-ki-*[*i*] AbB 2, 157: 10.

+ **Štn** OB lit. *mu-uš-te-ed-gi apluḫtim* JRAS Cent. Suppl. pl. 6 i 11 "he who constantly foments armor-bearing" (Papulegara), s. Streck/Wasserman 2008, 346f. (/*dk*/ > /*dg*/).

N 1. OB *taḫḫī ummātim id-de-ku-ú* AbB 3, 51: 18 "the replacements for the troops were summoned up".

2. LB *ša* PN *ultu* GN *id-da-ak-ka-am-ma kinaltu ša Esagila ina libbi itti* DN *u* DN_2 *ana* GN_2 *ūridū* YOS 3, 86: 7 "the ship of PN will be chartered from GN, and the staff of Esagila, together with DN and DN_2, may travel in it to GN_2"; pace CAD D 124b, not *dekû* G.

EZ (G), JW (G, D, Š, Štn, N), MPS (G, N)

dēkû "summoner (for taxes and corvée work); night-watchman"

1. MB *bēlī de-ka-a lišpuramma lidkēšunūtima lirdûma* JCS 19, p. 97ff.: 19 "my lord shall send the summoner and he shall raise them and they shall follow", s. Sassmannshausen 2001, 39.

2. MB *ana de-ki-i gugalli u šākin ṭēmi* PBS I/2, 20: 40 "for the summoner, the irrigation controller, and the commander", s. Sassmannshausen 2001, 38f.

3. "night-watchman" (hith. only lex., s. AHw 167): SB *de-ki-i ḫāʾiṭī šuknā* UAVA 12/2, 341 (Bab 36605): 4 "post night-watchmen (and) watchmen".

4. For *d.*s in the N/LB period, s. Stolper 1988, 135; Beaulieu 2005, 57f. JW

dēpu II "a thrusting weapon?"

1. For further LB ref. and disc., s. Beaulieu 2003, 380f.

2. CAD Ṭ *ṭēpu* "(a weapon)" and *ṭīpu* "attachment; addition" mng. 2 (a feature of the exta) belong to *dēpu* II.

derû, *darû* "to intercalate (a month or year)"

G NA [*ina muḫḫe*] *da-re-e* [*ša*] *šatte* [*ša šar*]*ru iqbûni* [*m*]*ā Elūl nid-ri* SAA 10, 253: 15–18 "[concerning] the intercalation [of] the year [about which the] king said: 'Let us add an intercalary Elūl'".

dešû "to be abundant"

D 1. OB lit. *attama mu-de-ši*!(text: *ti*)-*i-ma* CUSAS 10, 9: 19 "you are the one makes me flourish"; *mu-de-*{UD}*-ši*! *eqlim* ib. 13: 8 "who makes the field flourish".

2. SB *šeʾam lu-du-uš-šu* KAL 9, 7: 12 "may they (the rains) let grain flourish".

dēšû "abundant, flourishing"

1. OB lit. *wāšib ḫuršāni mēteqi de-šu-tim* OECT 11, 1: 3 "(Amurru) who dwells in the mountains, the abundant passages".

2. Borger 1962, 252: OB *nišī de-ša-*[*a-ti*] MDP 28, 12: 6 "the abundant people". EZ (2), JW (1)

diʾadānu s. *dadānu*

+ **diʾagiram** "royal regulation"; LB, Gk. lw.

LB *libbū ša šaṭṭār ina di-ʾ-gi-ra-am* van der Spek 1995, 229: 34, 38 "according to the writing in the *d.*" From Gk. < διάγραμμα, s. ib. 234.

NR/JW/MPS

dīʾānu "to judge"

G 1. OAkk. PN *u* PN_2 *i-dè-na-ma* BIN 8, 121: 3 "PN and PN_2 went to court", s. Edzard 1982, 29.

2. OB *aššum pūḫat bītim* ... *ša i-di-nu-ni-a-ši-im-ma kanīk šarrim lā innadnu* AbB 11, 62: 14 "concerning the substitute for the house … which they have adjudicated for us, but (for which) the tablet of the king has not been given", s. Stol ib. p. 37 n. a.

3. SB (you lift a vessel with clay figurines) *maḫar* DN *ta-dan*[*an*]*-šú-nu-te* KAL 2, 44 i' 10' "you convict them before DN" (Mayer 2016, 201).

4. NA 2 *summāti zikar u sinniš ina maḫar* DN *t*[*a*]*-da-an-ši-na-tú* SAA 8, 231: 4 "you convict two doves, male and female, before DN", cf. Livingstone 2000, 382f.

D 1. OB *ūmišam dīnātim ittīya tu-da-a-*[*an-ma*] AbB 11, 69 r. 3 "you have lawsuits with me every day".

2. OB PN *Ú-da-an-iš*$_8$*-tár* VS 18, 73: 1 (cit. AbB 11 p. 41 n. a); for DN-*mu-di-na-at* TIM 7, 92: 2 (cit. AbB 11 ib.), a reading *mu-ki-na-at* may be preferable (Durand 2005).

3. OB *mu-di-in-šu-nu ul ibbašī* FM 6, 89 no. 4: 27 "no judge(?) of theirs has occurred", s. Lafont ib. p. 97; Durand 2005.

4. Del ref. RÉS 1937 106 cit. CAD D 103 (now ARM 26/2, 161 no. 361: 20), read *ú-ki-in* (Durand 2005).

N OB *dīnam kīma dīnim ša inanna ina* GN *id-di-in-nu šūḫissunūti* AbB 13, 10: 10 "deliver a verdict in accordance with the legal practice that is currently applied in GN". JW (G, D), MPS (D)

dīʾāšu "to thresh"

G 1. OB *šeʾam šuʾāti di-i-iš zurūma* AbB 7, 170: 12 "thresh and winnow this barley!"; cf. *di-iš* AbB 3, 79: 35.
2. OB *aššum ... arḫiš di-a-ši-im* AbB 7, 171: 8 "concerning the quick threshing".
3. OB *ina di-a-ši-im qātam ninassaḫ* AbB 3, 54: 12 "we will be done with the threshing (by the 7th of Simānu)"; *ni-di-is-sú* ib. 15.
4. OB *ana de-ši-im* FM 2, 35 M.11030: 34 "for threshing", cf. *i-de-eš-šu* ib. 39; cf. ARM 14, 48 pass.
5. OB *ša kimissu ina maškanim da-ši-im alpum imḫaṣu* CUSAS 29, 23: 9 "(PN), whose lower leg an ox has hurt while (he was) threshing on the threshing floor".

D 1. OB *nu-da-aš* ARM 27, 37: 45 "we will thresh".
2. OB *aššum ... šê ēkallim du-úš-ši-im* ARM 27, 39: 15 "as to the threshing of the grain of the palace".
3. OB *ana maškanī ēkallim du-úš-ši-im* ARM 27, 94: 16; cf. 92 r. 2 "in order to thresh the (grain of) the threshing floors of the palace".

JW (G), MPS (G, D)

diʾ(a)tu, *daʾ(a)tu* "knowledge, information"; + SB

1. OB only in *d. šâlu* "to enquire after":
a) *diʾatu*: *di-a-ti-m[a?] ul išallū* AbB 10, 55: 19 "they never enquire after (me)". *di-a-at* AbB 5, 10: 7.
b) *diʾtu*: *di-iḫ-tam* AbB 5, 34: 3. *di-iḫ-ti* AbB 3, 88: 22
c) *daʾatu*: *da-a-ta-ma* AbB 12, 150: 6. *da-ḫa-at-ki* ARM 10, 46 r. 9; *da-ḫa-as-sú* ARM 10, 156: 18. *da-ḫa-ti* FM 2, 101 no. 60: 11', FM 7, 10 no. 2: 18 and pass.
d) *daʾtu*: *da-aḫ-ti-ma* AbB 7, 151: 8. *da-aḫ-ti* AbB 5, 160 r. 6. *dá-aḫ-ti* ARM 26/2, 59 no. 304: 43.
2. SB *šarru ana šarri da-ʾ-te-šú lā ipaššarū* KAL 5, 19 r. 43 "a king will not release information to a(nother) king".

JW (1, 2), MPS (1)

dibbatu "gossip, complaint"

1. OB *aššum amtim* PNf *di-ib-ba-tum māttum īlīʾamma* AbB 3, 2: 6 "there have been many complaints on account of the slave-girl PNf", s. Frankena 1978, 7.

2. In AbB 14, 158: 6 (cit. CAD D 131 as TCL 18, 80) *d.* is used synonymously with *dababābu* (ll. 12, 17, s. Veenhof 2005, 206). S. also *dibbu* 1.

JW

dibbu "words, utterance"

1. OB fem. pl. *dibbātu* (CAD D 131 s.v. *dibbātu* "agreement", AHw 168b s.v. *dibbu*):
a) *aššum di-ib-ba-tum lā šaknā* AbB 10, 148: 27 "because there has been no discussion".
b) OB *aššum di-ib-ba-at* ^{pa5}*namkarim* AbB 13, 64: 20 "concerning the discussion about the irrigation canal"; s. also AbB 13, 89: 45.
c) Some or all ref. might belong to the lemma *dibbatu* (Frankena 1978, 7).

2. OB masc. pl.:
a) *[kī]ʾam di-bu-šu-nu [umma]mi* FM 7, 20 no. 6: 14 "their words were as follows".
b) OB *ina di-bi-šu-nu* ARM 26/2, 259 no. 404: 13 "in their discussion", s. ib. p. 262 n. d.

3. NA *kīma ištēn ina libbišunu akī dibbi lammadūti ina libbi* GN *ētarbu* SAA 15, 199 r. 3 "as soon as one of them has entered GN by studied words (i.e. password?)", s. Fuchs ib.

4. Wr. NA *di-i-bi* StAT 1, 51: 25.
JW (1–3), MPS (4)

dibdibbu, + *diddibbu*? "water clock, clepsydra"; + NA

1. NA ^{giš}*di-di-⸢ib?-bu?⸣* StAT 2, 315: 9 in uncl. context. Note perhaps *bēt ša manê* "abacus" ib. r.1. If the reading is correct, lex. ^{giš}*dib.dib* is prob. *dibdibbu*/ *diddibbu* and not *ṣiṣṣippu* (AHw 1106).

2. Gen. disc. s. Brown/Fermor/Walker 1999/2000, 132ff. JW (2), MPS (1)

dibiru "calamity"; + Emar

SB (if the sun stands in the afternoon) *di*!*-bi-ri immar* Emar 6/4, 611: 134 "it will experience calamity"; cf. *mātu di-bi-r*[*a*...] Emar 610: 61; sim. 72, 193, 645: 3. Pace Pentiuc 2001, 44f., the ref. from Babylonia (AHw 168, CAD D 134f.) argue against a loan from NWSem., and the consistent spellings with a single *b* do not favor a form /dibbīr/. JW/MPS/NR

dibšu s. *dišpu*

didabû "scribal apprentice, pupil"

NA ⸢^{lú}⸣*di-da-b*[*i*] (broken context) SAA 13, 54: 2.

****diddigu** "chaff(?)"

Von Soden 1960, 489 ad CAD D 135: read ^{m}*Ḫa-*<*aš*>*-mar-gal-di id-di-in*! BE 14, 114a: 7. EZ/MPS

dīdu, *dādu* "female (under)garment"; + Emar

1. OB lit. *di-id kabatti* Ištar Louvre i 51 "undergarment of the mid-body".

2. MB Emar *mārat* PNf *ša lā išâmu di-i-di-i talaqqī* Emar 6/3, 33: 27 "the daughter of PNf will take the *d.*-garments without buying them", s. Durand 2009, 33.

3. SB [*ina naḫlapti na*]*kāsi du*[*dittu šeb*]*ēru u da-di batāqu* MIN [MIN] A 185: 50 (Frankena 1960, 174, nambur-bi) [for? ri]pping [a cloak, brea]king a p[in] or cutting off *d.*-garments ditto, [ditto] s. Simons 2017, 104.

4. For *d.* in CUSAS 10, 7: 6 s. Wasserman 2011 (s. *quddu*).
JW (1, 4), NR (2), FJMS (3)

diglu "vision, view; wish"

1. OB *šumma di-gi-il-ki* Iraq 38 p. 57: 12 "if it is your wish"; cf. AbB 6, 194: 13; AbB 13, 120: 14.

2. SB [*di*]*-ig-lu-ki littaṭṭalū kalu kibr*[*āti*] Lamaštu FsB 22 (Farber 2014, 267) "may your [gl]ances view the whole unive[rse]!" JW

diḫḫu s. *ziḫḫu*

diḫmennu s. *diqmēnu*

\+ **diʾiqetēsu** "controller, financial officer"; LB, Gk. lw.

LB *šipištu ša* ^{m}*di-ʾi-qé-te-e-su* BRM 2, 31: 8 "the legal document of the *d.*"; <διοικητής, s. McEwan 1988, 416.
NR

****dikkuldû** (CAD D 137a)

Borger 2008, 442: read DI NUMUN DI-*šu-ma* BBSt. 8 iv 11 and *di-in* NUMUN DI-*šu-ma* I R 70 iii 16.
MPS/NR

dikme/innu s. *diqmēnu*

dikmu s. *ṭikmēnu*

dikšu "bulge, swelling, wound "

1. OB *biltum ana gušūrīšu* ⌜*ikbitma*⌝ *gušūrūšu ittešberū u di-ik-ši aškunšum* ARM 27, 10: 18 "the load was too heavy for its (= the roof's) beams and its beams broke. Therefore, I installed 'bulges' (i.e. braces to stabilize the beam)".

2. SB *ana šarri di-ik-šu* MDP 57, 86 no. 4: 14 "the king will (suffer from) a wound", cf. CAD D 138 *d.* 3'.

3. SB *di-ik-šú* : *di-ik-ši* : *mur-ṣi* CT 41, 42: 37 (comm.) "wound = sickness".

4. On *d.* in math. texts mng. "outward/ inward extension (by a given fraction)" s. Friberg 1987–90, 564; Friberg/Hunger/al-Rawi 1990, 488ff. JW

diktu, *tiktu* "a type of flour"

1. Pace CAD D s.v. *diktu* ("a dairy product"), *d.* denotes a type of flour (s. AHw s.v. *t/diktu*(*m*); CAD T 404 disc. s.v. *tīktu*).

2. OB n SÌLA *di-ik-ta* PN *ublam* AbB 9, 165 "PN brought me n liters of *d.*"

3. OB *ti-ik-tum* FM 12, p. 216 M.9994: 2, 192 M.10106: 2, 158 M.10579: 2, 203 M.11134: 2, 144 S.79a, 120: 2; ARM 12, 350: 4, 385: 4, 393: 6; ARM 11, 2: 2, 290: 12; ARM 9, 98 v 28.

4. OB *aššum qēm dumqim u ti-ik-tim* ARM 10, 20: 5, 9 "concerning the high quality flour and the *t.*" JW

dīktu "fighting, slaughter"

1. OB *di-ik-ta-ni ša di-ka-nu linūḫma* FM 1, 83 A.3935+M.7557: 69 "the attack we are suffering shall calm down".

2. SB *di-ik-ta rabâ lū addūk* RA 76, 145 r. 37 "I truly inflicted a great massacre!" JW (1), NR (2)

dīku I "killed; crushed"; + OB, + MA

1. OB Said of sheep and cows: *di-ik-ti barbari/nēši* CUSAS 9, 316: 2; 317: 3; 321: 4; 326: 2; 328: 2; 337: 8 "killed by a wolf/lion".

2. OB lit. *di-ka naṭāl* CUSAS 32, 48: 1 "dead of watching" (said of a snake).

3. MA *mārē damqūte di-ku-ú-te* BATSH 4/1, 8: 42, 43 "killed elite (soldiers)".

4. OB said of sesame: *šamaššammū di-ku-tum* ARM 22, 276 ii 6, 14; iv 22. "crushed sesame", among *gurnu* "medium quality" and *sīkūtu* "pounded" sesame.

5. SB [*g*]*i gaz-za* = [*q*]*a-nu-ú de-e-ku* LKA 65: 10 // [*qanû di-*]*i-ku* AuOr. Suppl. 24, 54f.: 8 "cut off reed".

6. SB "crushed (?)" (in a stool diagnosis concerning constipation): *di-i-ki ša ultu durrišu lā uṣṣâ* SpTU 1, 36: 18 "*d.* (that is) what does not flow out of his rectum", s. Wee 2012, 646.

EZ (3), JW (4–6), MPS (1–3)

dīku II "lifting, raising"

1. On the *dīk bīti* ceremony s. Pongratz-Leisten 1994, 65 n. 139 and Maul 2000, 394 n. 58, 402ff. with further ref.

2. In VS 4, 96 (CAD D 140 mng. 1) read *ṭi-pi*, s. *ṭipu*. JW

dikuggallu s. *diqu*(*n*)*gallu*

dikûtu "corvée work"

OB *ḫadâšu* ⌜*u*⌝ *di-ku-sú illak* CT 45, 16 r. 4 "(the adoptive son) will carry out his (adoptive father's) workload (*adû*) and corvée", s. Goddeeris 2002, 342 and Stol 2004, 752ff. with further ref.

JW

+ **dilāru** "a chair"; OB

^{giš}*marḫuše* [*ana*] … 1 ^{giš}GU.ZA *di-la-ri-im* FM 1, 53 A.55: 17 "*m.*-wood [for] … 1 *d.*-chair", cf. Durand 1997, 79. JW

dilḫu "trouble"

OB lit. [*kīm*]*a* ⸢*girīti*⸣ *ina de-el-ḫi-ia* (// Sum.: *a lù-lù-a-ĝu*$_{10}$) *tabār*[*anni*] CT 44, 24 iii 4 "like a moray eel(?) you caught me in my troubled state (Sum.: troubled water)". JW

+ **diliḫtu** "trouble"; + MB

MB Susa *išītu u di-li-iḫ-tu*$_{20}$(DÙ) *ina māti iššakkan* MDP 57, 197 no. 9: 17 "there will be chaos and disturbance in the land". JW

dilpu "night attendance (on a sick person)" (CAD D 142b, hapax)

Von Soden 1960, 489 prefers to read *dīl pê* "watering of chaff", i.e. "nonsense" (s. AHw 170b s.v. *dīlu*). The original reading is probably preferable. Cf. Parpola, who translates "efforts" (SAA 10, 328 r. 7). EZ/JW

+ **dilû**, *dēlu* "the sign AŠ/DILI"; OB, SB

1. OB lex. (proto-Aa) *de-e-lu-um* Gong 2000, 84.

2. SB lex. *di-lu-u/ú* Gong 2000, 103.

3. SB DILI CUSAS 18, 33: 34f., cf. SAD B/P 22 s. v. *baṭṭu*.

dilûtu, *dulûtu* "bucket irrigation, a kind of canal, a water-drawing device"

1. OB *du-lu-ut-ka lū epšet* AbB 3, 65: 3 "(your field shall be in order and) your irrigation shall be carried out".

2. SB GN *ašar nāru lā īšû ina eb*[*li*] *ḫarḫarri kalkaltu mê būrti ina di-lu-ú-ti ṣābēya ušašqī* RINAP 4, 34: 18' "in GN, where there is no river, by means of ropes, chains, (and) sweeps(?) I provided well-water for (my) troops by drawing", s. Bagg 2000, 203f.

3. SB *mannu ikrikka kī pī di-*⸢*lu-ti*⸣ TCS 2, 2: 8 "who has dammed you up like an opening in a *d.*-canal?" (cit. CAD K 199). JW

****dimgallu** (CAD D 143a) s. *šitimgallu*

dimmatu "moaning, wailing"

1. OB lit. ⸢*bītī ana*⸣ *bīt* ⸢*di*⸣*-ma-tim uttēr anāku i-libbišu i-di-ma-tim wašbāku* OBO 278, 357: 10, 11 "he has turned my house into a house of wailing. I dwell in it while wailing", cf. *di-im-ma-tim* ib. 9 and *dim-ma-tim* K.4617: 15 // l. 10 (Guichard ib. p. 364). Cf. *dīmtum*.

2. SB *akal dím-ma-te* (var.: *-ti*) *u bikīti* Lamaštu I 189 (Farber 2014, 90) "food of wailing and weeping"; *de*$_{4}$*-ma-a-ti* Lamaštu Emar 32 (ib. 292). JW

dimtu "tower, fortified wall; district"

1. OAkk. "district": *in dì-*⸢*im-ti*⸣ [GN] CUSAS 27, 152: 5 "in the district of [GN]" cf. MAD 5, 87: 2.

2. "(movable) siege tower":

a) Early OB 10 ^{giš}*dì-ma-ti-*[*im*] … *liblam* AS 22, 9: 12 "(even if the Amorites) bring 10 siege towers".

b) OB *aššum eblī ebīḫī ša di-ma-tim u yāšibim* ARM 14, 45: 5 "concerning the rope for the girdles, for the siege towers, and for the battering ram".

c) OB *ana* ^{giš}*di-im-tim ana mīnim ītenellē* ARM 26/1, 479 no. 238 = ARM 10, 51: 14 "why does he keep going up the tower? (He must guard himself!)"

d) OB ^{giš}*di-ma-a-ti ana* GN *lū šūrudū* Shemshara 1, 7: 15 "let the siege towers be brought downstream to GN".
e) OB *yāšibum u* ^{giš}*[d]i-im-tum nadnūnikkum* ARM 26/1, 426 no. 199: 13 "the battering ram and the tower are given to you".
f) OB ^{giš}*di-im-ta-am uš-zi-iz* ARM 26/2, 298 no. 416: 5; cf. ib. 273 no. 407: 7 (cf. 6) "he had set up the tower".
g) ^{giš}*di-ma-at nakr[im]* ARM 27, 141: 9 "tower of the enemy", cf. ^{giš}*di-im-tim/tam* ib. 141: 5, 7.
h) OB *ana pan nakrim ina pan* ^{giš}*di-ma-tim u eperī wašbū* ARM 27, 142: 8 "they sit opposite the enemy in front of the towers and the earthwork". Cf. ib. 22, 23, 27.
i) OB *mušītamma di-im-ta-šu ipṭurma* ARM 27, 170: 27 "he withdrew his tower at night".
j) OB ^{giš}*di-im-tum* ⸢*šī*⸣ *ša ištū* GN *nilqûšu šaknat* ARM 28, 18: 6 "the tower that we took from GN is set up".
k) OB [^{giš}*di-im-t]am šâti* PN … *u akkâšum ina[ddi]nakkunūši ana* GN *[uš]erressim ištū ašrānum akkâšum inaddinakkunūši* ARM 28, 18: 22 "that tower PN will … and he will give it to you (pl.) for your (sg. masc.) benefit. He will let it descend to GN and from there he will give it to you (pl.) for your (sg. masc.) benefit". For add. Mari ref. s. Kupper 1997, 127ff.

3. Residential tower: OB *di-im-tam ša* PN … *ana wašāb* PN_2 *uštassiqū* ARM 27, 164: 6 "they put in order the tower of PN as residence for PN_2".

4. OB PNf *utūtu ša di-im-tim* ARM 9, 27 iv 26 "PNf, female gatekeeper of the tower" (in personnel list).

5. On the various mngs. of *d.* in Nuzi s. Koliński 2001 with prev. lit.

6. Cf. Soqotri *díme* "sheep pen", Mehri *dēmēt* "warehouse", Arab. (Yemen) *daymah* "cottage, small house" and sim. (Naumkin et al. 2016, 65). If these words are indeed cognates they suggest long *ī*: *dīmtu*. JW (1, 2, 4–6), MPS (2, 3)

dīmtu, + OA *dimʾu*, + OB lit. *dīmatu* "tear"; + OA

1. OA *[in]a dí-im-a-té-š[a] tasarraq bētam* CCT 5, 50e: 3 "with her tears she sprinkles the house" (Kouwenberg/Fincke 2012/13).

2. OA *dí-im-ú-tum u bikītum* kt 97/k 183: 6 "tears and mourning" quoted in Çayır 2015, 97 n. 4.

3. OA *dí-im-a-am* Prag 735: 22 s. *dummû* D.

4. Early OB *dì-ma-ti-a šuqqil* AS 22, 21: 45 "stop my tears".

5. OB *di-im-ti u di-ma-ti elīki* AbB 5, 160 r. 7 "my tears and wailing are on your account".

6. OB lit. *kīma ṣirpim iṣarrip di-ma-ti-[iš/ša]* UET 6/2, 395 r. 23 "she became red like dyed wool [through (her)] tears" (SEAL), diff. Lambert 1990, 293: "(he went…,) shedding tears like red dyed wool".

7. OB lit. *di-ma-tu-ša i-la-ka ṣa-ar-p[i-iš]* UET 6/2, 396: 13 "her tears were flowing bitterly"; *di-ma-tu-uš*! *ḫuṭṭupat* ib. 23 "her tear was shed".

8. Sg. *dīmatu*: OB lit. <*ina*> *bu-ur-mi-*⸢*ni*⸣*-ia di-ma-tum izannun* CunMon. 8, 110: 18 "a tear rains out of the iris of my eye".

9. SB *di-in-di indalâ īnāšu* SAA 3, 50: 28 "his eyes filled with tears".

10. NA 3 *ūmē pan* DN *di-at pani bikīʾā* Dornauer 2014, 5: 5 "cry tears of the face in front of DN for three days!"

11. LB *mūši u kal ūmu ina di-in-du u upāṭu ašbāku* AOAT 414/1 198: 15 "day and night I sit in tears and snot".

JW (4–5, 10–11), MPS (9), NJCK (1–3)

dinānu, + NB *di'ānu*, + NA *du'ānu*? "substitution, substitute"

1. For OA, s. *andu/inānu*.

2. OB *a-di-na-an mātišu u aḫḫīšu ittalak* ARM 28, 14: 26 "he will have gone as a substitute for his land and his brothers".

3. OB *ana di-na-ni-ka lū nadnū* AbB 3, 18: 19 "they shall be given as your substitute".

4. MA in letter opening formulas: *ultaka''in ana di-na-an bēliya attalak* BATSH 4/1, 2: 3 and ib. pass. "I (hereby) prostrate myself, I dedicate myself to my lord (lit. 'act as my lord's substitute')", s. ib. p. 56 and Streck 1997a, 271f.

5. NA *ša* n *šiqil du-a-ni i-ta-ni ša* n *kaspam du-a-ni ittannū* TCL 9, 62: 15, 17 "(witnesses) that n shekels were given (as) substitute(?) (and) that n silver was given (as) substitute(?)", s. Deller apud Fales/Jakob-Rost 1991, 135.

6. *ana d.* "in so.'s interest"

a) NB *ana di-a-nu bēliya lullik* OIP 114, 44: 2; 60: 2 "let me go in the interest of my lord".

b) LB ⌜*ad*⌝*-da-ni-ki mamma mimmašu ina panika lā inaššû* AOAT 414/1, 56: 6 "in your interest, no-one shall receive any of his property in your presence". Cf. ib. 212: 3.

JW (3–5, 6), MPS (2, 6), NJCK (1)

+ **dīniš** "justly, lawfully"; NA

SB *dummuqiš di-niš ša ina nikilti lē'ûtišu* [...] SAAB 8, 4: 2 "favorably, justly". JW

dinnû(tu) "bed"

SB *d*[*i*]*-in-nu-ut lalêki lū dakkan* ... Gilg. MB Ur 22 "may the bed of your delight be a bench of ...". Cf. George 2003, 303.

dīnu, + *dinnu* "legal decision; lawsuit, trial; legal practise"

1. OB lit. pl. *di-né-tim* CUSAS 18 p. 298: 46.

2. OB s. extensively Dombradi 1996, 2ff., 312ff. with disc. and ref.

3. OB *bēl di-ni-ša* AbB 8, 140: 19 "her legal adversary".

4. OB (PNN) *ina di-in-ni-i*[*a*] *izzizzū-ma u arnam ul īšû* MARI 3, 178 A.2518: 6 "PNN stood in my trial and were (declared) free of guilt".

5. On OB *d. šūḫuzu* "to deliver the verdict", i.e. to inform the parties about the judgement, s. Wilcke 1987, 101 n. 100.

6. NB *ašar di-nu īdû u lā di-nu idabbubū* OIP 114, 23: 9 "where one knows the law and one litigates without due process", cf. NA *ina lā dēnišu dabābu* (Cole ib. p. 82, cf. CAD D 155a).

7. NA *de-e-nu uzakkī* SAAS 5, 25: 6 "he has cleared the dispute". On the NA *dēnu*-texts s. Jas 1996.

8. For OA s. also *dīttu*. S. also *dīniš*.

MPS (1), JW (2–8)

dipāru "torch; a disease"

1. OB with *našû*, refering to military activity:

a) *di-pa-ar-šu inaššī* AbB 8, 23: 25 "he will raise his torch (and he has ordered provisions for his troops)".

b) *ina qablit mātim di-pa-ra-am našêta* MARI 7, 176 A.3206: 8 "you are raising the torch in the middle of the land", cf. ib. 11, 20.

2. OB lit. *šumšu kīma di-pa-ar muštʾāti im*⌜*mar*⌝ Iraq 78, 243: 2 "he looks at his offspring like a torch in the night".

3. OB lit. *liblī di-pa-ar zibbatišu* CUSAS 32, 49: 11 "let the torch of its tail be extinguished".

4. With determinative GI "cane, reed": OB ^{gi}*di-pa-ri-im* ARM 26/2, 85 no. 320: 8.

5. SB among diseases: ÉN *kirigiš di-pa-ri epqēnu kissatu* (var.: [*di*]-⌜*pár*⌝) Muššuʾu VIII/k 137; *di-pa-ar* (var. *di-pár*) ib. 147, 150.

6. Shortened PN: MB ^{m}*Di-pa-ru* CUSAS 30, 256: 24. For sentence names with *d.* s. AHw 172 *d.* 2.

7. Etym.: cf. Hebr. *lappîd* "torch" (Zimmern 1917, 36; Segert 1962; Salonen 1965, 139)?

JW (1–2, 5), MPS (3–4, 6–7)

diprānu s *daprānu*

dippu, *dibbu*, pl. *dippātu* "board; a kind of wooden door"

1. OB *aššum paššūrim ... di-ip-pa-t*[*u-šu*] *lū elammakkum u kablātūšu lū kamiššuru*[*m*] FM 8, 46 no. 6: 9 "about the table … (you wrote:) its top shall be *e.*-wood, its legs shall be pear wood", s. Durand ib. p. 48.

2. Mayer 2016, 202: OB 1 KA.GIŠ.KARÁ *di-pa-šu* […] ARM 22, 223 i *pass*. "1 *k.*-table, its top is […]".

3. OB lit. *qê di-ba-a-*⌜*šu*⌝ CUSAS 10, 1: 28 "its twin panels were copper".

JW (1–2), MPS (3)

diqāru "large bowl, tureen"

1. Plene *ā*: Lex. *útul* = *di-qa-a-rum* Emar 6/4, 537: 280 (Sa).

2. Early OB *dì-qá-ri ša ušēbilam adī matī ibaššī* AS 22, 12: 46 "how long will my bowl, that I sent, remain (there)?"

3. OB 1 *pīḫum di-qá-ru-ú ana* PN ARM 11, 12: 1 "1 beer-jar, a bowl, for PN"

4. MB *di-qa-ra-tum ša ana*! *lâši u maṣḫati* CUSAS 30, 342: 12 "bowls for(!) kneading and for *m.* flour".

5. On *šaman diqārātim* (*d.*-oil) s. Joannès 1993, 260f. and 266 with Mari ref.; s. also Sallaberger 1996, 111; Gaspa 2007, 150ff.

JW (2–3, 5) MPS (1, 4)

diqdiqqu, *duqduqqu* "wren"

1. SB *diq-diq-qu ina muḫḫi pēri kī uš*[*ibu*] *umma talīm idka an-a-a-ma ina šiqi mê erā*[*qma*?] *pēru ana diq-diq-qi ip*[*pal*] *kī tušibu ul īdēma kalāka mī*[*nu*] *kī tatbû ul īdē*[*ma*] BWL 216–218: 50–54 "when a wren sat on an elephant, he said: 'Brother, did I turn back (*nêʾu*/*naʾāʾu*) your side? I shall go [off] to the watering place.' The elephant answered the wren: 'I did not notice when you sat down. Wh[at] is all of you? I [also] will not notice when you have risen.'"

2. SB **a)** [$^{muš]en}$*du-uq-du-*⌜*uq*⌝ // *di-iq-di*!*-qu ina muḫḫi nīnî iltakan*! *pelâšu* Jiménez 2017, 334: 2 "a wren laid its egg on top of a *n.* plant".
b) ^{mušen}*du-uq-*⌜*du-uq*⌝ *akû lapnu* ib. 338: 38 "the forlorn, poor wren", cf. also ib. 334: 3, 5, 12; 336: 25; 338: 40.

3. OB *al-ti-ri-gu* // *si-bi-di-ga-ar* Jiménez 2017, 327 is perhaps corrupt.

4. On *d.* "wren" s. Veldhuis 2004, 217f.; Jiménez 2017, 357–360. On etym. (either *daqqu* "minute" or onomatopoeic) s. Jiménez 2017, 357 n. 822.

JW (4), MPS (1–4)

diqmēnu, *diq/ḫme/innu*, + *diq(i)mmu* "ashes"; + OA, + OB

1. Lex. *te-e* = NE = *di-qí-mu-um* CUSAS 12 p. 13 PAS 27 iv 49 (Ea).

2. Lex. *de-e* = NE = *di-qí-mu* CUSAS 12 p. 8: 29 (Ea).

3. OA *dí-iq-ma-am u nūram umallī* AKT 6A, 70: 27 "I have paid in full to the last penny" (lit. "ashes and light").

4. OB lit. *pâša mullīʾā di-iq-ma-a[m]* ZA 71, 63: 16 "fill (pl.) her (the evil eye's) mouth with ashes!"

5. OB lit. *di-qì-ma-am* BAM 4, 393: 24.

6. SB *šumma zība ina muḫ díḫ*(= UM)-*mi!-in innamerma* SpTU 2, 32: 17 "when a vulture is seen on top of ashes(?)".

7. Logogr. DÈ in a Sagig comm.: DÈ : *di-⸢iq⸣-me-ni* AOAT 43, 323: 5.

8. The combined evidence of the refs. 2 and 4 above favors /q/ as second consonant (s. *qí-iš-tum* CUSAS 12 p. 12: 221 (no example for GI, however), *zu-qì-qì-pu-um* BAM 4, 393: 19, but *ta-ša-qí-šu-ma* ib. 7, 18, *ru-qí-im* ib. r. 20). This, on the other hand, precludes /ṭ/ as first consonant (CAD Ṭ 110f.) but points to /d/ (AHw 169).

EZ (4–7), MPS (1–2, 8), NJCK (3)

diqu(n)gallu "chief justice"

Lex. *[di-ku₅]-gal* = *di-qu-gal-lu* Emar 6/4, 542: 20 (Ḫḫ).

+ **dirku?** s. *terku* 1c.

+ **dirištu** "downtrodden, pushed over"; SB

Mayer 2016, 202: *di-riš-ti uggūkka teleʾʾi kâša* AfO 19, 55: 9 "you can help the (one) downtrodden in your anger". Cf. *darāsu, dirsu.* JW

dirratu "lash, halter"

SB *nigkalagû qerdu* [gada]*dir-rat lūbaru sāmu* SpTU 4, 128: 28 "(one) *n.*-drum, plucked wool, a linen lash, a red garment", cf. ib. p. 27. JW

dirsu "pushing"; + SB

ina sīḫi siḫpi dir-si MesCiv. 13, 1: 49 "by disturbing, overturning, pushing". JW

dīṣtu s. *dāṣtu*

+ **dīšānu I** "spring harvest(?)"; MB

ummat tēlīti ālānī di-ša-an BagF 21, 66: 1 "bulk of the harvest from the towns, *d.*" (followed by the date), s. Sassmannshausen 2001, 253. Cf. *dīšu.* JW

+ **dīšānu II** "an official"; NA

nišē ša issīšunu allakanni anāku [lú]*di-ša-nu ina dūrānī [nuše]rrabšunu* SAA 15, 16: 6 "the people with whom I am coming – I and the *d.* [will brin]g them into the fortresses".

dīšāʾu s. *dīšāyu*

dīšāyu "of spring, born in spring"; + OB

1. OB n UDUxMÍ *di-še-tu* ARM 23, 219: 2 "n ewes born in spring"; n UDU A.LUM *di-še-tu* ib.: 4.; n UDU.NÍTA *di-šu-tum* n UDU.U₈ *di-še-tum* ARM 24, 41: 4–5.

2. Del. ref. HSS 15, 331: 4 (cit. AHw 1362a), read 2 *ku-du-u[k]-ti šá-ar-tu₄* (coll. Wilhelm 1985, 60). JW

diš/ziptuḫḫu "sweet beer"; + OB

1. OB *di!-zi-ip-tu-uḫ-ḫi-im* ARM 21, 106: 3, s. *ballukku*; *di-zi-ip-tu-ḫi* FM 3, 235 no. 64: 2, ib. 245 no. 95: 5

2. OB *šikāram sāmam di*!*-zi-<ip>-tu-*⸢*uḫ*⸣*-ḫa u šikāram* CUSAS 36, 95: 13 "brown ale, sweet ale and ale".

dišpu, + *dipšu* "honey, (date) syrup"

1. OB LÀL *ana inbī* ARM 12, 202: 1 "(6 *karpatu*-pots of) honey for (preserving?) fruit". For *d.* in OB recipes s. ARM 9–12 *pass.*

2. MA note the rare syll. spelling *di-iš-pu*^{m}[$^{\text{eš?}}$] MARV 6, 28: 2.

3. LB 1/2 SILÀ *di-ip-šú* AfO 38/9, 81 (BM 74504): 14, with metathesis (also found in Arab. and Hebr., Macginnis ib. p. 82).

4. LB *di-iš-pi u karāni* AOAT 414/1, 73: 5 "honey and wine".

5. On the mng. "syrup", esp. in Southern Mesopotamia, s. Volk 1999, 283ff.

JW (1–3, 5), MPS (4)

dīšu, *dišʾu*, *dašʾu* "spring"; + fem. pl. *dīšātu* "grass"

1. OA *ana da-áš-e išaqqal* AKT 8, 258: 36 "he will pay until spring"; further ref. s. AKT 10 p. 135.

2. OA *ina da-áš-e-šu kutānē nišâmma* AKT 9A, 3 r. 15 "in spring we will buy *k.*-textiles"; cf. *ana da-áš-i-šu* AKT 6A, 157: 31.

3. OB *ina d*[*i-š*]*i-im ūlū ḫaraptim gerram šâtu illakū* ARM 26/1, 113 no. 14: 19 "they go that route in spring or else in (early) summer" (cf. Streck 2009–2011, 597 § 2).

4. OB *ana pan di-ši-im* ARM 28, 83 r. 4 "(come) before spring!"

5. OB *kīma ša ūm di-ši-*[*im*] *Adad rigmātīšu* [*iddī*] ARM 23, 99 no. 102: 6 "Adad sounded his voice just like (on) a spring day".

6. OB (it is cold, therefore the sheep cannot be transported.) *ina di-ši-im anaddinakkim* ARM 10, 48: 13 "I will give them to you in spring"; cf. *inanna anūmma di-šu-um* ib. 15 "now it is spring."

7. Pl. *dīšātu* "grass":

a) SB *ṣērū di-ša-ta munamī malīʾū* SEM 117 iii 18 (Schwemer 2001, 169) "the steppes are full of grass, (full) of abundance".

b) SB *ē tašām alpa* [*š*]*a* ⸢*di-ša-ti*⸣ // *dì-i-ša-a-ti* Šūpê-amēli 96 "do not buy an ox (fed) with grass!"

JW (1–2, 5–7), MPS (3–4, 7)

ditalliš "into ashes"

SB *di*!*-tal-li-iš*! SpTU 4, 141: 11.

ditānu "wisent(?); a fish"

1. Lex. denoting a fish: *ku*$_6$*-saḫ*$_4$ = *ku-sa-aḫ* = … = ⸢*di-ta*⸣*-*[*nu*] MSL 15, fig. 3–4 (IM 124475) 23 (LB Diri).

2. Perhaps var. of *tišānu*, s. esp. SAD *tišānu* 1. JW

dīttu "lawsuit, trial"; OA

1. *i-dí-tí-im lašʾalka* Balkan 1992, 33 (kt c/k 581): 35, 36 "let me interrogate you in court".

2. PN *a-na dí-tim*! *išeʾʾēšunu* Larsen/Møller 1991 no. 2: 16 "he will sue them in court".

3. *ina dí-tim lā tušaʾʾalanni* AKT 6A, 264: 56 "do not question me in court!"; s. also ib. 268: 11 and pass. JW/NJCK

diʾu I "a disease affecting the head"

1. NA *takpertu* Á.SÀG.GIG.GA$^{di\text{-}ʾu}$ $^{marṣūtu.\text{meš}}$ KAR 44: 8 (incipit), s. Geller 2000, 235. Cf. *di-ḫu* : *šibṭa* (var.: *di-iʾ šibṭi*) ib. 20.

2. Disc. s. Scurlock/Andersen, 2005, 59ff.; Stol 2007a, 15ff. S. also *diʾû*.

JW

diʾu II "(deity's) throne-platform"

After Röllig 1996, *diʾu* "platform" is to be separated from *tuʾu* "room, cella" (cf. already the disc. in CAD D 167).

JW

+ **diʾu III**, *dû* (*duʾu*) "wattle-and-daub screen(?)"; Ur III

1. Ur III *dì-um* NATN 620 r. 2; MCS 7, 14: 2; AUCT 2, 343: 6. For further ref., s. Heimpel 2009, 177–179.

2. Ur III Garšana n GÉME *du-ú-um* AK CUSAS 3, 113: 11, 15 "n workwomen having made a *d.* (in construction of the foundation terrace of the brewery-kitchen-mill complex)", also in CUSAS 3, 115 and 121; "(for) construction of the of the brewery-kitchen-mill complex" in CUSAS 3, 128, 129, 131–133, 135, 138 and 141; "for construction of the enclosure wall" in CUSAS 3, 102 and 103. For further ref. s. Kleinerman/Owen 2009, 239ff.; Heimpel 2009, 250.

3. After Sallaberger 2011, 357, *diʾu* and *dû* (*duʾu*) might be var. of the same word.

MPS/NR

+ **diʾû?** "afflicted by *d.*-disease"; OB

OB *di-i-ḫa-ku-ú-ma am-ši-i-ma* AbB 10, 185: 7 "I was sick with *d.* and forgot", after von Soden 1986, 736 (nisba?).

JW

dû s. *diʾu* III

duʾānu s. *dinānu*

dūʾāru "to surround, enfold"; OAkk.

G OAkk. *du-ri-ni it-taskarinnī kī rēʾīʾu ì-du-ru ṣaʾnam* MAD 5, 8: 21, 24 "surround me among the boxwood trees, as the shepherd encircles the flock", s. Westenholz/Westenholz 1977; AHw 1551; Krebernik 1984, 166.

+ **dubābu** "complaint(?)"; OA

OA *amtam … ana ḫuluq ana du-ba-bé niddinakkum* kt 87/k.275: 9 "we gave you the slave-girl … for (nothing but) loss and complaints(?)", s. Hecker 1997, 165ff.

JW

dubāqu s. *tubāqu*

+ **duBBu** " a bronze implement"; OB

du-uB-Bu ARM 32 p. 261 M.18115: 6, *du-Bi-im* ib. p. 181 S.133, 40: 6, s. Arkhipov 2012, 132f.

JW

dubbubtu "(troublesome) negotiation(s), complaint(s); vexation"

1. OB lit. *kūṣam u du-bu-ub-tam elīya ittadī* ASJ 18, 21: 3 "he has cast chills and vexation upon me".

2. OB lit. *šumma ittanadlaḫ u du*!*-bu-ub*!*-tum šaknassu* YOS 11, 15: 22 "if he is constantly troubled and worry is set upon him".

JW

+ **duBBuru** "a metal implement"; MB Emar

1. 1 *pāšu* 1 *du-u*B-B*u-ru* ZABAR 1 *patru* ZABAR Emar 6/3, 33: 9 "1 hatchet, 1 bronze *d.*, 1 bronze dagger".

2. *kāsu* ZABAR *ša* [x x *d*]*u-u*B-B*u*-[*ru* ZABAR] 15 KI.LÁ.BI 2 *pāšta* ZABAR^{meš} CunMon. 13, 15: 10 "a bronze cup with, [n(?) bronze] *d.*, its weight: 15, 2 bronze hatchets".

3. Pentiuc 2001, 186 suggests, on the basis of the first ref., a reading *tuppūru* "an implement (sewing tool?) of bronze" and connects the word etymologically with Hebr./Aram. TPR "to sew together". The use of *tu* instead of *tù* throughout in Emar 6/3, 33 (*ú-nu-tu*^{meš} l. 11, *at-tu-ka-mi* l. 21, *tu-ta-ar* l. 23) and in CunMon. 13, 15 (*ú-nu-tu*^{meš} l. 21) does not favor that etym.

dubdubbu "a bird; a drum"; SB

arim dub-dub-bi SAA 3, 8 r. 16 "the *d.* drum is covered (i.e. tuned)". JW/MPS

dubgallu s. *tupgallu*

dubqu s. *tubqu*

dubsarmaḫḫu s. *tupšarmaḫḫu*

+ **dūdānūtu** "work of the kettle smith"; LB

LB *kaspu ša ana du-ú-da-nu-tú nadnu* CunMon. 3b, 129 no. 156: 7 "silver that has been paid for the work of the kettle smith", s. Wunsch ib.; cf. Jursa 1995/6, 260. JW

dudittu s. *tudittu*

duddû s. *dūtu*

dūdu I, + *tūdu* "kettle"

1. MB Qaṭna n *du-du* (URUDU) QS 3, 12: 3; 17: 2; 18: 3 "n (copper) kettles".

2. MB Emar 1 *tu-ú-du siparri* 1000 *šuqultašu* Emar 6/3, 283: 1 "1 bronze kettle, its weight is 1000 (shekels)".

3. MB Nuzi *kukkubu siparri ša tu-u-ti* HSS 14, 247: 72 "bronze *kukkubu*-vessel of *t.*; cf. *ša du-ú-ti* HSS 15, 130: 42; *ša du-ú-te* ib. 52, s. Schneider-Ludorff 2009, 517f. (a set of two vessels?). JW (3), MPS (1–2)

dugānu, *tugānu* "a stomach disease"

For disc. and lit. s. Stol 2006, 111. JW

duggūru s. *tugguru*

duglu s. *tuklu* II

duḫḫu s. *batabtuḫḫu*

duḫnu, *tuḫnu* "millet"; + OB

1. OB n *du?-uḫ-nu ša* MÙNU CUSAS 9, 177: 1 "n millet(?) for(?) malt". Dalley 2009, 121 suggests emendation to *duḫḫu* "residue, pulp".

2. EA *ana* ŠE.IM^{meš} <*du*>*-uḫ-ni* : *mu-ḫu-ṣu* EA 224: 9 "concerning the millet: it has been spoiled". Note that after this interpretation *mu-ḫu-ṣu* is not a gloss. Cf. CAD M/1, 83 ([*u*]*ḫ-ni* (or -*ir*) : *mu-ḫu-ṣu* 'it is … (gloss) spoiled'"), s. Na'aman 1975, 78 n. 78.

3. MA *tu-uḫ-ni u šamaššammī … lēru-šū* BATSH 4/1 r. 14 "they shall cultivate millet and sesame".

4. LB n *mašīḫu ša duḫ-nu* PN *ittašu* BM 114788: 2, 5 "PN has brought n measures of millet (instead of sesame)", s. Da Riva 2002, 95ff. for disc. and ref.; add CT 55, 737: 1.

5. For etym. s. Kogan 2012, 247.

JW (3–5), MPS (1), NR (2)

duḫšû s. *dušû* I

+ **duKKutu**(?) "a garment"; OA, OB

1. OA 2 *du-Ku-tù* 2 ^{túg}*kusīʾātum* 1 *šiknum* Prag 429: 63 "2 *d.* cloaks, 2 *kusītu*-garments, 1 *šiknu*-garment".

2. OB ^{túg}*du-Ku-tu-t*[*u*] T. 101: 1; GÚ! *du-Ku-tu* T. 110: 4 "*d.* cloak", s. Durand 2009, 33. JW (1), NR (2)

dulāqu "mng. uncert."

Also in OB Susa PN *Du-la-qum* MDP 28, 431: 1.

+ **dulbānūtu** "(long-)distance(?)"; NB

PN *qīpi ša* GN *ina pēthalli* [*d*]*ul-ban*!-*nu-ti iktalda* SAA 17, 120: 10 "PN, the messenger of GN, arrived on a (long)-distance(?) horse". Dietrich, ib. p. 106 "passageway horse". Cf. *da/ulbānu*.

dulba/ātu "a part or product of the plane-tree(?)"; OA

1. *ḫuršīʾānum ša du-ul-ba-tim* AKT 5, 58: 5 "a package of *d.*" (followed by *kamāru*-fish).

2. 15 *du-ul-ba-tum u mu-lu-ḫu-um* AKT 6A, 239: 11 "15 *d.* and *m.*-wood(?)"; s. also AKT 6A, 144: 27.

3. Conventionally parsed as fem. pl. of *dulbu*; exclusively attested in OA, whereas the sg. *dulbu* is not (s. CAD D 172 s.v. *dulbātu* "a foodstuff that could be counted, as well as measured by capacity"; AHw 175). Perhaps better understood as *dulbatu*, pl. *dulbātu*, referring to a part or product of the *d.*-tree (cf. *terinnu* and *terinnatu*).

JW (2–3), MPS (1)

dulbu, *dilbu*, + *dalbu* "plane-tree (*platanus orientalis*)"; + Ur III, + OB, + MA

1. Ur III Garšana n ḪAR ^{giš}*dú-ul-bu-um* CUSAS 3, 1256: 29f.; 1375: 31 "n plane tree seedling(s)".

2. OB [x] *lēʾu rabû ša du-ul-bi* FM 7, 114 no. 30: 18 "[x] large boards of plane".

3. MB Ekalte [*d*]*u-ul-bá … umalli* WVDOG 102, 77: 5 "he has fully paid for(?) the [pl]ane".

4. MB lex. ^{giš}*dal-bu-um* KBo. 25, 5 + 26, 6 b i 16 (list of trees); cf. Emar 6/4 p. 59 Msk 74163b v 4; Emar 6/1 p. 105ff. Msk 731030 iv 51.

5. MA 2 ^{giš}*dul-bu* 2 *erû adi narki*[*bī-šina*] StAT 5, 72: 1 "2 (poles of?) plane trees, 2 lower millstones with [their?] upper mill[stones]".

6. The fem. *dulba/ātu* is only attested in OA, s. above. S. also Postgate 2005, 591.

JW (2, 4–6), MPS (3), NR (1)

dullu "trouble, ritual, work, service"

1. OA *ištū bulut abīya du-⸢lam⸣ ašdud u ūmam a-du-⸢li⸣-im-ma ē taṣba‹-tī›ni* AKT 9A, 75: 23f. "I have endured hardship because of my father's health and now you shall not keep me in hardship", s. ib. p. 122.

2. SB *ana dul-lu ša* PN *šarri u mārēšu* TCS 5 p. 284 Chr. 13b: 7 "for the *d.*-ritual of PN, the king, and his sons".

3. LB on *bīt dullu* s. van Driel 1990, 221 (land under cultivation that has reached full productivity), s. also Jursa 1995, 126 n. 256.

4. LB *dul-lu gamru* BM 74682: 1 "completed work", s. Bongenaar 1997, 359.

5. On *d.* as corvee work, s. van Driel 2002, 260ff.; Abraham 2004, 36f., with disc. and ref.

JW

dulluḫ̮iš "quickly"

SB ⸢*du*⸣-*lu-ḫi-iš nasḫa bari ul up*[*puš*] ZA 102, 204: 10 "copied in a hurry, collated, not finis[hed(?)]", s. Maul ib. p. 207.

dul(l)uḫ̮tu, + *dul(l)iḫtu* "hurry, despatch; confusion, anxiety, trouble"; + OB

1. OB *du-li-ḫa-tim annêtim* PN [*īpuš* (?)] FM 7, 125 no. 35 r. 6 "PN [caused] this trouble".

2. OB *du-lu-uḫ-tum lā ibbaššī* ARM 26/1, 175 no. 39: 47 “trouble must not develop!”

3. OB *du-lu-uḫ-tum ina libbi mātim iššakinma* ARM 26/2, 278 no. 409: 42 “trouble was made in the land”.

4. OB *ina libbi mātim mimma du-lu-uḫ-tam lā tašakkanā assurri du-lu-uḫ-tam tašakkanāma* ARM 28, 65: 6f. “do not make trouble in the land! I fear that you will make trouble”.

5. Moran 1992, 22f. n. 24: corr. CAD D 179a to *ki-i du-ul-lu-uḫ-t*[*i-iš*] EA 11 r. 27 “as soon as poss[ible]”.

6. NA For the ref. Iraq 18 in CAD D 179a *d.* 2 s. now SAA 19, 144 r. 7: DNf u DNf_2 *lū īdâ kī ūmussu itti du-lu-uḫ-ti-a* “DNf and DNf_2 really know that he is daily among my concerns”.

JW (1), MPS (2–4, 6), NR (5)

+ **du-lu-qa-ri-ta-an** (mng. unkn.); Hurr. word in MB Qaṭna

QS 3, 2: 8; cf. disc. ib. p. 49.

dulûtu s. *dilûtu*

dumāmu I “leopard”

Lex. [... = *mašak*] *du-ma-mi* Emar 6/4, 546: 4 (Ḫḫ) “[skin of] a leopard”.

dummû, + OA *dammuʾu* “to bring to tears”; + OA

D OA (in a good year shipments from you come to me, but) *annī dimʾam tù-dá-mì-a-am* “now you have brought me to tears” Prag 735: 22 (diff. ib. p. 309, Reiner 2007, 56: *tí-im-a-am tutammi-am* “now, you swear an *oath* to me”).

NJCK

+ **dummuqiš** “well, favorably”; NA

SB *du-mu-qi-iš dīniš* SAAB 8, 4: 2’ “favorably, justly”, s. *dīniš*. JW

dummuqtu “good deed, benevolence”

1. OB *du-um-mu-uq-ta-ka ... ittabšīʾam* AbB 13, 158: 5 “your benevolence ... has been imparted to me”, cf. *rēš du-um-mu-u*[*q*]-*t*[*i-ka*] *ana bītini* ib. 7 “the beginning(?) of your benevolence towards our house” (broken context).

2. OB *kīma īnī imaḫḫarū ina du-um-mu-uq-ta-ka ammar* AbB 7, 140: 10’ “I shall see that (the textiles) will be pleasing (to the merchants) through your good work” (note *dummuqtaka* instead of expected *dummuqtika*, cf. Kraus ib.). For *d. amāru* cf. *dummuqu*. JW

dummuqu “good quality; good action”

1. OB *ša ṭūb libbiki lūpuš u du-um-mu-qí amrī* AbB 11, 41: 16 “I want to do what pleases you – see (how I shall do) my best!”

2. OB *panīšu aṭṭul u du-um-mu-qá-am elīšunu artašī* OBTR 131: 9 “I saw him personally and I received more kindness (or: higher quality goods?) than they”.

3. OB *ittī* PN *šuʾāti dabābam du-um-mu-qá-am dubub* AbB 7, 167: 8 “speak well-chosen words with that PN!”, cf. ib. 25. JW

****dumqiš** “well” (CAD D 180a)

Von Soden 1960, 489: del. CAD **dumqiš*, Alalakh 109: 3 $SIG_5^{gí\text{-}iš}$ = *damqiš* “well”, s. AHw 157a. EZ

dumqu, *dunqu* “goodness, good (thing), favor; jewel”

1. OAkk. *lū dum-qú-uk* CUSAS 27, 73 r. 10 “let (this) be your favor (to me)”.

2. OB *ēpiš du-um-qí* UET 7, 73 iii 111 “who prepares choice food”.

3. OB *ana paššūr du-um-qí* ARM 11, 2: 5 "(food) for the table of choice food" (referring to an offering).

4. OB Susa PN *Ea-du-um-qí* MDP 28, 412: 3 "Ea is my favor".

5. MB Qaṭna "jewel" (cf. *dumāqū*): 1 *du-un-qú ḫurāṣi* QS 62: 32 "1 gold jewel". JW (1, 3), MPS (2, 4, 5)

dumuqtu "good deed, favor, welcoming gift"

1. OB *du-mu-uq-[tam] [u]šēṣûniššunū-š[im]* M. 5009: 7 (Fs. Garelli p. 19) "they sent out a welcoming gift for them".

2. OB *[an]nītum ana* [PN *l*]*ū du-mu-uq-[tum]* A. 3185 (Durand 2000, 401f.) "this shall be a welcoming gift for PN". JW

dunānu "decorative disc of a chariot(?)"

1. NA *amēlu ša* É.ḪÚB *ša* DN *amēlu ša pan ēkalli šanû isse* ᵈGAŠAN *du-na-ni irakkubū* SAA 20, 18: 35 "the man of the É.ḪÚB of DN, the *ša pan ēkalli*, and (his) deputy are riding (the chariot) together with the lady (i.e. Ištar?) of the *d.*"; *bēlat d.* also SAA 20, 37 r. 22; SAA 20, 15 r. ii 41.

2. NA PN *ša* ᵍⁱˢ*du-na-ni* pass. in CTN 3, s. p. 286 "PN of the *d.*", cf. Kinnier Wilson 1972, 54f. ("standardbearer").

3. Disc. s. Deller 1992, 296f. JW (1–3), MPS (1)

dun(n)āʾū pl. tant. "increase, surcharge(?)"; OA

1. *balūm dunāʾē* "without surcharge(?)":

a) (n silver) *balūm du-na-e ištē* PN TPAK 1, 200: 1 "without surcharge(?) is owed by PN" (cf. ibid. 25; AKT 7A, 141: 8; AKT 8, 199: 3; TC 3, 211: 12).

b) (n silver) *balūm du-na-e ina* 1 *ma-na-i-a* PN *iddinam* TPAK 1, 200: 25 "PN gave me (n silver – weighed) with my 1-mina weight – without surcharge(?)" (cf. CCT 1, 26b: 5).

2. *d. nadāʾu* "to lay down *d.*": *ina* 1 *manāʾim ša* PN *ilqeʾū du-na-ú ulā nadʾū kaspum takīttam na-ší-e* kt a/k 516b: 13 quot. in Dercksen 1996, 83 "they have received it (a loan of silver) – weighed with the one-mina weight of PN; *d.* have not been laid down and the silver is the correct amount", s. also *takīttu*. S. Veenhof 2015, 261f. for add. ref.

3. The conventional transl. "increase, surcharge" is based on the etym. proposed by Veenhof 1972, 67: a *PuRuS-Sāʾ* form of *danānu*, "to be(come) strong", hence "increase (of an amount to be paid, agio)". However, this is semantically tenuous, and the only attested *PuRuSSāʾ* derivation of a II/gem. root shows a diff. pattern (*qalullāʾū* "discredit, dishonour" from *qalālu* "to be(come) light", a rare var. of *qulālū*). Another suggestion, based on the expression *du-na-e nadāʾu*, is that *d.* are small weight stones that could be placed on a balance to compensate for a deficiency in weight (Veenhof 2015, 261f.). The etym. remains uncertain. NJCK

dunnu pl. *dunnāti* "power, strength; (fortified) farm(stead); a type of bed, furniture; part of the lung"

1. OB in transf. mng. *dunni panim* "hard of attitude": *ša īrišūma ūṣû ana mê du-ni panim īšû* AbB 10, 42: 43 "(those) who cultivated and went out have a strong attitude about the water"; cf. *danānu*, *dannu*.

2. “fortified farmstead”:

a) OB *kīma du-un-ni ḫabtu* AbB 7, 116: 4 “that my farmstead has been plundered”; s. ib. 12, 19, 28.

b) OB *tenēštam ša du-un-na-a-tim u dimātim* AbB 10, 150: 22 “the population of the forts and watchtowers”; cf. AbB 7, 49: 8.

c) On MA *d.* as a type of settlement similar to *dimtu* in the Nuzi texts s. Koliński 2001, 30ff.

3. NA *qirsi ša* [giš]*du-un* ⌜*ma*⌝-*ḫi-i*-⌜*ri*⌝ SAA 19, 207: 8 “take a cart(?) with benches(?)!”, cf. CAD D 185 *dunnu* B.
JW (1–2), MPS/JW/FJMS (3)

dunqu s. *dumqu*

+ **Dup(p)aššu I** “a type of dyed wool”; MB Ugar., Hurr. lw.(?)

1. SIKI.ZA.GÌN *ḫašmāna* SIKI.ZA.GÌN : *ḫandalāti ù* SIKI.ZA.GÌN : DU-*pa-aš-ši u aban gabî maʾdiš bēltiya lišēbi-la* Ug. 5, 48: 9–13 “may my lady(?) send me a great deal of *ḫašmānu*-type blue wool, *ḫandalātu*-type blue wool, *d.*-type blue wool, and alum”.

2. For the interpretation as a type of wool, s. CAD U 194; for a color or hue, s. van Soldt 1990, 344; Lackenbacher 2002, 297; Thavapalan 2018, 12. Heltzer 1978, 58 n. 129 proposes a connection to *dbš* “honey”, which is unlikely.
MPS/NR

+ **Dup(p)aššu II** (mng. uncert.); MB Ugar., Hurr. lw.(?)

1. *šar* GN 50 *manā ḫurāṣa ištu* 10 *ḫarrānī ša bīt du-up-pa-aš-ši ana Šamšī ittadin* PRU 4, 151, 17.59: 18 “the king of GN has given 50 mina of gold from 10 caravans of the house of *D.* to my Sun”.

2. Perhaps to be understood as *bīt tup-paššì* “house of tabletship, accounting house, sealed storehouse”, s. Sasson 1966, 135 n. 52; Archi 1973, 213; Arnaud 1996, 60; Beckman 1999, 183; Lackenbacher 2002, 102. It remains uncertain whether *-šši* is a Hurr. suffix (Sasson 1966, 135 n. 152). Heltzer 1978, 149 proposes a connection with Akk. *duppussû* “younger brother”. Sivan 1984, 215 connects the passage with D*up*(*p*)*aššu* I.
JW/NR

duppu s. *duBBu*

duppuru I “to move away, withdraw; stay away” s. *dapāru*

duprānu s. *daprānu*

+ **duqdu** “almond”; NA

1. [[giš]*zi*]*q-pu* ⌜*ša* [giš]*duq*⌝-*di* [*ša*] *supur-gillum* [*ša*] *angāšē* [*i*]*mattuḫū* SAA 1, 226 r. 1 “they are collecting saplings of almond, quince and plum(?) trees”.

2. 1 *kappi duq-di ṣarpi* SAA 7, 81: 1 “1 bowl of almond wood (and) silver”.

3. *duqdu* is the NA form of *šiqdu*/*šuqdu* elsewhere in Akk. For further ref. cf. AHw 561 and CAD L 238 **luddu*.
MPS (1, 3), JW (2)

duqduqqu s. *diqdiqqu*

+ **duqqu** “crushed, pulverized”; OA

ḫusārum du-qú-um “crushed lapis lazuli” TC 3, 49: 41; Prag 623: 8. S. Michel 2001a, 348f.; cf. *daqāqu* D and *daqqu*; GOA § 7.2.3.
NJCK

durāru s. *andurāru*

durāʾu, + *adrāʾu*? "arm, foreleg"; Aram. lw.

NA *ina muḫḫe ad-ra-ʾ ša nā[re ša šarru bēlī] išpuranni mā ḫu-ú-ṭ[a-šu?] libbi ad-ra-ʾ ša pitte* [x x] *nārātu ša ana libbe* […] *kaqquru matiḫ* SAA 19, 88: 4, 6 "as to the arm(?) of the ri[ver, about which the king, my lord], had written me: 'Dig [it!]' The inner part of the arm(?) in the area of […] (and) the rivers, which […] into it – (its) ground is elevated". Luukko ib. p. 92 interprets *ad-ra-ʾ* as var. of *durāʾu*, a loan from Aram. Note, however, that the word is not used with rivers in Aram. On etym. s. Cherry 2017, 100f.

+ **duraʾuʾannu** "a leather or woolen object"; Nuzi

^{kuš}*du-ra-ú-a-an-nu*, Santag 4, 92 no. 29: 3 (among parts for a chariot), s. Müller ib. p. 93; cf. HSS 15, 208: 2, 6 (cit. AHw 1373a s.v. *turāʾu*). JW

durru "anus" s. *ṭurru* II

dūru I "wall, rampart, fortification, fortress"

1. Early OB *maṣṣartum ina dú-ri-im lā urradam* AS 22, 7: 15 "the guard shall not come down from the wall".

2. OB *šarrūtum nalbanassu u palûm du-ur-šu* ARM 10, 51 = ARM 26/1, 479 no. 238: 13 "kingship is his brick-mold and regnancy his wall" (cf. Heimpel 2003, 268).

3. On *dūr libbi* (cardiac septum?) in extispicy s. Durand 1988, 277 on ARM 26/1, 109: 11.

4. LB PN *Nabû-dūr-e-di* OECT 12 A 105: 4, 8 "Nabû is the wall of the lone one".

5. On *dūr šinni* "gum" s. disc. Kogan 2003, 128f.

6. *samān dūri* AHw 178b belongs here and not to *dūru* II.

JW (1–3, 5), MPS (4, 6)

dūru II "permanence"; + OA

1. OA *adī dūrimma* "forever": *ša ištē aḫḫuʾātēšunu izanniʾūni adī du-ri-ma izanniʾū* AKT 4, 63: 5 "do people who get angry with their sisters have to stay angry forever?", s. Veenhof 2008/9: 201.

2. OB *kīma lā kûm ina du-ri-im ul tīdē* AbB 3, 63: 7 "will you never understand that it is not yours?"

3. OB *ištū dūrim* "long-since":
a) *ina lā mašqītim ištū du-ri-ka ammīni mê tereddē* AbB 10, 171: 20 "why have you long-since been funneling water (even) when there is no irrigation?"
b) *ištū* [*d*]*u-ri-im matīma šeʾam ina panīya ul ikmisūnim* AbB 12, 31: 10 "never before have they brought the barley in before my arrival".
c) OB *qaqqad kirîm šuʾāti ištū du-ri-ma* PN AbB 5, 219 r. 7 "the head of that garden has long-since been PN".

4. For *samān dūri* AHw 178b, s. *sāmānu*; belongs to *dūru* "wall".

5. NA/SB *murṣu ša du-ur ūmē* SAA 2, 14 ii 14 "sickness forever".

JW (2–3), MPS (4–5), NJCK (1)

dūru III "a lance"; + OB

1 *du-ur kaspim* ARM 32, 203 A.1389: 3, 6, 11, 14, 18, 22 "1 silver lance", s. Arkhipov 2012, 106. JW

durummu "a bird"; + Ur III

Ur III *dur-ru-um*^{mušen} FLP 145: 15, s. Owen 1981, 37. JW

duruššu "foundation"

SB *du-ru-*⸢*uš-šú*?⸣ Jiménez 2017, 379 iii 8 (in broken context).

dusinnu s. *tuzzinnu*

dušmû "(house-born) slave"

1. OB lit. *du-šu-um-šu* (Sum.: *i-mi-du-du*) *anāku* OBO 278, 357: 5 "I am his slave" (Guichard 2015, 368).

2. SB *du-uš-mu-u pāliḫku* AMD 8/1, 431: 11 "the servant who honors you".

JW

duššû "abundant, copious"

1. Borger 1962, 253: Lex. *du-uš-šu-u* RA 17, 174 K 14889: 1. Joined with K. 4165+ by Fincke 2015 (Nabnītu).

2. Lex. *lu-ú* = LU = *ú-du-ú* = *du-uš-šu-u* MSL 14, 186: 189 (Ea).

3. SB *nīqūka nindabūka du-uš-šú-tum* RA 82, 160: 41 "your lavish sacrifices and offerings". JW (2–3), MPS (1)

+ **duššuptu**, *daššuptu* "sweetness, sweets"; OB

1. Early OB (sesame) [*i*]*š da-šu-pá-tìm* ARM 19, 393: 4 "for sweets".

2. OB lit. [*li*]*bbī ītegram du-*⸢*šu-up-ta*⸣*-ka* CUSAS 10, 9: 8 "your sweetness coiled around my [hea]rt".

3. For the PNf *Duššuptu* s. AHw and CAD D s.v. *duššupu*.

JW (1, 3), MPS (2)

dušû I, + *duḫšu*, + *duḫšû*, + *tuḫšu* "a mineral, quartz, (blue) frit, beadwork, faience; dyed leather or wool"; + MA, Hurr. lw.

1. Lex. *za-gìn-na* : *uq-ni-tum* : *tu-uḫ-šu* Emar 6/4, 556: 18 (Ḫḫ); [^{siki}]⸢*sag-gil*?-*mud*⸣ : *ḫa-aš-ma-nu* : *tu-uḫ-šu* ib. 20, s. Pentiuc 2001, 47.

2. OB LÁ.U^{ḫá} DUḪ.ŠÚ.A ARM 21, 232: 14; ^{siki}DUḪ.ŠÚ.A ARM 22, 50: 14, cf. ARM 22, 51: 14; ^{siki}*tu-uḫ-ši-im* ARM 23, 545 no. 580: 12; ^{siki}*du*!*-uḫ-ši-im* ARM 18, 30: 5.

3. OB [*pat*]*innu ša du-uḫ-ši-im* ARM 10, 18: 7 "sash of blue wool".

4. OB 100 *gištuppī* ^{na4}DUḪ.ŠÚ.A ARM 25, 404: 1 "100 platelets of *d.*-quartz". For additional Mari ref. s. Arkhipov 2012, 33f.

5. OB PN *Du-uḫ-ša-tum* ARM 23, 572 no. 607: 18; *Du-úḫ-šu-*⸢*um*⸣ YOS 14, 132: 10.

6. SB *kubša ša uqnî du-še* HS 1886: 3' "a *kubšu*-headdress of lapis (and) quartz".

7. MA (dyed leather) s. Wiggerman 2000, 200 (T98-7, T 98-30).

8. NA *ina amtim ša ana* PN *iddinuni ina* ⸢*duḫ-ši*⸣ BATSH 6, 2: 8 "concerning the slave-girl whom he gave to PN for(?) *d.* (i.e. for crafting beadwork?)".

9. NA ^{kuš}*duḫ-ši-i* Ass. 2001.D-377: 5 (MDOG 134, 48) "*d.*-leather", cf. Radner 1997, 301 + n. 1691 ("green kid leather") with further ref.

10. LB ^{siki}*du-šu-ú* CT 57, 255: 15.

11. On the NA profession *ṣārip du*(*ḫ*)*še* s. Dalley 2000, 6, 15f. ("a refiner of frit, faience and glass", not connected to red-dying); in LB also a tanner of colored leather (s. dubsar 3, 77: 19).

12. For lit. and etym. s. Dalley 2000 and Richter 2012, 466.

EZ (6), JW (2, 4–5, 7–12), MPS (1, 4), NR (3, 1)

dūšu I "a silver object"; OAkk.

2 *du-śa-an* KÙ.BABBAR CNIP 3, 25: 2 (among other silver objects), s. von Soden 1990, 136. JW

dūtu, + *duddû* "virility, manliness; codpiece; secret place"

1. Lex. *du-ú-ti/tú/tum* = *mašḫandu*, DU$_8$.UD.DA // *du*$_8$-⌜*ud-du*!-*u*⌝ // *du-ud-du-ú* = *mašḫandu* AOAT 50, 375: 211f. (malku) "codpiece = warming cloth". Cf. Hrůša ib. p. 237.

2. OB lit. *du-ta turram* CunMon. 8, 110: 11 "restoring manliness".

3. SB *du-ut-ka lūmid* ORA 7, 285: 58 "let me take refuge in your secret place", s. ib. p. 294.

JW (2, 3), MPS (1), NR (3)

duʾu II s. *diʾu* III

+ **duʾʾudu** "to fondle, to make love(?)"; SB

(*namrirrašu*) *ú-da-ʾ-as-si-ma ittanas-ḫarši* Fs. Kraus p. 200 iv 12 "(its brilliance) fondles (?) her and seeks her welfare"; *Ebardurgarra bēltum ú-da-ʾa-si-ma* ib. 14 "E. fondles(?) the mistress", s. Lambert ib. p. 216 (denom. from *dādu*?). JW

duʾummatu s. *daʾummatu*

+ **duZZuru** "a textile"; OB

1. 2 *du-Zu-rum* ARM 22, 324 iv 5 (between bridles and slings).

2. 2 ^{túg}*du-Zu-ru* SAG ARM 22, 110: 4 "2 first-quality *d.*" (between textiles).

3. For further ref. and disc. s. Durand 2009, 33f. MPS/NR

T

tabākatta

1. For TC 3, 97: 14 cf. Dercksen 1996, 74f. (*t. nadā'u* "to solder").

2. For *ta-ba-ku-tum* AKT 5, 65: 25 s. *tabku* I 2, below. MPS (2), NJCK (1)

tabāku "to pour (out), lay flat, heap up"

G 1. OB lit. (of an apple tree) *it-bu-ku inibšu* ALL no. 1 i 9f. "heaped up its fruit", s. *ḫašḫūru*.
2. OB lit. *it-bu-uk imassu am-mātā*[*tim*] FM 14 i 29 "he poured his poison over the lands".
3. In transf. mng. "to pour s.o. out", i.e. "to weaken s.o." (CAD T 7 *t.* 3d), s. also D 1, below:
a) SB *it-bu-ka-an-ni u īsipanni* Oshima 2011, 210: 38 "he poured me out and gathered me up".
b) NA *ina muḫḫi mīn ta-ta-ab-kan-ni* SAA 13, 190 r. 25 "(I have no house, no maid, no servant … I am finished) why have you 'poured me out'?", s. Kouwenberg 2005, 100.

D 1. "to weaken" (CAD T 8 *t.* 6, s. also G 3, above): OA *ina awātim ú-ta*!*-bi-ik-šu-ma al'ēšuma* TPAK 1, 70: 7 "I weakened him and triumphed over him in a lawsuit" (after Dercksen 1997/8, 336b).
2. For *ú*-TAB-*bi-qa-an-ni* Ugaritica 5, 162 = Oshima 2011, 210: 37 s. *dabāqu*.

N 1. OB lit. (of a dog foetus) *e-ṣe-em-ṣe-ri-šu it-ta-at-bi-ku-ma* CUSAS 18 p. 319: 28 "its backbone becomes limp". Note *ittatbikūma* instead of *ittat-bakūma*.
2. NB *nišū māti gabbi … it-ta-at-ba-ku* SAA 17, 120: 23 "all the people of the country were crowded together".

Ntn SB *it-ta-na-at-ba-ak* Lamaštu MB I 16 (Farber 2014, 121) "she keeps 'spilling out' (i.e. appearing) constantly." JW (G, D, Ntn), MPS (G, N)

tabālu "to take away, carry off, bring along"

G 1. Early OB GN *ikkirma ana* PN *gerram i-ta-ba-al* RIME 4, 708: 11 (Simurrum) "GN turned hostile and waged war against PN"
2. LB *kaspu ta-ba-la … ša* PN *i-ta-ba-la* BM 75617 (MacGinnis 2008, 83): 2 "stolen silver ... which PN stole" (s. also *tablu*).
3. LB *kaspu ša* ⌜*ta*⌝*-bal* Bēl rēmanni p. 251 BM 79128: 11 "silver which was stolen/of stealing", s. Jursa ib. 252.
4. On the mng. "to bring/take along" s. Kouwenberg 2005, 89f. with ref.
5. On use in math. texts s. Høyrup 1993.

D Stol 2010, 171: OB *zēram ú-tab-ba-lu-ú-ma* Anbar/Stol 1991, 19 no. 8: 16 "they shall take away the seed".

Š OB *ṣabassunūtima šu-ut-ba-al-šu-nu-ti* Haradum 2, 70: 38 "seize them and have them taken away!"
JW (G, Š), MPS (G), NR (D)

tābalu "dry land"; + OB, + LB

1. OB *ḫalaṣ nārim u ta-ba-li-im lū dunnun* ARM 28, 10: 14 "may the river district and the dry land be reinforced".

2. LB *kī naptanu ina ta-*⌜*bal-lu*⌝ *aṣab-batma adî ina būrāti* ITI 2-*ta naptanu aṣabbata* AOAT 414/1, 48: 12 "(I swear:) I will not take the meal from the dry land, rather I will take the meal twice per month from the ponds".

tabarru, + *tubarru* "red wool, a garment"

1. OB ^{túg}*tu-ba-ru* ARM 30, 205 M.5681 i 39; ^{túg}*ta-ba-ru* ib. iii 28; GÚ *ta-ba-ru* ib. iii 29. Cf. Durand ib. 120f. and CAD T 470 s.v. *tumāru*.

2. OB lit. *nazzūssu irīmki ina ta-ba-⌜ar-ri-im⌝ lamī* Or. 87, 20 ii 21 "your love-charm stands by him (= the performer), wrapped in red wool".

3. MB (1/2 mina of) DA-*ba-ru* MBLET 20: 4 "1/2 mina of *t.*-wool" (after *šīpātu* "wool"). Spelling with DA- is also attested in OB Mari (CAD T 21). Gurney 1983, 73 translates "*dabāru*-wood" (mistake for "wool"?).

4. MA n *qimmātu ša ta-bar-ri* MARV 4, 138: 16 pass. "n loads of *t.*-wool" for wrapping weapons in the context of a ritual, s. Dercksen 2005b, 123ff.

5. NB ^{siki}ḪÉ.ME.DA.KUR.⌜RA⌝ OIP 114, 45: 10, 13 "foreign(?) *t.*-wool".

6. LB ^{siki}GÚ.È *šá* ^{siki}*ta-bar-ru* YOS 17, 307: 3 "1 coat of *t.* wool". For add. LB ref. s. Zawadzki 2006, 47; dubsar 3, 43: 32.

7. On the LB reading of the logogram ^{siki}ḪÉ.ME.DA (*tabarru* rather than *nabāsu*) s. Beaulieu 2003, 384 and 388f.; Zawadzki 2006, 41. YOS 17, 307: 1 apparently uses both terms side by side: 1 ^{siki}ḪÉ.ME.DA *na-bal-su* "1 *tabarru* garment made of *nabāsu* wool(?)"; the exact interpretation of the line remains, however, unclear, s. Zawadzki 2006, 41 n. 84. The same text has syllabic *tabarru* in l. 3, s. 6, above.

8. For etym. and further lit. s. Richter 2012, 440f. S. also *takiltu*.

JW (2, 4–6), MPS (3, 6, 7), NR (1)

tabāštānu, + *tabāštēnu* "excrement"

1. Lex. *ta-ba-áš-te-nu* = *zû u šīnātu* AOAT 50, 368: 137 (malku) "excrement = dung and urine".

2. SB *ina ta-ba-aš-ta-n*[*i*] *šutbī*[*šu*] CT 58, 70 r. 7 "lift [him] from faeces".

JW (2), MPS (1)

tabbibu s. *tapp-*

+ **tabbukku**, *tabku*, pl. *tabbukkātu* "a container for heaping up grain(?)"; SB, MA

1. Lex. [*nabārum*?] = *ta-ab-bu-uk-ku* : *ta-ab-ku*$_8$, [*na*]*bārum*? = MIN, [*na*]*bārum*? = MIN Emar 6/4, 545: 117 (s. Y. Cohen 2010, 829) "[cage(?)] = *tabbukku*, *tabku*, [ca]ge(?) = ditto, [ca]ge(?) = ditto".

2. MA *ana* 4-*i-šu tab-bu-ka*$_4$(QA)-*tu* VS 19, 58: 11 "(n bowls and) 4 times as many *t.*", cf. ib. 6 *ša kabli* ib. 6 "with feet", *ša pani kutalli* ib. 8 "with front and back"), s. Farber 2004. The spelling with *ka*$_4$ is, however, unusual.

JW/MPS

taBḫištu "a container"

The etym. remains unclear, s. Streck 2000, 118 with prev. lit. If the word is original Akk. the orthography allows a derivation from either *beʾēšu* "to mix" ("mixing vat", Dalley 1976, 151) or *paʾāṣu* "to grind" ("grinding vat"). However, since the container is used for *azamru* fruits both derivations are questionable. JW/MPS

tābila "in dry form, in a dry state"

On the eye disease (keratoconjunctivitis sicca?) s. Fincke 2001, 210f. JW

tābīlu "dried plants"

1. Mayer 2009, 423: SB *ta-bi-lu īnīšu teqqi* SpTU 2, 50: 7, 9 "you rub his eyes with (an ointment prepared from) dried plants".

2. Reiner 2007, 48: LB PN *ta-bi-lu mala ina eqli ... illûn(u) ana makkūri anamdin*[(*u*)] Jursa 1995 p. 133 no. 43 BM 74439: 21 "I will deliver all the dried plants that grow in the field to the (temple) stores." NR

tabku I "poured out, spilled"; + OA, + NA

1. Part of the date-palm: Lex. [^{giš}LAGAB?]-*nimbar* = *tab-ku* CUSAS 12 p. 105 iv 6; for restoration s. MSL 9 p. 165 ad l. 382.

2. OA *tuppū ša išassû ta-ba-ku-tum* AKT 5, 65: 25 "tablets to be read, thrown away(?)". Cf. *tabākatta*.

3. NA *ṭēḫ mê ta-bi-ku-te ša* GN StAT 2, 60: 10 "adjoining the poured out water (= water reservoir?) of GN".

tabku II s. *tabbukku*.

tablīttu, + pl. *tablīṭātu* "sustenance, victuals, fodder"; + MB

MB (fodder for) 10 UZ.TUR^{mušen} *esrūti* ... 20 UZ.TUR^{mušen} *tab-li-ṭa-ti* MBLET 7, 71: 3 "10 caged ducks and 20 fattened(?) ducks (lit. 'ducks of fodder')". Reiner 2007, 48 transl. "free-range", Gurney, MBLET p. 175f. "domestic". MPS/NR

tablu "stolen goods"

1. LB *kaspu ta-ba-la* MacGinnis 2008, 83 BM 75617: 1 "stolen silver", s. *tabālu* G 2.

2. LB *ta-bal ša* PN Iraq 54, 123: 3 (cf. CAD T 28 s.v. *tablu*, quoted as Durand Textes babyloniens 6) "(goods) stolen by(?) PN"; *ta-bal* ib. 12; *ta-bal itbalu* ib. 15 "the stolen goods that he stole". MPS (2), NR (1)

tabnītu I "beautification, arrangement of a sacrificial table"; + NB

1. NB *mamma tab-ni-tu ina bīt ili ul ubann(u) ... laḫru ... lušēbilamma* ⌜*tab-ne-e*⌝*-tu ina libbi lubennû* OIP 114, 17: 37 "(for a long time) no-one has arranged the sacrificial table in the temple. (Have PN) transport a ewe here so that they may arrange the sacrificial tables therewith".

2. LB *ta-ba-*⌜*ni-tum*⌝ MacGinnis 1995, 52: 5; *tab-ni-*⌜*tú*⌝ ib. 63: 6; *tab-*[*ba*]*-ni-t*[*ú*] ib. 156: 10 "(oil for) the table-arrangement".

3. LB *tab-ni-ti* TCL 6, 38: 49, s. Linssen 2004, 142.

4. MacGinnis 2008, 83: *t.* is not a type of offering (pace CAD T) but designates the arrangement of offerings for a deity, carried out by the *mubannû*. JW (1), MPS (1–4)

tabrītu s. *tebrītu*

tabrû "a type of produce"

In Nuzi: barley *ša t.* = "fodder?", s. Negri Scafa 2009, 451f. for disc. and lit. JW

taddīʾatu, + *taddīyatu* "a luxury garment"

1. AHw 1300 *taddītu*, CAD T 33 *taddiātu*. Durand 2009, 71 and 122f. with further ref. CAD supposes a plurale tantum, and Durand analyses the word as pl. of *taddû*/*taddīʾu*. However, many ref. show that the word was understood as sg., e.g. 1 ^{túg}*ta-ad-di-a-tim*/*tum* ARM 23, 44: 1; 45: 1; ARM 30, 481 M.11892+: 13; 1 ^{túg}*ta-ad-de-tum* ARM 18, 41: 1. Moreover, in

ARM 30, 338 M.12201, we find both 1 ^{túg}*ta-ad-di-ú* (l. 12, 18?) and 1 GÚ.È.A *ta-ad-di-a-tum* (l. 22) side by side. Cf. *taddītu*.

2. The unique spelling ^{túg}*ta-ad-di-a-ia-tum* ARM 30, 289 M.12522: 1 is obviously a mistake: the scribe started to write *-di-a-* and then added *-ia-* to render a glide between the vowels: *taddīyatu*. Pace Durand 2009, 122, ARM 30, 481 M.11892+: 13 does not have *ta-ad-di-a-ia-tum* but rather *ta-ad-di-a-tum*.

taddī'ātu s. *taddī'atu*

taddītu "layer, course (of bricks)"

1. In math. "laying number" of bricks, i.e. "the number of bricks of a given type needed to cover a unit of area with a single layer of bricks" (Friberg 2001, 72f.).

2. For the garment in OB texts s. *taddī'atu*. JW (1), MPS (2)

+ **taddû**, *taddī'u*, early OB *taddā'u* "a garment"; OA, OB

1. OA:
a) 1 ^{túg}*ta-di-im* KTS 54b: 2, s. CAD T 38 s.v. *tadu*.
b) *ta-dí-im* Kt c/k 811b: 15 (cit. Michel/Veenhof 2010, 245).

2. Early OB *ta-da-u* ARM 19, 318: 2.

3. OB (Durand 2009, 122f.):
a) *ta-di-im* ARM 22, 233: 3, s. CAD T 38 s.v. *tadu* adj.
b) 1 ^{túg}*ta-ad-di-ú* ARM 30, 338 M. 12201+: 12, cf. 18? "1 *t.*-textile." This text also has *taddī'atu* (s. *taddī'atu* 1, above).

4. OB lit. *erišti ta-di-im* (var.: *ta-di-i*) DN *lubuštam irriš* YOS 10, 51 i 27 (cf. MARI 8, 281 § 7) "a wish for a *t.* – DN desires a garment".

5. Derivation from *nadû* remains uncertain. The uncontracted form *taddī'u* is remarkable.

JW (1–2, 4), MPS (3, 5), NR (3)

****tadduntu** s. *taduntu*

tādirtu "darkening of mood"; + NB

NB *bikītu agâ ša* MN *ša nišī māti gabbu* ⌜*ta*!⌝*-dir-tu ukallū* SAA 21, 33: 7 "this weeping of month MN which all the people of the land maintain as a (rite of) distress".

tadnīntu "strengthening, enhancement"

1. OB AL.DÙ *ta-ad-ni-in-ti ù nudunnê* BM 80939: 6 "(grain) quota for *t.* and dowry".

2. OB *ta-ad-ni-in-ti īkim* OECT 13, 263: 7 "reinforcement of a dyke", cf. *ta-ad-ni-in-ti bīt* DN ib. 8 "reinforcement of the temple of DN", cf. ib. 9, 13, s. von Soden 1992.

3. For disc. s. Stol 2010, 171.

JW (2), NR (1, 3)

****tadu** adj./s. (CAD T 38), s. *taddû*

+ **taduntu** "gift"; SB

1. Lex. *ta-du-un-tum* MSL16, 154: 42 (Nabnītu), s. AHw 1300 and CAD T 34 s.v. *tadduntu*. But instead of *taPRuSt* from *nadānu* the form rather derives from *tadānu*.

2. Pentiuc 2001, 176: *ina* 3 *ūmi isin ta/tá-ad-na-ti ēnti* Emar 6/3, 369: 48 "on the 3rd day of the festival of the gifts of the ēntu-priestess".

MPS (1–2), NR (2)

taggamānu, s. *tagmānu*

tagmānu, *taggamānu* "a type of impost or rent"; Gk. lw.?

1. LB (dates) *ša tag-ma-nu ša* MU 55^{kam} Hackl 2013, 120: 5 "from the *t.* of year 55".

2. For disc. s. Jursa 2006, 149ff. with prev. lit. Perhaps a loan from Gk. τάγμα "that which has been ordered or arranged", s. already von Soden 1981, 295. JH/JW

****tagrību** (CAD T 39)

MacGinnis 2008, 83: in CT 55, 243: 8 read [*n*]*a-ak-ri-ma-nu* (a leather bag). NR

taḫāḫu "to soak(?)"

SB *raḫāmu* : *ta-ḫa-ḫa* SpTU 3, 99: 43 (comm.) "*raḫāmu* : to soak", s. CAD R 69.

+ **taḫakka** "man"; Hurr. word in MB Qaṭna

1. *rab šekkāte ša* : *ta-aḫ-a-ka-še-na* QS 3, 51: 9 "*rab sikkati* officials of the men".

2. *bītāt* : *ta-aḫ-a-ka-še-na* ib. 15 "houses of the men"; cf. *ṭābiḫu*.

3. For etym. cf. Richter 2012, 427 (derived from Hurr. *taḫe* "man"). JW (3), MPS (1–2)

taḫaltu, + *teḫiltu* "a type of cereal"; + OB

1. Reiner 2007, 48: OB *ina* n *eqlim ša* PN ... *kinītam u te-ḫi-il-tam* ... *izrū* FM 2, 38 no. 11: 29 "he sowed *kinītu* cereal and *t.* in PN's field of *n* size", cf. ib. p. 40 note n.

2. MA [...] NINDA *ta-ḫal-ta* BATSH 9, 63: 26; 67: 32 "*t.*-bread"; [NINDA *t*]*a-ḫal-te* 82: 30. JW/MPS

taḫapšu "felt, (felt-)rug"; + MB Emar

1. MB Emar *ēpiš ta-ḫap-še* Emar 6/3, 132: 3 "felt maker".

2. For etym. and lws. in Ugar. and Eg. s. Manassa 2012, 99–110; Richter 2012, 425f.

3. For the meaning "felt" cf. Cancik-Kirschbaum 1999, 85f.; Postgate 2000, 213–217. Further disc. and ref. Zawadzki 2006: 134f.; 2013, 562f. JW (2–3), MPS (1)

+ **taḫartu** "a metal object"; OB

1 *ta-ḫa-ar-ti kaspim* ARM 25, 149: 3, s. ARM 32 p. 396 M.8647 and ib. p. 126 and Durand/Marti 2004, 124. JW

tāḫāzu "battle"

OA *Ištar bēlat ta-ḫa-zi-im atmā* kt j/k 97: 12 "I swear by Ištar, lady of battle", s. Günbattı 1997: 133. NJCK

+ **taḫḫittu** "addition, supplement, complement"

1. n $ÁB^{ḫi.a}$ *ta-aḫ-ḫi-it-tum* ARM 26/1, 190 no. 47: 8 "n additional cows".

2. *šīm ta-aḫ-ḫi-it-ti* ARM 25, 630 = ARM 31, 54: 9 "(n gold,) additional/complementary price (for slaves)", cf. Guichard ib. p. 384 n. 61.

3. n GÍN KÙ.GI *ta-aḫ-ḫi-it-tum* ARM 25, 263: 4 "n shekels additional gold".

4. [*ta*]-*aḫ-ḫi-tu*[*m*] ARM 27, 156 r. 1 in broken context.

5. See Durand, ARM 26/1, 191 n. b ad no. 47. The ref. booked in CAD T 48 under *taḫḫitu* also belong here. Etym.: Sum. *daḫ*+*ed*-? To be distinguished from *ta*ʾʾ*ītu*. JW (3), MPS (2, 4–5), NR (1–2)

taḫḫitu (CAD T 48) s. *taḫḫittu*

taḫīqtu "mixing, blending (of wine)"

Stol 2010, 171: OB *inūma ta-*[*ḫi-*]*iq-ti šarrim* ARM 21, 101: 4 "on the occasion of mixing (wine) for the king". Cf. Durand ib. p. 105f. MPS/NR

taḫlaptu "cloak"; + NB

NB [túg]*taḫ-lap-ti* OIP 114, 86: 16 in broken context. Therefore, pace CAD T 51, the lex. ref. is not an error.

taḫlīpu, + pl. *taḫlīpānu* "covering, armor"

NA [[giš]GIGIR] [ta]*taḫ-líp*!*-a-ni* BATSH 6, 35: 6 "(for) an armored [chariot]". JW/MPS

taḫluptu "armor"

SB *ša lā taḫ-lu-up-tum ana nakri ittardū* SpTU 4, 121 iv 7 "they came down upon the enemy without armor". MPS/NR

taḫnuḫlu s. *taluḫlu*

+ **taḫrīru** "a technique in textile production(?)"

OB ⌜4⌝ TÚG SI.SÁ ÚS *ta-aḫ-ri-ru ana epēšim* ARM 30, 458 M.8605: 2 "4 unbleached garments of second quality, in *t.* technique(?), for manufacturing". S. Durand, ib. p. 42 note d: a treatment of fabric, perhaps tufting or trimming. Cf. *ḫa*/*urruru* "a garment" ib. p. 40f. MPS/NR

taḫsīstu, + *taḫšīštu* "reminder, memorandum"

1. OB *aššum ḫišeḫti ēkallim ša ina ta-aḫ-sí-sa-tim ina qāt* PN *šaṭru* FM 8, 161 no. 45: 34 "concerning the requirement of the palace that is written down in the memorandum by/in the possession of PN".

2. MB Ekalte *ṭuppi taḫ-ši-iš-*[*ti-*]*im* WVDOG 102, 71: 1 "tablet of memorandum". The spelling with *iš* is also once attested in a lex. text from Emar (CAD T 52; Mayer 2009, 424). JW (1), MPS (2)

+ **taḫtānu** "under"; NA, Aram. lw.

ēribtu taḫ-ta-n[*u-ni*? …] *mā anīni niḫaṣṣin* SAA 15, 116 r. 14 "we will protect the entrants under [our own(?)] (responsibility)". Cf. Fuchs/Parpola, ib. p. 80 n. ad r. 14; Cherry 2017, 260f.

taḫû "side(?)"

With *ana*: SB *at-ta-aḫ* PN *abīšu uštēbil* Astronomical Diaries 3 p. 274 no. 124 B: 20 "he was brought next to his father PN". NR

taḫûtu "young ones"

On *ša ta-ḫu-ti-ki* (E_1 *ta-ḫu-*⌜*ti-ki*⌝, Z_1 [*ta-ḫ*]*u*?*-ti-ki*, f [*ta-ḫu-t*]*i-*[*ki*]) in Gilg. SB VII 107 (AHw 1303; CAD T 57) s. George 2003, 847. Lambert 1979, 273 had suggested to del. the entry (read *ta-*RI*-ti-ki* in RA 62, 124: 14a after coll.). JW/MPS

taʾʾīttu, + *taʾʾīdu* "information, notification, instruction(s), order, (official) ruling"

1. OA "instruction" rather than "information" (Larsen 1976, 248 n. 2):

a) *ištē* PN *ta-ḫi-tám ašpuršim … ammākam naḫḫidāšima ina ḫuršiya šillatum lā ibaššī* AKT 6A, 225: 20 "I sent her instructions with PN … . Instruct her there so that nothing untoward occurs in my storeroom".

b) PN *šiparni ana ta-ḫi-tim ana* GN *šaper* AKT 5, 75* B 11 "our envoy PN has been sent to GN to convey an order".

c) *ti*ʾʾ*irtaka ta-ḫi-tum lillikaššunūti* KTS 2, 11: 9 "let a message from you (with) instructions come to them".

d) *ṣuḫārka ša ta-ḫi-tim* Cole 2: 14 (quot. Michel 1991c, 30) "a servant of yours with instructions".

2. Mayer 2017b, 250: OB *ta-ḫi-da-am ṭurdīma* AbB 14, 163: 35 "send (the letter) with a warning (that he must not come here)!"

3. OB *malā ta-i-ti ša tašpuram utakkal* MHEO 1 p. 103 Di 616: 16 "I will trust all information you have sent me".

4. OB (PN has died:) *ta-ḫi-tum* PN_2 ARM 23, 523 no. 551: 5 "(this is) information from PN_2".

JW (2–4), NJCK (1)

takāku "to (op)press"

G Stative "to suffer": OB lit. *šerʾānū-šu*/*ṣibtūšu ta-a-ku* CUSAS 18, 15: 39, 41 "his sinews/his tumors are suffering"; cf. ib. 6, 36. Cf. George ib. p. 89, quoting [*šumma n*]*akkaptāšu qātāšu u šēpāšu it-ta-ku* Sagig IV r. 29 "[if] his [te]mples, hands and feet suffer", s. Mayer 2017b, 231.

takāltu "trust"; + OB

1. Mayer 2917b, 250: OB lit. *ṣīrum dūrkun šu ta-ka-la-tim* MesCiv. 7, 214 iv 15 "august is your wall, (it is) of trustworthiness".

2. SB *ta-kal-tam* SpTU 5, 246 iv 7, s. *tāqurtu*. Diff. Mayer 2017b, 232: *tarībtu*. JW (1), MPS (2)

tākaltu "bag, sheath; stomach; part of the exta"

1. Containing seed for the seeder plow (cf. CAD T 63 *t.* A 3):

a) Lex. ⸢*ta-kal*⸣*-tum* = *epi*[*nnu*] AOAT 50, 363: 65 (malku) "bag = p[lough]".

b) Lex. *ziqqu* = [*t*]*a-kal-tú ik*[*-ka*!*-ri*!] AOAT 50, 364: 67 (malku) "*z.* skin = bag of the pl[oughman]".

2. OA *ta-kà-al-tum ša* 15 GÍN KÙ.GI kt 00/k 14 r. 6 "a bag/sheath (with, or: worth?) 15 shekels of gold (weighing 2 1/3 minas)", in a list of precious objects, s. Donbaz 2004, 186.

3. Stol 2010, 171: OB 2 [dug]*našpakū ša ta-ka-al-t*[*im*] YOS 8, 174: 12f. "two storage vessels with (i.e., in) a bag".

4. Mayer 2017b, 231: OB *ta-ka-al-ta-šu u himissu teleqqē* YOS 11, 4: 5 "you take its (= the frog's) stomach and fatty tissue (and boil them)". For mng. "stomach" here and in YOS 11, 23: 16 s. Glassner 2002. On med. usage s. Stol 2006, 107ff.

5. OB "sheath": *ta-ka-al-ti kaspim* ARM 25, 154: 6; cf. ARM 32, 126.

6. OB lit. DN *bēl ta-ka-la-tim* DNf *bēlet rēmim* DNf_2 *asūt awīlē* CUSAS 32, 25: 9 "DN, lord of the stomach, DNf, mistress of the womb, DNf_2, doctor of men".

7. For *t.* in ext. s. Jeyes 1989, 76; Leiderer 1990, 113f.; Koch-Westenholz 2000, 267ff.

JW (4–5, 7), MPS (1, 3, 6), NJCK (2), NR (3)

takālu "to trust"

G 1. Imp. *tikal*: OAkk. *ana dayyānī ti-kà-a*[*l*] FAOS 19, Gir 5: 5 "trust the judges!", s. ib. p. 72. The imp. is *takal* elsewhere in OAkk., *tikal* from Ur III on (Hilgert 2002, 202f.; Kouwenberg 2010, 135 + n. 31). In OA, both *tikal* and *takal* are attested in PNN (GOA p. 500 n. 28).

2. Imp. *tikil*: MB PN *Enlil-ti-kil* CUSAS 30, 372: 11 "Trust in Enlil!"

3. On the colophon formula NIR.GÁL-ZU (read: *atkalka*) s. Mayer 2009, 424.

Gtn Mayer 2009, 424, s. id. 1976, 497: SB *ša ana kâša it-ta-ka-lu-ka* (// *it-ka-lu-ka, tak-lu*) *tukān išdīšu* STT 58: 3 "you will firmly establish the foundations of him who always put his trust in you".

D 1. OA PN ᵈIŠKUR-*tá-ku-ul* AKT 7A, 76: 8 "Adad inspires confidence", s. ib. p. 181.

2. OB ⸢*karānum*⸣ *ina ālim* [*t*]*u-uk-ku-ul-ma* MARI 6 p. 79 n. 202 A. 3362: 10 "the wine in the city was promised".

JW (G, D), NR (Gtn)

takāpu "to prick, puncture, speckle, dapple, stitch"

G 1. OB lit. *tarbu'tašu i-*⸢*ta-ki*⸣*-ip šamê* Gilg. OB Harmal$_1$ 5 "his (the bull's) cloud of dust was thrusting into (or: speckling) the sky".

2. OB lit. *i-ta-ak-ki-ip kīma alpim*! MHEO 2 p. 82 IM 95317: 33 "(pain) is goring me like a bull".

+ **N** SB *šumma sinništu tikpī ina rēmiša i-tak-kip* SpTU 5, 253 r. 1 (s. also obv. 19) "if a woman is covered with dots on her womb". Pace Mayer 2009, 424 and Stol 2010, 172 not G-stem.

JW (G), MPS (N)

takiltu, + *tikiltu* "blue-purple (wool)": + MB Emar

1. Reiner 2007, 48: MB Emar *qimmatu ša* ˢⁱᵏⁱ*ti-kíl-ti* Westenholz/Ikeda 2000, 24: 3 "a tuft of blue-purple wool", followed by a tuft of ˢⁱᵏⁱḪÉ.ME.DA "red wool".

2. For disc. s. Thavapalan 2018, 4–13 with prev. lit.

JW (2), NR (1)

tākiltu "an algebraic square"

For disc. s. Høyrup 2002, 23 (etym.: *kullu*; also CAD T 73); Robson 2008, 113–115 (etym.: *šutākulu*); Britton/Proust/Shnider 2011, 527ff.

JW/MPS

takīttu, + *tikīttu* "corroboration, confirmation"

1. OA always regarding the accuracy of a weight stone:

a) 8 *manā kaspam ina* 1 *manā'iya ta-ki-tám* PN *isniqam* Prag 608: 3 "PN transferred to me 8 minas of silver, (weighed) with my one-*mina* stone – verified" (also TC 3, 171: 14; VS 26, 134: 3; AKT 8, 209A: 4).

b) *t. našī*: *ina* 1 *manā'im ša* PN *ilqē'ū* ... *kaspam ta-ki-tám na-ší-e* Dercksen 1996, 83 kt a/k 516b: 13 "they have received it (a loan of one mina of silver) on the basis of the 1-mina weight-stone of PN ...; the silver carries *t.*", i.e. represents the correct amount.

c) *kaspam ina abnem ni'ā*[*'im*] *ta-ki-tám išaqqulū* Dercksen 1996, 84 kt 91/k 518/b: 3 "they shall weigh the silver with our weightstones – verified". S. also *la ta-ki-tám* Fs. Veenhof p. 2 kt 92/k 328.

d) "(send a message to your representatives to give me tin and textiles ... worth about 1 talent of silver)" *i-ta-ki-it annī'ātim* 10 MA.NA^{ta} *kaspī lilli-kakkum*(*ma*) TC 1, 26: 10 "then from the *t.* of these (goods) silver acquired by me will come to you in quantities of 10 minas at a time" (translated by Dercksen 1996: 84; one would expect a stat. cstr. *takītti*).

e) Uncert.: 1/3 *manā* PN *ša tí-ki-ta lā īšû* Dercksen 1996, 84 kt 91/k 140: 60 "1/3 mina (of silver due by) PN, who does not have a verified weight-stone" (translated by Dercksen, atypical context).

2. Cf. Dercksen 1996, 82–83; Veenhof 2015a, 262 n. 89.

NJCK

+ **takkaltu** "plotting, slander"; SB

DN … *ša ta-ka-la-at ni-ši-im* (var. *ta-ka-lat*) *ibarrû kajjānim* SANER 3, 58: 9; 94 i 16 "DN … who regularly observes the plottings of the people", s. da Riva ib. p. 99 with different translation and index ib. p. 203. Derives from *nakālu*, cf. *takkīlū*. JW/MPS

takkannu s. *dakkannu*

takkapu "peephole, opening, window"

OB *dūram qablê ša ta-ak-ka-pí ša … ibbalkitūma* FM 2, 12 no. 1: 15 "(they did not leave through the city gates,) they climbed over the central wall with(?) openings" (cf. ARM 13, 26, quot. CAD T 75: *dūram ša ašar ta-ak-ka-pí imqutū*). JW

takkassu, *dakkassu* "(small) block of stone; a bead"

1. OB 1 *kišādu ták-ka-sí* ŠÀ.BA 14 *ták-ka-sú qutītum* 15 *da-du-ri ḫurāṣi* 1 *kisibirru pinku* ARM 25, 55: 1f. "1 necklace of *t.*, containing: 14 Gutian *t.*, 15 golden *da-du-ri*-beads, 1 coriander (as) knob", s. also *tutturu*. Cf. ARM 32, 44 for further ref. and disc.

2. Reiner 2007, 49: MA *ina abnī ša tàk-ka-si ša* GN … *ḫīṭ* MARV 4, 114: 15 "checked with the *t.*-stones of GN", s. Freydank ib. p. 21 and Radner 2003 (a weight stone?). JW (1), NR (2)

takkasû "a type of baked goods"

1. LB as income from a prebend: *tak-ka-su-*⸢*ú*⸣ *mamma ul iklu* AOAT 414/1, 130: 10 "no-one has retained the *t.*"

2. In LB Uruk also a collective term for baked goods (Kessler 1991, 84). JH/JW (1), NR (2)

takkīlū pl. tant. "unfounded talk, slander"; OA

awātūšina sarrā u ta-ki-le taštanammēʾī AKT 3, 79: 7 "their words are false, yet you keep listening to the slander"; cf. ib. 80: 3, 8. Cf. *takkalātu*. JW

takkīru I "a type of irrigation canal"

1. OB *inanna ta-ki-rum ša* ^íd^⸢…⸣ *teptēma* AbB 13, 180: 9 "now you have opened the *t.* of the ⸢…⸣-canal".

2. LB *mê ša tak-ki-ri-ka* PN *kī iššû ana* PN_2 *ikkarišu ittadissunūtu* BIN 1, 44 = dubsar 3, 124: 8 "PN, having taken water from your *t.*, gave it to PN_2, his ploughman". JW

takkīru II "a garment"

1. Ur III Garšana "a heavy, valuable cloth":

a) ^túg^*gú-è tá-ki-ru-um bar-si ĝar-ra tur lugal* CUSAS 3, 824: 1 "small royal *t.*-cape fashioned with bands".

b) ^túg^*sagšu tá-ki-ru-um* PN CUSAS 3, 563: 2 and passim (s. CUSAS 4, 156) "*t.*-cap of PN".

c) ^túg^*tá-ki-ru-um tur* DN 3^kam^ *ús* CUSAS 3, 608: 5; 796: 4 "small 3rd-quality *t.*-textile of DN".

2. For further ref. s. CUSAS 4, 191. Cf. Sallaberger 2011, 358; Waetzold 2010, 203f. and 206. NR

takkussu "reed-stem, tube, cut of wood"

LB 3 *tak-ku-us-su ša* 18^àm^ KÙŠ *arrakū* Isimu 2, 87: 5 "3 (freshly-cut) logs (of wood), which are 18 cubits long". JW/MPS

takkuštû, + *takkuštātu* "a textile"

1. OB ^túg^*ták-ku-uš-tu-ú* ARM 30, 121 T.346: 5; ^túg^*ta-ku-uš-tu-ú* ARM 30, 121 M. 11665: 1, 2; 4 ^túg^*ta-ku-uš-tu* ARM

30, 380 M.11563: 1. For further ref. s. Durand ib. p. 121.

2. OB 1 ^{túg}*ták*!-*ku*!-*uš*!-*tá*!-*tum* ARM 7, 251: 7, s. Durand 2009, 121.

3. For disc and add. OA ref. s. Michel/ Veenhof 2010, 221, 245 (from a GN "Takkušta"?, cf. *tuttubû*).

JW/NR (1, 3), MPS (1, 2)

taklīmtu "revelation, instruction; display"; + OAkk.

1. Reiner 2007, 49: OAkk. *in ták-lim-ti* DN RIME 2, 139: 37 "by the order of DN".

2. OAkk. *ták-lim-tum šu sanga* CUSAS 25, 125 r. 3 "(by) the order of the Sanga-priest"; ib. obv. 3; 119 r. 2.

3. Reiner 2007, 49: OB lit. *ta-*⸢*ak-lim*⸣*-tu-uk-ka ikannušū* OECT 11, 1: 44 "by your orders they prostrate themselves".

4. OB lit. *šērī ta-ak-li-ma-a-tim ītawūšum* CUSAS 10, 1: 15 "he told him songs of revelation".

5. Mayer 2009, 424: For mng. "display of grave goods" rather than "of the body", cf. Scurlock 1991; Nasrabadi 1999, 62–64; s. also *taklīmu*.

JW (2, 4–5), MPS (4), NR (1, 3)

taklīmu, + *takallimu* "displayed offering"

1. Mayer 2009, 424: SB *lā innamdinu tak-li-mu* Mayer 1990, 462: 12 "(DN without whom) no displayed offering is given".

2. Stol 2010, 172: NA *ta-kal-li-mu lā imaḫḫar* Fadhil 1990, 461: 17 "he shall not receive displayed offerings (in the underworld)". NR

+ **taklūtu** "trustworthiness"; OB

OB *bēlī ták-lu-ti ū lā ták-lu-ti līmur kīma aḫī lā nadêku* ARM 26/2, 493 no. 520 r. 8 "may my lord see my trustworthiness or my untrustworthiness, (and) that I am not negligent". Cf. Heimpel 2003, 400.

takmīsu "a slaughtered sheep"

1. MA *ták-mi-su* MARV 3, 16 i 20; VS 21, 29: 10; cf. Llop 2011, 23.

2. NA *šarru bēlī akī tak-mis iptaqdannâši* SAA 16, 43: 7 "the king, my lord, gave us orders as if (we were) *t.*-sheep". MPS (2), NR (1–2)

taknītu s. *teknītu*

takpīrtu "purification (rite)"

SB *am*[*ē*]*la māmīt lā īdû itmû tak-pir-ta-šú turru ... itti* DN SpTU 3, 67 iii 19 "a man who has sworn an oath that he does not know – to bring about his purification is with DN".

takpītu, *tukpītu* "a bead"

1. LB 4 ^{na4}*tuk-pa-a-ta* OIP 122, 120 ii 8.

2. On *t.* in LB Uruk s. Beaulieu 1999, 154f. with further ref.

3. Cf. ARM 32, 54f. with add. OB ref.

JW (1), NR (2, 3)

takpu "a basket"

1. NB ^{gi}*tak-pi rēḫēti* SAA 18, 9 r. 17 "a reed basket of leftovers".

2. LB 1-*en tak-pu* AOAT 414/1, 91: 14 "1 *t.* basket".

takpurtu "clearance allocation, payment to equalize"

Reiner 2007, 49: LB *bītu* PN *šupêlti ina qātīya itēpuš u kasap tak-pu-ur-ti maḫrāk* Gehlken 1995, 167 no. 1: 10 "PN exchanged the house with me and I have received the silver of the *t.* payment." NR

takrībtu, *takrību* "a prayer; (performance of) an Emesal lament"; + Ur III

1. Refs. for a ritual (CAD T 200f., AHw 1324 s.v. *taqribtu* and *taqrību*) belong here (= Sum. *ér* "(Emesal) prayer, lament", s. Gabbay 2011, 71 and n. 35). For OA/B refs. to commodities, s. *taqrībatu*. S. also *teqrūbatu*.

2. Ur III Garšana in circumambulation rituals (Gabbay 2011, 70f.):
a) ^{dug}*útul-šè gala-e-ne tak-ri-ib-tum* CUSAS 3, 437: 13 "(provisions) for the tureen of the lamentation singers (for their performance of) *t.*"
b) *tak-ri-ib-tum iri*^{ki} *ne-ne-*de_4 CUSAS 3, 1016: 21 "(performance of) *t.* (involving) circling around the city".
c) *gala ù ama-gal-e-ne íb-*gu_7 u_4 *tak-ri-ib-tum bàd* CUSAS 3, 1035: 11 "the lamentation singers and the female mourners ate … on the occasion of their *t.*-performance at (?) the (enclosure) wall".

3. Mayer 2009, 430: OB *kīma tebê ta-ak-ri-ib-ti* MHEO 1 p. 103 Di 604: 5 "when the *t.* started (I had the various priests stand in the gate of the choir-master)". NR

+ **takrīmātu** "time of heaping up, autumn"; NA

ina tak-ri-ma-⸢*a*⸣*-*[*ti*] *ina Tašrīt* (vii) SAA 16, 90 r. 3 "in the autumn, in month Tašrīt (ca. October)", s. also Reiner 2007, 49.

takṣâtu, *takṣīʾātu* s. *takṣītu*

takṣītu, pl. *takṣīʾātu*, *takṣâtu* "cold weather, frost, cold season, cooling"

1. OB lit. *luttaddī ana libbika šurīpam ta-ak-ṣ*[*i-a-tim*] ALL no. 25: 27 "let me throw on your heart ice (and) frost".

2. SB *ana tak-ṣa-a-tú ša arīti … ina libbi šīrūšu ikaṣṣû u damū ikkallû* SpTU 4, 153: 7 "for cooling the pregnant woman … by means of (it) her body will cool off and bleeding will stop".

3. Reiner 2007, 49: LB 3 *sūt ša tak-ṣi-ti* ^{lú}UM.ME.A YOS 19, 138: 29 "3 seah (of dates) of/for(?) the cold season(?), for the master". Mayer 2009, 425 tentatively suggests "for (the) 'cooling-off' (ritual)". Cf. *ana tak-ṣi-tú* YBC 11324: 6 (Jursa apud Reiner 2007, 49).

MPS (1, 2), NR (2, 3)

****takšakku** s. *taktaku*

+ **takšī/ērtu** "repairs"; OA

Reiner 2007, 49: 10 GÍN *annakum a-ta-ak-šé-er-tim* CTMMA 1, 96: 11 "10 shekels of tin for repairs"; n silver *ta-ak-šé-er-tum* Prag 804: 15. Cf. *kašāru*, *takšīru*. MPS/NR

takšīru "repair"

1. Ur III Garšana:
a) 3 *guruš šidim* 6 *guruš ták-ší-ru-um šà é-gal gub-ba* CUSAS 3, 35: 33 "3 builders (and) 6 workmen employed (for) repair in the palace".
b) du_{10}*-ús é-didli ták-ší-*[*ru-um*]*-šè* CUSAS 3, 1260: 4 "for repair of the bathrooms of various houses".
c) 1 *guruš šidim ták-ši-ru-um é* Gi-*na-tum šà* ^{giš}*kiri*$_6$ *gub-*[*ba*] CUSAS 3, 92: 18 "1 builder employed (for) repair of the barracks in the garden" (s. also G*i-na-tum*).

2. For further ref. s. CUSAS 4, 192, 676 and 679; Heimpel 2009, 285ff.

NR

takšītu "profit"

1. OB *ḫarrānātūšunu ana ta-ak-ši-tim ... uṣṣû* ARM 26/2, 526 no. 532: 11 "their caravans will go out for profit".

2. OB *matī ta-ak-ši-i-tum lā ibaššû* CUSAS 36, 174: 10 "whenever there is no profit".

takšû I "triplet"

A constellation of 3 stars (CAD T 89 *t.* 3): SB [mul]*ta*[*k-š*]*á-a-tum* Iraq 63 p. 171: 5. JW/MPS

takšû II, *takši'u*, + *šakšû* "a leather bag, saddlebag"; + OB

1. OB 2 *nādāt kaspim* 6 *ta-ak-šu-ú iḫḫabšūma ana nādātim rabī'ātim u ta-ak-ši-i innepšū* M.11267 (quot. ARM 26/1, 197 n. b.) "2 silver pouches (and) 6 *t.*s, that had been damaged, have been turned into large pouches and *t.*s"

2. OB var. *šakšû*(?): *ina libbi ša-ak-ša-tim akannak ša-ak-ša-am ana libbi ša-ak-*[*ši*]*-im anāk*[*uma*] *ašakkanš*[*u*]*ma* ARM 26/1, 196 no. 54: 7 "I will seal (the silver) inside *š.*-bags. I will place (each?) *š.*-bag inside (another) *š.*-bag myself", s. Durand ib. p. 197; cf. Stol 2010, 172. Note the fem. pl. whereas the previous attestation shows masc. pl. forms.

3. The ref. CAD D 35 s.v. *dakšiu* "donkey saddle" and AHw s.v. *dasû* belong here. JW (1–3), NR (2)

taktaku "part of a chariot (made of bronze)"

The ref. cit. CAD T 89 s.v. *takšakku* belongs here (s. ARM 32, 161). JW

taktīmu "a blanket"

1. OB 1 [túg]*ta-ak-ti-mu* ARM 30, 334 M.11777: 21; p. 343 M.5490 i 15. Cf. Durand ib. p. 122.

2. MB 1 *šūšī* [gada]*tak-tim-mu lā damqū*[*tu*] RSO 14, 239 RS 88.2158: 37 "60 woolen blankets of bad quality". JW/MPS

takulatḫu "candleholder, candelabra"; Nuzi, Hurr. lw.

Cf. Schneider-Ludorff 2005 with disc. and etym.; Richter 2012, 429. JW

tākullû "itch, pain"

1. Reiner 2007, 49f.: LB *ana sinništi ša tulûša*!? *ta-kul-lu-ú ikkaluši* Finkel 2000, 158 5C r. 4 "(medicine) for a woman whose breast(?) hurts" // [...*t*]*a-kul-la* ib. A16 // *ta-kul-*⌜x-x⌝ ib. B_1 19.

2. From *akālu*, hith. not attested noun pattern *taPRuSSā/ī*? MPS (1–2), NR (1)

tākultu "(ceremonial) meal, banquet"

MA *ana ta-kúl-te ša līmē* PN Fs. Röllig p. 129ff. VAT 19194: 27 "(barley) for the banquets of the eponymy of PN", s. Freydank ib. p. 133f. JW

ta/ākulû (AHw 1309, CAD T 91) s. *tākullû*

****takunnātu** (AHw 1309b)

Lambert 1979, 273: In RA 29, 98: 4 read with Sommerfeld 1985 *ta-ku-un-*x x*-nu*. JW

takurassu, *takurazu* "a profession"

Nuzi LÚ[meš] *ta-ku-ra-z*[*i*] SCCNH 7 p. 123ff. ERL 82+: 15. JW

tal'abu "a reptile(?)"

S. Sjöberg 1996, 227 + n. 8: "a fast moving/creeping animal, perhaps some kind of reptile". JW/MPS

talālu I "to stretch out"

Disc. s. Mayer 2009, 425f.

+ **talālu II** "to support, to form an alliance with"; OB, SB

G 1. With *ittī*: *ana ṣēr šarrī ša panānum ittī awīl* GN *ta-al-lu lištappar* MARI 8 p. 364: 28 "may he repeatedly send messages to the kings who were formerly allied with the man of GN". Cf. CAD T 92 *talālu* 2b.

2. With acc.:

a) OB *kīma* PN *aḫī* PN_2 *u* PN_3 *it-lu-lu-ma* ARM 27, 71: 17 "as my brother PN supported PN_2 and PN_3".

b) OB *kīma šū šarrī šunūti it-lu-lu yâti abī*! PN *li-it-lu-la-an-ni* ARM 27, 71: 25f. "just as he made an alliance with those kings, may my father PN make an alliance with me".

c) OB *ištū anāku* PN *u* PN_2 *ta-a[l-l]a-nu-ma qātam ana qātim tiṣbutānu* ARM 26/2, 391 no. 468: 7 "since I, PN, and PN_2 made an alliance and took each other's hands." Cf. CAD T 92 *talālu* 2b.

d) OB PN *u* PN_2 *šarram ayyêm it-lu-lu* ARM 26/2, 317 no. 423: 46 "with which king have PN and PN_2 made an alliance?" Cf. Heimpel 2003, 361, pace Joannès, ARM 26/2, 317f. (*dalālu*).

e) Add here SB CT 20, 5: 10, 23, 25 (CAD A/1, 331 s.v. *alālu* A 2c; Reiner 2007, 50; Streck 2003 41 and n. 20).

D "to make an alliance" (Reiner 2007, 50): PN *ú-ta-la-al* ... *idam ištēn ú-ta-al-la-al* ARM 26, 483 no. 513: 20, 22 "PN wants to make an alliance … together he wants to make an alliance".

MPS/NR

talammu "a container of standard capacity"

1. LB for ghee: *ta-⸢lam⸣ ša ḫimēti* dubsar 3, 127: 7.

2. N/LB measure for beer, s. Stol 1994, 168f. JW

talannu, *telannu* "dice, astragal; a footwear"; + OA

1. Lex. *zi-in-gi gìr-ra-ra* = *mēlulu ša ta-la-[an-ni]* MSL 17, 219: 246 (Antagal) "to play, with an astr[agal]"; cf. the copy in CT 19, 31 iv 21, with coll. by Finkel 2007, 29. S. also Stol 2016. Cf. CAD T 327 *telannu* "a stone object". The word is probably related to Latin *talus* "ankle bone, astragalus", s. Finkel ib.

2. OA "a footwear":

a) *tá-lá-né-e-e[n] damqātim aš-šēpēya šēbilam* TPAK 1, 69: 17 "send me a pair of good *t.* for my feet!"; *šēnēn ta-lá-né-e-en* ib. 8 "a pair of *t.*-shoes"; *tá-lá-né*!*-en* ib. 20: 30.

b) 1 *ta-lá-né-en šinīšu šuḫuppatān* AKT 6A, 239: 6 "2 pairs of *t.*-shoes, a pair of boots" (in list of cloths, objects, and logs), s. also GOA 288f.

c) *ta-lá-né-en ana* 2 *šinīšu damqātim* DIRI ib. AKT 6A, 508: 1 "2 pairs of *t.*-shoes, extra-fine quality".

3. *t.* "dice, astragal" and *t.* "footwear" are probably the same word: both belong to the semantic field "foot".

JW/NJCK (2), MPS (1, 3)

talbītu "circumference"

NA *tal-bit māt* GN AfO 25, 62: 33 pass. (Sargon Geography), with Horowitz 2011, 86 and Liverani 1999–2001, 68ff. (with prev. lit.) not to be read as *ribīt* (pace CAD T 93, CAD R 318, AHw 1310). JW

talbuštu "issue of clothing, a textile"

LB *iltēn* ^{túg}*tal-bu-uš-tum ša bīti* RA 97 p. 99 BM 54655+: 11 "1 *t.*-textile 'for the house' (for 1 mina of silver)", s. Jursa ib. p. 100 (a curtain or carpet?).

JW

talḫadī'u "textile from Talḫad/t"

S. Michel/Veenhof 2010, 221; 223; cf. textiles *ša Talḫad/t*, ib. JW

talīmu I, + *talimmu* "favorite brother"

1. Lex. *tam* = *tá-li-im-mu* Emar 6/4, 537: 380 (Sa).

2. Early OB *ta-li-im* Enlil CUSAS 17, 38: 18 "(Išme-Dagan) brother of Enlil".

3. In NA a high-ranking family member of the king, s. Bartelmus 2007 for disc.

4. Del. SpTU 2, 6: 1 and 6, read U_4-*ma* "storm(demon)" (Mayer 2009, 426; Borger 2010, 345).

JW (2–3), NR (1, 4)

+ **talīmu II**, pl. *talīmātu* " a (quality of a) garment"; MA

1. 6 TÚG *ša*!? $^{túg!}$*ta*!?-*li*!?-*ma-a-tu*^{meš} *ša ṣer*!?-*pi* StAT 5, 82: 2 "6 garments of *t.* of red wool".

2. 2 TÚG *ša* ^{túg}*ta-li*!?-[*m*]*a-tu*^{meš} *ša* UGU?^{meš} […] StAT 5, 36: 3 "2 garments of *t.* whose upper side […]".

3. Prechel/Freydank ib. 103 suggest to connect this term with *atulimānu*, *talīmānu*, *tulīmātu* "both hands". JW

tālittu "offspring of animals"

1. MA "breeding quota": 1 *šūši*$^{ta.àm}$ *ta-li-tu-šu ana* 80$^{ta.àm}$ *ta-li-te* 2 *alpū mūrū maṣī'ū* BATSH 9, 39: 17–19 "60 each is (the quota for) his offspring; for 80 for each offspring, 2 male calves are substracted." For disc. and further ref. Freydank 2010, 87–97.

2. Mayer 2009, 426 suggests to parse this word as *talīttu* (*taPRīSt* of I-w). Cf., however, the var. *tamlittu* (MA onwards, CAD T 97). JW/MPS

tallaktu "walkway; way (of life); cart"

1. Mayer 2009, 426: SB *bītu ša tal-lak-ti* BagM Bh. 2, 97: 9 "house with walkway" (in list of temples).

2. Mayer 2009, 426: SB *anna tal-la-ka-tum ša mēlulika* AulaOr. Suppl. 23, 186: 13 "behold, the walkway where you play".

3. NA **a)** *alpu ša* ^{giš}*ta-lak-te* SAA 14, 23: 2 "wagon-ox".

b) *adu tal-lak-tú-šú* ib. 439 r. 1 "(a donkey) with its wagon".

4. In SA.GIG XVI 80 read *pi-rit-ti/u* instead of *tál-lak-* (pace AHw 1311a s.v. *tallaktu* 3b), s. Heeßel 2000, 192.

JW (3–4), NR (1–2)

tallu I "dividing line, beam, diameter"

1. Ur III? lex. *dal sík-ĝu*$_{10}$ = *ta-al-li pērtiya* CUSAS 12 p. 154 ii 6 (Ugumu) "part of my hair".

2. OB 20 *urnī* ... 1 *ammā u ūṭā ta-al-šu-nu* ARM 28, 17: 11 "20 cedars … their diameter is 1 and a half cubit each".

3. OB also as part of jewelry and carrying pole of a palanquin, s. ARM 32, 161 with add. ref.

4. Mayer 2009, 426: SB *i-na* <*bi*>*rit* GN *u* GN_2 *kīma* ^{GIŠ}DAL *parku* TCL 3: 65 "(a district that) lies across between GN and GN_2 like a cross beam".

5. LB *ana bitqa ša tal-lu erê ša narkabti* MacGinnis 2008, 83f. BM 64023: 6 "(silver) for the repair of the bronze pole of the chariot".

6. For GIŠ RI as body part of the sheep s. *isru*. JW (3), MPS (1–2, 6), NR (4–5)

tallultu s. *tullultu*

talmīdu "apprentice"

1. Lex. *šu-i zu-zu*= *ta-lam-*[*id/di gallābī*] Emar 6/4, 602: 139 (= MB Lu 186) "apprentice of the barbers", s. Y. Cohen 2004, 84.

2. Mayer 2009, 426: MB PN GÁB.[ZU.Z]U *ša* PN_2 Emar 6/4, 604.12: 7 "PN, apprentice of PN_2" (colophon).

3. On *t.* as an age-category in MA s. Bloch 2008, 160–165 (corresponds to NA *ṣaḫurtu*). JW (1, 3), NR (2)

talmīttu "female apprentice"

1. MA 2 [f]*tal-mi-da-tu* Chuera 70: 77.

2. On *t.* as an age-category in MA s. Bloch 2008, 160–165 (corresponds to NA *batussu*). JW (2), MPS (1)

talmu "large"

MA ÙZ[meš] *tal-mu* BATSH 9, 11: 4 "[…] large goats". JW

talmuttu s. *tilmuttu*

talpīttu "application, coating; an irrigation technique(?); storage(?)"

1. OB in agriculture (referring to the irrigation technique *mê lapātu*?):
a) *ina šipir ta-al-pí-t*[*im*] *ša* 2 *iniʾātim* YOS 12, 221: 5 "during the irrigation(?) work with 2 plow-oxen".
b) n *iniʾātum ta-al-pí-it*!(IK) BM 97939: 7; n *iniʾāt ta-al-pí-it-ti* BM 97133: 1 "n plow-oxen of/for *t.*" (quot. Stol 1995b, 212 n. 193; s. ib. p. 200).

2. Reiner 2007, 50: MA *ana šipar talpi-te* K.11823: 3 "for the smearing work" (Postgate 1994, 6). Cf. *ripītu*.

3. NA uncert.: A.ŠÀ *ta-al-pi-u-te* BATSH 6, 37 = SAAB 7, 110 no. 1: 17, s. Postgate ib. p. 113. Radner 2002, 62f. understands this as *talpittu* "storage, silo", listed in the dictionaires as *ripītu* (s. also ead. 1997, 252). JW (1, 3), NR (2)

+ **taltallakku** "an object"; NB

tal-tal-lak-ku-ma ... *ša ḫurāṣi epu*[*š*] SAA 21, 134: 2 "a *t.* …: make it of gold!" Cf. *tallakku* A "a wooden carrier for food?" (CAD T 97)?

taltallu "(male) inflorescence of the date palm"

1. SB *tal-ta-lu* KAL 3, 75 ii 6.

2. SB *irīšu tal-tal-lu yar*[*uttu* ...] *lirīšū-ka* KAL 9, 33 ii 6 "may fragrance, inflorescence, *yaruttu*-aroma rejoice over you".

tālu "young date palm"

SB 2 *qimmātušu kīma ta-lim* AulaOr. Suppl. 23, 44: 11 (Gilg.) "his 2 locks were like a young date palm".

taluḫlu, *taḫnuḫlu* "a class of person"

1. In Nuzi HSS 14, 597: 34 read *ta-aḫ*$_4$-*nu-uḫ*$_5$-*li* (= AdŠ 3, 122: 34).

2. For disc. and lit. s. Zaccagnini 1990, 41f.; Richter 2012, 435. JW

tamalākum "a sealable container"; OA

ta-ma-lá-kam ša maškam sāmam naktamšu<<*nu*>> *ḫa-ar-mu* Fs. Donbaz 157 left 4 "a *t.* of which the lid is covered with red leather", s. Veenhof 2010, 174. NJCK

tāmartu "view(ing); audience-gift"

1. OA *ta-ma-ar-tám damiqtam* 80 TÚG[hi.a] *ša ālim u* 20 TÚG[hi.a] *ša Akkidiʾē ana litabšika nuštēbilakkum* kt 01/k 217: 61 "we have sent you a nice audience-gift: 80 textiles of the city (Assur) and 20 Akkadian-style textiles for you to wear', s. Günbattı 2014, 90.

2. Early OB 12 *tá-ma-ra-tum* KTT 52: 1 "12 presents".

3. OB *ta-ma-ar-ti* PN TLT 153: 2 "(1 *qû* first-rate oil), a gift from PN". On *t.* and its relation to the *igisû*-tax in OB, s. Stol 2004, 771–3.

4. OB *aššum ta-ma-ar-ti ana šarrim ṣamādim* Haradum 2, 68: 27 "concerning the packing of the audience-gift for the king".

5. OB *ta-ma-ar-tam kuṣṣudākuma ina lā ta-ma-ar-tim alākam ul ele''ī* Haradum 2, 77: 5, 7 "concerning the audience-gift, I have been detained, and I cannot go without the audience-gift".

6. OB 30 DUG GEŠTIN *u* 10 *amarāt taskarinnim ta-ma-ar-ta-šu-nu ušarkibūma* ARM 26/1, 272 no. 105: 19 "they loaded 30 jars of wine and 10 boards of boxwood, their audience-gift, (onto a boat)".

7. OB *ta-ma-ar-t*[*i*] *ša* PN [*i*]*rdūnimma* MARI 8, 405 no. 5 [A.964]: 10 "they brought (1 horse, 2 goats, 8 rams, 10 ewes), the audience-gift from PN", s. Joannès ib. n. b for add. Mari ref.

8. OB/MB lit. *ta-ma-ra-tu našû lalêki* ALL 11 r. 6 "they bring gifts to please you", cf. Mayer 2017b, 231.

9. Mayer 2009, 427: NB *bāb ta-mar-ti* LUGAL x [...] BagM Bh. 2, 97 r. 2 "gate viewing(?) the king".

10. Reiner 2007, 50; Stol 2010, 172: in *bīt tāmarti*, "house of observation, theater": SB *puliṭānu ša ina Bābili šaṭrū ina bīt ta-mar-tú šasû* Astronomical Diaries 132D_2 r. 15 "[the...which] were written for the citizenry of Babylon were read out loud in the theater", wr. É IGI.$DU_8^{meš}$ ib. 161A.25, 140A r. 6, and passim. A calque on Gk. θέατρον, s. van der Spek 2001.

11. LB "meeting?": *libbū* ⌜*ša ta-mar*⌝*-tum ittiš*[*u* ...] AOAT 414/1, 129: 16 "just like the meeting with him [...]".

12. On *t.* as a (diplomatic) gift in OB Mari, s. Lerouxel in FM 6, 423ff. On *ana t.* in colophons (CAD T 111 mng. 1b) s. Pearce 1993, 186–8. For *t.* in Ugar. in comparison with *šulmānu* "gift" s. Malbran-Labat 2010, 86.

JW (3–5, 7, 8, 11–12), MPS (2, 6), NJCK (1), NR (9, 10)

+ **tamḫāṣu** "battle, combat"

OB lit. *uzzum*! *ta-am-ḫa-ṣú šibbatu u nâḫu ... kûmma Ištar* Or. 87, 16 i 21 "anger, battle, glow and calming ... are yours, Ištar". Cf. *tamḫuṣu* CAD T 118f.

JW/MPS

tamīmu, *tammīmu*, + fem. *tammatu*? "complete, perfect, healthy (said of cattle)"

1. Stol 2010, 172: LB $KÙ^{me}$ *u ta-mi-me-e* AUWE 5, 48: 10 "(cattle) pure and healthy". Hence KÙ is not a logogr. for *t.* (pace CAD T 119).

2. LB *ta-mi-im*!*-ma-tum* FLP 1482: 2 (quot. BagM 21, 588ff.), s. also van Driel 1995, 220.

3. LB GU_4.MUNUS ... *ta-am-ma-tum* OECT 10, 188: 2 (coll.) "(1) healthy heifer" (for *tamīmtu*; incorrectly read *ta-me-mi-tum* in CAD T 119 as BM 47354). JH (3), JW (2), NR (1)

tamirtu s. *tawertu*

tāmītu s. *tāwītu*

tamkāru "merchant, businessman"

ṣābī tamkāri "people of the merchant" (CAD T 132 *t.* c 3'): OB lit. *ṣa-bi* DAM.GÀR UET 7, 73 v 183 (s. Westenholz 1997, 168).

tamkārūtu "business, commerce; merchants"

1. OA *umma* DAM.GÀR-*ru-tum-ma* Donbaz 2001 p. 111 kt 98/k 118: 2 "thus speak the merchants".

2. OB [*ta-am*]-*ka-ru-tu-um lā itabbalū* AbB 14, 135: 9 "lest the creditors take them away", s. Veenhof ib. p. 219.

3. OB *imērī u ṣābam ša ana tam-ka-ru-tim illû* MARI 6, 63 no. 129: 10 "(they are detaining) the donkeys and people who come up to trade".

JW (2–3), NR (1)

+ **tamku(?)** "estate(?), tenure(?)"; Ugar.; NWSem. lw.(?)

PN … *maškana* : *ta-am-kí ša* PN_2 … *ana* PN_3 … *ittadinšu* PRU 3, 169a: 2 (leg.) "PN … gave PN_3 … the estate (gloss:) *t.* of PN_2". Cf. Sivan 1984, 278 and Huehnergard 1987, 185: <? TMK "to hold, grasp". MPS/NR

****tamliš** s. *tamšīlu*

tamlītu "filling"

1. For uncert. *tam-la-tum*, quot. CAD T 142 *t.* 1 in broken context, s. the PN *Tam-la-*[*tum*] CUSAS 29, 38: 9 (cf. also Stol 2010, 172). The mng. and etym. of the name are unclear.

2. OB 60 *iku eqlam ta-am-li-*⌜*it*⌝ [*i*]*škār* ^{giš}APIN^{há} *ša ēkallim i*[*na* GN]… *eleqqē* FM 2, 72 no. 37: 23 "I will receive a field of 60 iku (as) fulfillment of the work assignment of the plow teams of the palace i[n GN]".

JW (2), MPS/NR (1)

tamlīʾu "filling; terrace; inlay"; + OAkk.

1. OAkk. Girsu "a category of workers": (PNN) *tám-li-um*^{me} ITT 2, 4669 ii 6; *tám-li-um* ib. 4683 and 5869 (court. E.-M. Huber, Mainz).

2. Early OB [*t*]*ám-li-am* [*ad*]*ī qanūʾim šupuk* AS 22, 4: 21 "erect a terrace a full reed high!".

3. OB PN *ina tam-li-i-im ša bāb ēkal-*[*lim*] ... *ub*[*lam*] FM 11, 151 no. 132: 3 "(wine, which) PN has received on the terrace of the palace gate".

4. OB "stone inlays": For add. OB ref. s. ARM 32, 69.

5. MA *ina bīt karme ša tam-le-e ša pī bābi ša ana ta-am-li rabê* BATSH 9, 87: 9f. "in the granary on the terrace in front of the gate that (leads upstairs?) to the big terrace"; cf. 86: 3f; 91: 6; s. Röllig ib. p. 26 § 6.1.3.

6. Mayer 2009, 428: SB *sikkat karri* [.].. *u uqnâ tam-la-a umalli* BagM 21, 393 iv 19 "I had the knob-pegs inlayed with […] and lapis lazuli."

JW (1–5), NR (6)

tamlû s. *tamlīʾu*

tamrīru "bitter"

Instead of *ta*?-*am*?-*ri-ra-am* ARM 10, 133: 25 (CAD T 146), read with Durand 2000, 336 n. 102 GEŠTIN *re-ša*!-*am*. MPS/NR

tamru "camel", pl. *tamarātu*; SB, s. *ud-ru* 2.

+ **tamṣītu** "opening(?)"; SB

[*e*]*ptēki*? *ta-am-ṣi-a-tim u miṣrātim* ALL no. 11: 3 "[I] opened(?) the openings(?) and borders for you". Cf. CAD U 287 *uṣṣû* b "to open wide doors, openings".

tamšāru "whip(-thong)"

1. CAD T 147 *t.* 1a: Instead of *ṭi-rì tam-še-e-ri*, von Soden 1991, 190 suggests to read *de-ku-ut še-e-*[*ri*] "who wake up in the morning".

2. OB *tam-ša-ru* JCS Suppl. 2, 61: 2 (list of objects).

3. For disc. s. Stol 1995b, 187 and 205 n. 77 (ref. to cattle) and Streck 2004, 269 (a rope made from palm bast or fibers). JW (2–3), MPS (1)

+ **tamšīḫu** "area"

Reiner 2007, 51: 3 *šar u pitir Uruk tam-ši-ḫu* Gilg. SB I 23; XI 328 "3 1/2 square miles is the area of Uruk". Cf. *mašāḫu.* JW

tamšīlu "image, likeness"

1. Mayer 2017b, 232: Lex. *tam*-LIŠ (read *tam-šil*$_4$), s. AHw 1315b s.v. *tamlīš*, CAD T 149b ad 2c; cf. MB [*tam*]-*šil*$_4$ DN Or. 80, 141: 1 "image of DN".

2. Ur III *tám-še-lum* SAT 3 1613: 3; *tám-ši-lum* NBC 524: 3 "figurine". S. Sigrist 2004, 251ff. on wax figurines. JW

tâmtu s. *ti᾽āmtu*

tamṭītu "diminution, scarcity"

Del. 4R 28* no. 4 r. 43f. (CAD T 158a), read with Reiner 2007, 51 and Borger 2008, 442 *uṭ-ṭe-tum.* NR

tamû II "to swear"

G 1. OB *ālī ina abnika ta-mi-im izzīzamma* ARM 28, 44: 18 "my city stood up in order to swear by your stone".
2. Mayer 2009, 428f.: MB [*nīš* D]N *u* DN$_2$ *ta-mi* UET 7, 1 r. 3 "he will be subject to the oath of DN and DN$_2$".
3. NA *lā it-me-i-u* BATSH 6, 123: 6 "(if) they do not swear".
4. Stol 2010, 172: Logogr. KUD in NU KUD (= *lā itamma*) Iraq 21, 52: 52 (= CTN 4, 58).
5. On the expression (*māmīt*) *atmû* (*u*) *lā atmû* "be it any oath I have sworn" s. Mayer 1989, 166f.; id. 2017b, 232.

Gtn LB *it-te-nim-mu* AOAT 414/1, 224: 12 (PSBA 31, 169ff.) "they swear continuously".

+ **Dtn** Mayer 2009, 428f.: SB *mu-ut-ta-am-mu-ú-a š*[*uḫ*]*miṭ* GN ORA 7, 320: 43 "burn those who constantly bind me by oath, o Marduk!".

Dtr "to swear mutually":
1. Early OB [*an*]*āku šūt* [*n*]*u-ta-ma-am-ma* AS 22, 23: 23 "I and he will mutually swear"; cf. *ú-ta-ma-ma-a* AS 22, 50: 3 (broken context).
2. Cf. Kouwenberg 2010, 440.
JW (G, Gtn, Dtr), MPS (G, Dtr), NR (G, Dtn)

+ **tamu᾽᾽ātu** "oath(?)"

Mayer 2009, 429: MA PN [*ša*] *a*[*na*] *ta-mu-a-ti illi*[*kuni*?] Subartu 14, 14: 7 "(PN) who went to (give) an oath".

+ **tan-** "to do"; Hurr. word in MB Qaṭna

5 ref. in Akk. context, cf. QS 3 p. 194 (index). S. also Richter 2012, 436f.

+ **tanaḫlatu?** "inheritance, possession"; MB Emar; NWSem. lw.

1. *mimmūya kīma ta-na-aḫ-la-ti-ia* AulaOr. Suppl. 1, 35: 10 "all my goods are like my inheritance". Pentiuc 2001, 177 corrects to {*ta-*}-*na-aḫ-la-ti-ia.*

2. Cf. *naḫālu* II "to share out, transfer property" and *niḫlatu* "transferred property" in OB Mari. Etym.: Streck 2000, 106f. s.v. *naḫālu.* JW/MPS

tanattu, pl. *tanadātu* "praise, glory"

1. Mayer 2009, 429: OB lit. *ta-na-da-ti-ia mātum ana šutanūdim* BagM 34, 150 xiv 12 "so the land may sing my praise".

2. Mayer 2009, 429: MB Bogh. *ana multarriḫutti ana tá-na-a-ti-šu ilqû* KBo. 1, 3: 9 "(doors, which PN) boastfully had taken for his glory". NR

tanēḫtu, + *tenēḫtu* "pacification, mollification, relaxation"; + MB

1. OA *té-né-eḫ-tí libbika ... ašapparakkum* AKT 6A, 176: 45 "I will send you relief of your heart".

2. OB *ta-[n]é-eḫ-ti libbika liqē* ARM 26/1, 174 no. 39: 9 "obtain the relief of your heart!"

3. OB *mīnam inanna ta-né-eḫ-ti libbim ana ṣēr šarrim i nišpur* ARM 26/1, 267 no. 101: 10 "what now? let us write to the king for the relief of (his) heart!"

4. OB lit. *akāl* ⸢*ta*⸣*-ne-eḫ-tim* MARI 5, 258 FLP 1674: 21 "the food of peace".

5. OB pl. (garments and wine) *ana ta-né-*⸢*ḫa-tim*⸣ FM 11, 166 no. 155: 6 "for leisure".

6. MB n *aklu ta-né-eḫ-ti ša* DN CUSAS 30, 275: 11 "n loaves of bread for the appeasement of DN".

JW (1, 4–5), MPS (2–3, 6)

tānēḫtu "moaning, distress"

SB *ina ta-né-eḫ-ti ṣurrupat* ... AulaOr Suppl. 23, 33: 23 "... burns in distress".

tanēḫu "quieting, pacification"

SB *addīki šipta ša ta-né-ḫi* Lamaštu II 4 (Farber 2014, 95) "I have cast a pacifying spell against you" (alternatively *tānēḫu* "wailing, moaning"; ambiguity perhaps intentional, s. ib. p. 224f.).

JW

tānēḫu "wailing, moaning"

S. also SB Lamaštu II 4 cit. s.v. *tanēḫu*.

tanēštu s. *tenēštu*

tangussu "a metal pot"

LB [2]-⸢*ta*⸣ ^{urudu}ŠEN.TUR^{meš} AOAT 414/1, 110: 8 (in list of copper objects).

tanīḫtu s. *tanēḫtu*

tānīḫtu s. *tānēḫtu*

tanīḫu s. *tanēḫu*

+ tanpīḫtu "fire, conflagration"; OB

OB lit. *pūtam ta-an-pí-iḫ-tam is-ri-[im?] išāt qablim* FM 14 i 32 "in front, the fire of battle has opened up(?) conflagration", cf. *napāḫu* D "to ignite". S. Guichard ib. p. 39. JW

tanūqātu pl. tant. "battle cry"

1. SB *alālama kīma arīti ta-nu-qa-tum!?-ma* KBo. 36, 27: 17 "there is an *alāla*-cry, there is a battle cry like that of a pregnant woman!"

2. Mayer 2009, 429: SB *ana ta-nu-qa-ti-šá dūr šadî* <*i*>*quppūši* AfO 50, 22: 17 "at whose battle cries the wall of the mountain buckles."

JW (2), MPS (1)

tāpalu "pair, set of two"

1. For OB ref. from Tell Leilan (pairs of shoes and boots) s. Vincente 1992, 262f.

2. OB uncert.: *ēpiš ta-pa-li*!(TU) AbB 10, 197: 12 "(PN,) maker of pairs" (a profession?).

3. MB referring to chariot teams, s. Vita 2010.

4. In Ugaritica 5, 20: 5 quot. CAD T 177 read *lik-ta-an-ni-*na*.

5. In peripheral Akk. *t.* is also used as a pl. marker (s. Reiner 1999). JW

tapātu s. *dappātu*

tapḫaru "entirety"; OB

Mayer 2009, 428: OB lit. *tabikkum râmī ta-ap-ḫa-ra-am* ALL no. 15 i 25 "my love is poured on you entirely".

taphīrtu s. *tapḫurtu*

tapḫīru "collection"; OA

1. *ší-kam ana šumi* PN … *ana ta-áp-ḫi-ri-im ašqul* AKT 6B, 492: 10 "I paid (15 minas of *šikum*-copper) on behalf for the *t.*".

2. *ana tap-ḫi-ri ašqul* AKT 8, 327: 2 "I paid (5 minas and 22 shekels (of copper?)) for the *t.*" (sg. without mimation).

3. [n] *kutānē ana ša tap-hi-ri-im ša Šar-ra-ma-té-en nuraddī(ma)* VS 26, 43 r. 28 "we added [n] *kutānu*-textiles to (the amount?) of the *t.* of Šarramātēn".

4. *aṣṣēr gamrem ša tap-ḫi-ri-kà ša Šar-ra-ma-té-en₆ nuṭaḫḫī* VS 26, 43 r. 7 "we have added (5 shekels of silver which were left over from the sale of 3 *kutānu*-textiles) to the expenses of your *t.* for Šarramātēn".

5. Obscure: *ana aššitika ana niqê/ niqīʾe tap-pá-ḫi-ra-am ša pá-ar-ṣí taddin(-ma)* AKT 7A, 249: 15 "for the sacrifice(s?) you gave your wife a *tapḫīru*(?) for the cult(?)".

6. Traders contribute relatively small amounts of silver or copper to a *t.* If the god's name is specified, it is always Bēlum or Šar(ra)-mātēn. The *t.* can be described as a debt and as belonging to the person who pays for it. S. Veenhof 2010, 97f. for add. ref. NJCK

tapḫu "cauldron, kettle"

1. NB 5 *batqa ana tap-ḫa-a-nu* BagM 28 p. 388: 4 "(material for) 5 repairs (to be done) on the kettles"

2. (silver) *ana ta-ap-ḫa-a-nu petiq* ib. 12 "is cast for kettles". JW/MPS

tapḫurtu, + *tapḫīrtu* "assembly, company, collection"

1. OAkk. *tap*ₓ(URUDU)-*ḫir-tum* Subartu 2, 59 ii 4 "collection?", s. ib. p. 98 and p. 177 for further ref.

2. Stol 2010, 172: OB uncert. *i-na t[a-a]p-ḫur(!)-tim* TIM 4, 33: 27 "(they have not hidden the sesame), in *t.*, (in straw)". JW (1), NR (2)

+ **tapp-** "to strengthen"; Hurr. word in MB Qaṭna

GN *dunninkunu* : *da-ab-be-eš* QS 3, 3: 11 "strengthen GN (gloss:) strengthen!" Cf. disc. ib. p. 56. Cf. ref. cit. CAD T 24 s.v. *tabbibu*. S. Richter 2012, 440.

tappaštu, *t/dappastu, dapastu* "a woollen rug, blanket"

1. NA *tap-pa-⸢as!⸣-tú* SAA 7, 66 r. 1; 64 r. 7 (with golden ornaments, s. ib. p. XXV).

2. NA *eršu adi lēʾi* 3 ᵗᵘ́ᵍ*tap-pa-sat qarrāru* SAA 16, 53: 9 "a bed including a wooden board, 3 *t.*-blankets, and a *q.*-fabric".

3. NA 4 ᵗᵘ́ᵍ*tap-pa-sat* ḪÉ.MED StAT 3, 1: 18 "4 *t.*-blankets made of red wool".

4. SB 2 ᵗᵘ́ᵍ*tap-pa-šá-a-ti ša muḫḫi erši* 3 ᵗᵘ́ᵍ*tap-pa-šá-<a-ti šá> muḫḫi kussî* SpTU 4, 128: 90 "2 *t.*-blankets for over the bed, 3 *t.*-blankets for over the chair".

5. LB 1-*et* TÚG.MAḪ *da-pa-*<*sa*>*-at* Roth 1989 no. 42: 12; cf. Roth 1989/90, 32 n.141. Cf. *tapātu*? JW (1), MPS (2–5)

tappātu "(female) companion, counterpart"

1. Early OB *awīltum tap-pá-ti* AS 22, 53: 8 "the woman, my associate".

2. OB lit. *ina īn ta-ap-pa-ti-*[*ia*] ALL no. 15 i 12 "(I have gained so much value) in [my] girlfriend's eye".

3. OB uncert.: *ana ḫa-su*?-[*tim*] *ša tap-pa-*[*ti*]*m*? ARM 32 p. 283 vi 42 "(1/2 mina bronze) for the ... of a *t*.", s. Durand 1990b, 175. JW (1, 2), MPS/NR (3)

tappīlātu s. *tappīltu*

tappīltu "compensation"

1. Stol 2010, 172: Early OB 5 GUR *iš* ÉREN *tap-pil-ti* PN ARM 19, 414 r. 2 "5 kor for the workers, balancing payment of PN", coll. Durand apud Charpin 1989/90, 104b.

2. Mayer 2009, 429: MB *ana idī tupšarrūti tap-pil-ti qīšti arêšu* BBS 5 ii 6 (Kudurru) "as payment for his scribal craft, as compensation for the wages for his multiplications". Diff. Paulus 2014, 442).

3. Pace AHw 1321 and CAD T 182, the word is not pl. tant. MPS/NR

tappû "friend, colleague"

SB *tap-pa lā tap-pa-šu ē tappulšu* Šūpê-amēli 23 "do not give a friend as compensation to somebody who is not his friend!"

****tappû II** "to collaborate"

In the only ref. CCT 3, 20: 30 (AHw s.v. *tappû* II, CAD T s.v. *tuppû*) read *ú-ta-pá-áš*! (*epēšu* Dt), s. Michel 2001b, 434f. and AKT 6B p. 297f. JW

+ **tapsu** "a cake"

Lex. *tap-su* = *mersu* AOAT 50, 375: 224 (malku) "*t*. cake = *m*. cake".

tapšuḫtu "rest"

Lex. *é-*⸢*ní-dúb*⸣ = *bīt tap-*⸢*šu-uḫ*⸣*-ti* CUSAS 12 p. 40 i 35 (Kagal) "house of repose".

taptû "land newly prepared for cultivation"; + MB

1. Mayer 2017b, 251: MB Ekalte *ša dūrim ša tap-te* WVDOG 102, 20: 16 "(the building) at the wall of the land prepared for cultivation".

2. For disc. and add. LB ref. s. Jursa 1995, 140f. JW

tapṭīru "castrated bull"

S. van Driel 1995, 221 and 213 for add. ref. JW

taqānu "to be in order"

D MA *ṭēma táq-qu-na lā ubbala* BATSH 4, 12: 10 "he does not send a proper report". JW

taqbû "(song of) praise"

1. Lex. *tàq-bu-u* // ⸢*táq*⸣*-bu-*[*u*] // ⸢*nàr-bu*⸣*-*[*u*] = *nu-*ʾ*u-*[*du*] AOAT 50, 404: 160 (malku).

2. Mayer 2009, 429: SB [*l*]*īpuš āmerī táq-bi-*M[U] KAR 68 r. 1, cf. BMS 4: 4 "who beholds me shall praise me(?)". Cf. Foster 2005, 652. JW/NR

+ **taqdīšu** "purification, clearing of claims(?)"; OA

1. Reiner 2007, 51: *urram ta-aq*!(IQ)*-dí-ša-am muḫurniʾātima* ICK 1, 2: 12 "accept the *t*. from us tomorrow (and the day after tomorrow take your textiles)".

2. *ta-aq-dí-ša-am liqyam ... ta-aq-dí-ša-am alaqqē᾽akkum* k/k 75: 4, 7 (quot. Hecker et al. 1998, 265) "obtain a *t.* ... I will obtain a *t.* for you". S. also Stol 2010, 172 ("purification (before the oath)"?). Cf. *qadāšu*, *qadiš*.

NJCK (2), NR (1)

taqrībatu, *teqrūbatu* "(military) escort; available goods(?); an offering"

1. "escort":

a) For *teqrūbatu* "escort" in AbB 10, 67: 6 and AbB 12, 119: 7 (CAD T 348) s. AbB 10 p. 73 n. 67c and AbB 12 p. 99 n. 119b.

b) Mayer 2009, 430: OB [*t*]*a-aq-ri-ba-tam idiššumma ḫarrān šulmim lillikam* Shemshara 1, 45: 14 "give him an escort so that he can travel safely".

c) OB *ṣābum ta-aq-ri-ba-tum ... eleppē ana* GN *ušallimūnim* MARI 8, 354 no. 4: 14 "the escort troops delivered the ships safely to GN".

2. "available (goods)(?)": OB (silver and garment) ŠÀ *te-eq-ru-ba-at aplūtim* JCS Suppl. 2, 86: 3 "as(?) *t.* of the estate", s. Richardson ib. p. 63.

3. "an offering":

a) OA *ša ta-aq-ri-bi-tí-šu* kt 94/k 538: 4; *ta-aq-ri-ba-tám* kt a/k 339: 37 quot. GOA p. 131.

b) OB Some OB ref. (CAD T 200 s.v. *taqribtu* a2') seem to refer to temple offerings (cf. *qerēbu* D).

JW (1–3), NR (1)

****taqribtu** "a ritual" (CAD T 200f.)

For ref. to a ritual or prayer performance, s. *takrībtu* (Gabbay 2011, 71). For ref. to an offering or type of goods s. *taqrībatu*. JW/NR

****taqrību** s. *takrībtu*

taqtītu, + *tagdītu* "end, termination of a time period"; + LB

LB *kī tág-di-tum* MN *ina libbi ittašbu* UET 4, 36: 13 "if he (still) resides in (the house) by the end of MN", s. Popova 2018. JW

taqumtu s. *tuqumtu*

+ tāqurtu "appreciation(?)"; SB

aššum kīma nēši ta-qu-ur-tam lā tīšû aššum kīma barbari takāltam lā tīšû šamrū kakkūka assapanka SpTU 5, 246 iv 6 "because you, like a lion, do not possess appreciation(?), because you, like a wolf, do not possess trust – your weapons are fierce –, I have destroyed you". Diff. Mayer 2009, 430; 2017b, 232: *taqqurtu*.

taraḫḫu "bank, embankment, slope on the earth heap"

1. SB *bābu ša ana ta-ra-aḫ-ḫa petû* OLA 40, 6: 29 "the gate which opens on to the bank" cf. George 1992, 398f.

2. SB Made of wood: SB *imaḫḫaṣ ta-ra-*⌜*aḫ-ka*⌝ Jiménez 2017, 172 Ic 36 "he beats your (= the poplar's) revetment". Cf. ib. p. 189f.

3. LB *bāb ta-ra-aḫ* PN GCCI 2, 395: 14 "gate opening to the embankment of PN". Cf. the attestation 1, above. Pace AHw 1324, CAD T 203 s.v. *taraḫu* not a loan from Aram., cf. Abraham/Sokoloff 2011, 54.

4. "The earth dug out from the sides or bottom of a canal or irrigation ditch to create extra water capacity", s. Powell 1988, 170 (in math. texts.)

JW (1, 3–4), MPS (2, 3)

****taraḫu** s. *taraḫḫu*

tarāku "to beat, thump; to be dark"

G 1. OB *kīma ḫudušším ta-ri-ik* ARM 26/1, 276 no. 109: 13 "(the heart) was darkened like a frog".

2. OB *ḫattum elīšunu ta-ar-ka-at-ma* ARM 27, 161: 9 "fear is pounding them".

3. OB *ištū qātum ina akālim ta-ar-ka-at* FM 7, 151 no. 45: 31 "after the hand had become dark during the meal" (unclear).

4. OB lit. *ta-ri-ka-at palḫatma* CunMon. 8, 110: 36 "she is pounding frighteningly".

5. S. also *tasāḫu*.

D OB *libbum ḫašûm imittam u šumēlam ṣulmam tu-ur-ru-ka* ARM 26/1, 276 no. 109: 8 "the heart (and) the lung were darkened by black spots".

JW (G), MPS (G, D)

tarammu I "grain heap"

Stol 2010, 172: OB 4 *ta-ra-am ana zarêm* OBTR 163: 13 "4 grain heaps for winnowing" with Anbar 1978, 212; Langlois 2017, 166 (st. abs.) JW

tarāmu "beloved one"

OB Susa PN *Ta-ra-am-Adad* MDP 28, 431: 13 "Beloved one of Adad".

tarāmu s. also *šarāmu*

tarannatu s. *terinnatu*

tarānu "roof"

SB [...] *ta-ra-an* SAG.GÌR [*tar*]*tâ ta-ra-an* SAG.GÌR Šūpê-amēli 116 "... a roof of ..., [you s]et in place a roof of ...".

taraphu "a material, a wood?"; Nuzi, Hurr. lw.

Schneider-Ludorff 2002 translates "a type of upholstery", noting the word could also be read *ta-*⌜*ḫa-ap*⌝*-šu*) (s. *taḫapšu*). JW

tarāpu "to be covered in paint, (dis)colored"

AHw *tarāpu*, CAD *tarāpu*, *turrupu*.

G Del. OBTR 124: 5 (CAD T 207), read ⌜*na*⌝*-ru-ub-ma*, s. *narābu*.

D SB *šumma lētāšu tur-ru-pa* SpTU 4, 150 iii 23 "if his cheeks are discolored".

\+ **Dt** SB [*mūšu*] ⌜*ú*⌝*-tar-ra-pu* MesCiv. 13, 2b: 23 "(ignore that ...) [the night] is discolored". JW (G, Dt), MPS (D, Dt)

tarāqu? (mng. unkn.)

Neither the root nor the mng. are established. Cf. the disc. in George 2003, 888 ("to relent"? after A. Westenholz) and Streck 2007, 420. For the PN listed in CAD T 207 cf. Hilgert 2002, 193 (interpretation remains uncertain). For *li-tá-ar-*GA*-am-ma* RTC 78 cf. CAD T 205 *tarāku* 6 (N-stem?). The name of the demon *La-ta-ra-*AK/RAK (Lambert 1987–1990, 163) can well be derived from *tarāku* "to beat": "Unbeatable"; pace George ib., the commentary BM 62741: 23 *lā ta-ri-*KUM does not decide the last consonant since a reading *ta-ri-kum* instead of *-qu* is possible. For *it-ta-*RAK in Gilg. XI 131 cf. Streck ib.: *ittarak* "schlug nieder"?

JW/MPS

tarāṣu I "to stretch, to spread, to extend"

G 1. MA *panī ana bēt qaqqere ta-ri-iṣ* BATSH 4/1, 2: 14 "I was facing the ground" differently Mayer 2017b, 232: "they were facing ...".

2. On *ubāna tarāṣu* "to point a finger" (CAD T 213) s. Magen 1986, 94ff. with refs.

D SB *ina abulli nēreb ilia tu-ur-ru-ṣa dalātū'a* Jiménez 2017, 250: 25 "in the gate, the entrance of the gods, my (= the palm tree's) doors are set in place". JW (G), MPS (G, D)

tarāṣu II "to be(come) in order, correct, pleasing"

1. Stol 2010, 172f.: MA [*ša*] *ina bērišunu ta-ar-ṣú-ma* [*kaspa ušallam*] KAJ 39: 15 "whoever is appropriate among them shall reimburse the silver" (s. Saporetti 1979, 113).

2. MB Ugar. *ana panī šarrim bēlika tar-ri-iṣ!-ma* RSO 14 p. 259 (RS 86.2236): 20 "(if) it is right in the eyes of the king your lord", cf. *šumma tar!-ṣú* ib. 15. JW (2), MPS/NR (1)

+ **tarāṣu IV** "ritual arrangement"

1. Reiner 2007, 51: SB 21 *ta-ra-ṣu ša* DN *u* DN_2 *ša ina lib*[*bi* 6 *t*]*a-ra-ṣu gappī arû ša* DN *u* DN_2 George 2000, 284: 20, 24 "21 arrangements for DN and DN_2, six of which are arrangements of pruned foliage for DN and DN_2." (referring to palm-fronds, s. the comm. ib. p. 288).

2. MacGinnis 2008, 84: LB *qēme ša ta-ra-ṣu ša* MN BM 62195 r. 3 "flour for the ritual arrangement of MN".

3. Lexicalized inf. of *tarāṣu* I. For use of the verb in context of ritual preparations s. CAD T 212, 5. JW/NR

tarbāṣu "animal stall; courtyard; an ornament; halo (of the moon)"

1. OB an ornament: [...] *ḫurāṣu ša tar-ba-ṣi* ARM 25, 644: 12 "gold for the *t.* ornament"; cf. 118 r. 25; 612: 3. On *t.* as part of GUR_7(.ME) jewellery in Mari (CAD T 220) s. Durand 1990c, 145f.; ARM 32, 94.

2. Mayer 2009, 430: SB *akulī alpa ina tar-ba-ṣi* LKA 153 r. 3 "eat a bull in the animal stall!"

3. MB Ugar. *bītu* : *ta-ar-bá-ṣí u bītu alpī ana šâšuma* PRU 3, 91: 17 "the house, (gloss:) the cattle-pen and the house of the oxen are his". Cf. Huehnergard 1987, 176; Sivan 1984, 279. The gloss mark seems to denote *ta-ar-bá-ṣí* as a foreign word. Cf. alphabetic *trbṣ* Olmo Lete/ Sanmartín 2004, 877.

4. MB Ekalte *ḫarrānu ša ana tar-ba-ṣi ša āli urrad* WVDOG 102, 11: 5 "the street that leads down to the city square", s. Mayer ib. p. 10.

5. For NA ref. s. Radner 1997, 261f.

6. NB *alluttu ina* ⌜TÙR⌝ *Sîn* [*izzīz*] SAA 18, 124: 3 "cancer [stood] in the moon's halo". JW (1, 4, 5), MPS (1, 3, 6), NR (2, 3)

tarbītu "enlargement; child rearing; rearling"

1. OA *ana ta-ar-bi₄-tim ukultim u qubūrim ša mer'u'āt* PN AKT 5, 40: 1 "for upbringing, food and burying of the daughters of PN".

2. MB Emar *ištū* KÁ *tar-bi-ia-ti lipṭu-rūšu* RA 77, 18 no. 3: 7 (Emar) "may they remove him from the gate, (from) among the adopted children". Cf. Pentiuc 2001, 179 and 236. Differently CAD T 224 *t.* A 1. MPS (1–2), NR (2)

tarbu'tu, *turbu'tu*, *turbu'u*, + *turrubû*? "dust, sandstorm; turmoil"

1. Stol 2010, 175: poss. var. SB [...] DIB = *tur-ru-bé-e* 5R 12 no. 5: 11 (Sm 305, comm. on meteors), between celestial events. Cf. *tu-ru-bu* Igutuh I 284, cit. CAD T 485 *t.* lex. sect.

2. SB *lubār isinnātika šakru ina tu-[ur]-⌜bu-i⌝ liballil* Gilg. MB Ur 17 (// *[tur]-⌜bu!⌝-[ʾ!?]-⌜ú⌝* Gilg. SB VII 110) "may the drunkard smear with dust your festive gown". Cf. George 2003, 302.

3. In transferred mng.: MB *puḫur tur-bu-ti annīti ina ṭuppāti iltaṭar*! BAF 21, 309: 10 (coll. Brinkman 2004, 301) "he wrote down all that turmoil(?) on the tablets". JW (1), MPS (2–3)

tarbûtu "adoptive child, foster child"

1. SB *mārāt ili urabbâ tar-bu-ta* Gilg. SB III 126 "the daughters of the god will bring up the foster child".

2. Mayer 2009, 430: LB PNf *tar-bu-ú-tu ša ... urabbû* TBÉR 69: 5 "the adoptive child PNf, whom … they raised". MPS (1), NR (2)

tardennu, + *terdēn/ennu* "second(ary)"

1. Reiner 2007, 52: OB 10 GÚ.È.A *té-er-de-nu* Shemshara 2, 138: 4 "10 *naḫ-laptu*-garments of second quality"; 57 TÚG$^{\text{ḫi.a}}$ *té-er-de-nu* ib. 2 "57 textiles of second quality".

2. Reiner 2007, 52: OB 36 ^{giš}*tiyārī damqūtim* 14 ^{giš}*tiyārī te-e[r-de]e-nu-šu-nu ... ušark[abam]* ARM 26/2, 532 no. 540: 15 "I will load (onto that boat) 36 good quality *tiyāru* logs and 14 *tiyāru* logs of a quality inferior to them" (coll. Marti 2001).

3. Pl. fem. in LB *naptanu ⌜tar⌝-de-na-a-tú* AUWE 8, 68: 9 "second courses".

4. Cf. *tartānu*; Richter 2012, 448 with prev. lit. JW (2, 4), MPS (3), NR (1)

targumannu, *targumiy/ʾannu* "interpreter, dragoman"

1. OA *ana* PN *ta-ar-gu-me-a-nim* AKT 5, 6: 40; Kt d/k 1: 8; Kt 92/k 194: 40. Cf. Veenhof apud Reiner 2007, 52.

2. For etym. s. Starke 1993; Dercksen 2007, 37. For bibliography s. Richter 2012, 445. JW/MPS/NR

tarḫu "a vessel"; OB

Guichard 2005, 315 suggests to connect this term with *te/irḫu* "a vessel" (AHw 1348, CAD T 425). JW

tarībtu "replacement"

Stol 2010, 173: OB Elam ⌜*tár*⌝*-íb-tum* MDP 55, 30: 12 (uncert. context), s. de Graef ib. p. 118 (for *tarbītu*?). JW/NR

tarīḫu, pl. *tarīḫātu* "a vessel"

MA ^{dug}*ta-ri-ḫa-te* GIBIL *kī mūšišu liškunū* Chuera 12: 13f. "they shall place new *t.*-vessels for the night".

tarīmtu "gift, award"

1. Stol 2010, 173: OB 1 *ta-ri-im-tum* ZABAR DCS 115: 11 "1 bronze-*t.*".

2. LB *ta-ri-ma-a-ta* KÙ.GI dubsar 3, 18 (= YOS 21, 86): 15 "golden *t.*". JW (2), NR (1)

tārīmu "a door or attachment for covering a door"; + MB

MB (Reiner 2007, 52; Mayer 2009, 430): **1.** *ana* ^{giš}⌜IG *ta*⌝*-ri-m[i]* Sassmannshausen 2001 no. 376: 2; 378: 2 "(paint) for *t.*-doors."
2. *ana šagammī ša* 2 ^{giš}IG *ta-ri-m[i]* … *ana šamāti* Sassmannshausen 2001 no. 380: 3 "(paint) to mark the hinges of 2 *t.*-doors", s. ib. p. 411. NR

tarinnu II s. *terinnu*

tāriru “a profession”; + OB

1. OB *mannum ina ḫalṣim annîm wašib ul ta-ri-ru-ú wašbū* FM 8, 64 no. 14: 28 “who dwells in this district? Are there no *t.* dwelling (there)?”, s. Durand ib. p. 67 n. h.

2. On ^{lú}*ta-ri-ru-ma* (*qātil* or *qatīl*?) s. Huehnergard 1987, 186. Cf. alphabetic *trrm* (DUL 880, etym. uncert.).

JW (1), NR (2)

tārītu I “nurse, nanny”

1. OB lex. $^{\text{e-me-da}}$UM.ME = *ta-ri-tum* MSL 14, 96 :186 (Proto-Aa).

2. Lex. *eme-da* = *ta-ri-tum* = *ta-ri-ʾ-tum* Emar 6/4, 191: 373 (Lu). Cf. Pentiuc 2001, 178 (3rd radical /ʾ/ or /h/?) and Cohen 2010.

3. OB *amtum šī ta-re-et* ARM 27, 85: 13 “this slave girl was a nursemaid”.

4. Mayer 2009, 430: OB lit. *tušta*ʾ*dir ta-ri-ta-am* OECT 11, 2: 9 “you (baby) have startled the nurse”.

5. SB *tuštabki ta-ra-ti-ka* CUSAS 30, 448: 6 “you (baby) brought your nursemaids to tears”.

6. Mayer 2009, 430: SB *šattišamma ušabkû ta-ri-ta* SpTU 3, 84: 92 “(the bandit, who) year after year, brings the nurse to tears”.

7. SB *irabbaṣ ta-a-ri-tum* Lamaštu Emar 30 (Farber 2014, 292) “the nurse is resting”.

8. *lū ta-ri-i-tum ša Adad … atti* ib. 34 “may you be nurse to Adad”.

JW (1, 7–8), MPS (2, 3, 5), NR (4, 6)

tārītu II “offshoot”

OB [n] GUR *ta-ra-tim* AbB 13, 55: 12 “[n] kor of offshoots”. JW

tarkīstu “obligation”; + MB Emar

MB Emar uncert.: *ta-ra-ki-sá-ti-šu-nu liddinma* AulaOr. Suppl. 1 p. 122 no. 72: 14 “he shall give (60 shekels of silver), their *t.*”, s. Arnaud ib. p. 12. JW

tarkīsu, *taškīsu* “an ornament”

LB 8 $^{\text{na4}}$*taš-kis*^{meš} NBC 4894 (Beaulieu 1999) “8 *t.*-stones/beads”, s. ib. p. 154.

JW

tarkullu “wooden post, pole”

Stol 2010, 173: “palisade” in ARM 14, 13: 23, 27 (CAD T p. 236 mng. c), s. Durand 1998, 579 on no. 804.

tarkumassu, *tarkumasḫu* “an officer(?)”; Nuzi

For disc. s. Dosch 1993, 21ff. (a handler of horses and chariots?). JW

tarlugallu “a wild bird, rooster”

1. OB DAR.LUGAL^{meš} Edubba 7, 100: 1 (in list of birds).

2. SB […] DAR.LUGAL^{mušen} *irâš qīšti nuḫši* JCS 66, 76: 23 (Gilg.) “[at the cry of(?)] the rooster the forest of abundance exulted”.

tarmītu “release, discharge, relaxation”; + OB

1. OB […] *ta-ar-mi-tam lā ir*[*aššī*] Amurru 3 p. 91 A.4280: 7 “(the troops) shall have no leave”.

2. Mayer 2009, 430: *tar-me-ta irtaš*[*û*] RIMA 2, 57: 22 “(when the wooden logs in the palace) become loose”; cf. [*ta*]*r-mi-ta irtašû* KAL 3, 13: 3 and s. Frahm ib. p. 40. JW (1), MPS/NR (2)

+ **tarmu** in *tarmumma epēšu* "to provide drink"; Nuzi, Hurr. lw.

Reiner 2007, 52: Nuzi *zazulumma ipuš ù ta-ar-mu-um-ma īpuš* SCCNH 7, 19 IM 73390: 8 "provide food and drink", s. Fincke ib. 20f.; Richter 2012, 446.

JW

tarmuš "lupine(?)"

1. MA ^{ú}*tar-muš*$_8$ StAT 5, 68: 1 (medicinal recipe).

2. Stol 2010, 173: ^{ú}*tar-muš šammi api* BAM 1, 92 ii 31 "*t.*, the plant of the swamp". JW (1–2), MPS (2)

tarnannu, *tarnaš* "a vessel; measure of capacity"; Hitt. lw.

Cf. Hitt. *tarna-* "a vessel, a dry measure of capacity", in Emar also for liquids, s. Pentiuc 2001, 179f. NR

tarnappakku, *turnipakku* "a large basin"

OB 2 *tu-ur-ni-pa-kum* ARM 25, 493 (= ARM 31, 268) ii 9. Cf. Guichard 2005, 324f. for add. ref. JW

tarnaš s. *tarnannu*

+ **tarni/eneḫ̮u** "a textile"; OB, Hurr. lw.(?)

1 ^{túg}*ta-ar-ni-ne-*⸢*ḫu*⸣ Shemshara 2, 118: 4; ^{túg}*ta-ar-*⸢*ne?-ne?*⸣*-ḫu* ib. 132: 5, 7, s. Durand 2009, 111. MPS/NR

tarnu s. *tīrānu*

+ **tarpi** "enemy(?)"; MB Emar, Hurr. lw.?

ina šatti ERIM^{meš} *tar-pi āla lami* AulaOr. Suppl. 1 p. 25 no. 3: 2 "in the year when the enemy's(?) troops besieged the city". Cf. Wilhelm apud Zaccagnini 1995, 97f. n. 15: < Hurr. *tor*(*u*)*bi*? Richter 2012, 446f. with diff. proposals in prev. lit. MPS/NR

tarpisu "a medicinal plant"; + NA

Reiner 2007, 52: *ina* 80 *tar-pi-su ša* 1 *šatti* MDOG 134, 69 Ass. 2001.D-1502: 8 "from 80 *t.* of 1 year (... n were carried off ...)" (among plants).

MPS/NR

tarpu s. *tarwu*

+ **tarpuštu** "cloak"; LB

Reiner 2007, 52: 1-*en* ^{túg}*tar-pu-uš-tum ša zikari* 2-*ta* ^{túg}*tar-pu-uš-tum ša amīltu* Waerzeggers 2002, 332 no. 4: 5f. "one men's cloak, two women's cloaks"; < *rapāšu*. MPS/NR

tarqu s. *daraggu*

+ **tarrapītu** "dyeing works(?)"

MB Ekalte (an estate) *panīša tar-ra-pí-tum* WVDOG 102, 16: 11 "in front of it the dyeing works(?)". Mayer ib. p. 10 connects the word with *tarāpu* "to be covered with paint(?)" AHw 1325 (CAD T 207 mng. uncert.) and *turrupu* "discolored" CAD T 489.

tarṣu III "extent, duration"

Reiner 2007, 53: LB *ana* ⸢*tar*⸣*-ṣa dumqi ša ī*[*pušu*] *mādiš ḫadâka* API 6, 4: 17 "to the extent of the good he did I am well pleased", s. Borger apud Hinz 1969, 157. JW

tartāmu "mutual love"

1. SB *ina bītim lumaḫḫ̮ḫ̮irka nawār kabattim kuzbam ta-ar-ta-ma-am* ALL 11 r. 7 "in the house, let me make you accept happiness, attractiveness, mutual love".

2. SB *ušarbiṣ za-ru tar-ta-ma* AnSt 33, 147: 11 "he caused (them) to rest in mutual love" (s. von Soden 1984, 213, with n. 4; Mayer 2009, 430; reading after E. Bischoff).

3. For the noun pattern *taPtaRS* s. Streck 2012.

tartānu, *tartannu*, + *turatānu* "deputy, second in command"; + MB, Hurr. lw.

1. Lex. [*ug*]*ula é-du*[*b-ba* = MIN *bīt*] *tuppī* = *tu-ra-ta-nu* // [*tur*/*tar*?]*-te-en-nu* Emar 6/4, 602: 217 (Lu) "head scribe". Cf. Pentiuc 2001, 181; Cohen 2010, 830.

2. MB Ekalte *tu-ur-ta-*⌜*na*⌝*-am* WVDOG 102, 44: 6 in broken context (cf. Mayer 2009, 436).

3. MB Emar: In filiation ("son of *t.*"): *tar-ta-an-ni* Emar 6/3, 118: 12; (lú)*tar-ta-ni* ib. 128: 27; 221: 12; RE 10: 13, 34, 38. S. also Beckman 1996, 19; Pentiuc 2001, 181.

4. For MA ref. s. Jakob 2003, 191ff. For bibl. s. Richter 2012, 448.

JW (3–4), MPS (1–2)

tarû II "to turn upward"

G The ref. quot. CAD T 249 s.v. *tarû* C "mng. uncert." might belong here, s. already AHw 1336 and George 2003, 890 (referring to a jerky movement of animals?).

D Reiner 2007, 53: SB *qannīšu ana patīʾa sibbassu ana tu-ur-ri-i ul addin-šu* KBo. 1, 18 iv 18 "I did not allow it (the scorpion) to open its pincers, to raise its tail upward", s. Ford 2001 204f. JW (G), NR (D)

târu "to turn, return; become (again)"

G 1. OAkk. *in tù-a-rí-śu* GN *nakirma* RIME 2, 48: 45 "upon his return, GN was in revolt".

2. "to return from a river ordeal":

a) MB *ana ḫuršān išpurūšuma ina ḫuršān i-tu-ra-am-ma* Sassmannshausen 2001 no. 458: 11 "they sent him to the ordeal and he returned from the ordeal".

b) Disc. s. Mayer 2009, 431 (pace CAD T 257 s.v. *târu* 3d rather "to return from a river ordeal" than "to refuse the river ordeal").

3. On *ša taturru*/*iturru* in LB personnel lists ("PN, who was/had become …") s. Joannès 1997, 123; Jursa 2001; Mayer 2017b, 233 with add. ref.

D 1. Stol 2010, 173: OB *awāssu la tu-ta-a-ar* StEb 2/4–5, 50: 19 "don't set his matter aside".

2. "to avenge": MB DN … *mārī* GN *ana tu-ur-ri* ... *napištašu kīma mê itbuk* CUSAS 17, 61: 18 "DN … in order to avenge the sons of GN … spilled his life(-blood) like water".

3. For MB *qāt* PN *turru* "to undo the control of PN(?)" s. *tūrtu* and disc. van Soldt, CUSAS 30 p. 31f.

4. Mayer 2009, 431: NB *ina patê up*[*pi*] [*ad*]*i tur-ru bābi* SAA 17, 34: 6 "from the unbolting of the door until the closing of the gate".

JW (G, D), MPS (D), NR (G, D)

taruallinnu "a household utensil"

Cf. Hitt. giš*taruyāli* (Watson 2008). S. also Richter 2012, 449 with further lit.

JW

tarušḫu "brazier"; MA, + MB Qaṭna

1. 1 *kubbillu* URUDU : *ta-ru-uš-ḫé* URUDU QS 3, 13: 15 "1 copper *k.* (gloss): 1 copper *t.*"; cf. disc. ib. p. 89.

2. Cf. Hitt. (kuš)*tarušḫa* (Watson 2009). S. also Richter 2012, 445 with further lit. JW (2), MPS (1)

+ tasāḫu "to beat"; SB

tarāku : *ta-sa-ḫu* SpTU 4, 143 r. 25 (comm.) "*tarāku* 'to beat' means *t.*". Etym. unclear.

tasdīru "supply of offerings(?)"

Delete var. *taldīru* (Mayer 2008, 101, s. SAD *piṭru* 4). NR

\+ **tas/šḫultu** "drilling stone"; SB lex.

In MSL 10, 9: 189 (= UET 6, 406 r. 5) read $^{\text{na4}}$*bala* = *ab-nu tas-ḫul*!-*t*[*um*!] "stone for drilling". Cf. the disc. in Kleber 2016, who rightly discards the reading *tas-niq-t*[*i*] (AHw 1337, CAD T 283). Kleber proposes a reading *ta-ši-ri-t*[*um*] instead, but *tas-* instead of *ta-* is clear, and the second part of *ḫul* does not resemble *ri* but is clearly UR (see also the reservations made in DCCLT). In Emar 6/3, 553 annexe IV 3 read [$^{\text{na4}}$*ba*]*la* = NA$_4$ *ta-aš-ḫu*!(copy: RI)-<*ul*>-*ti*. Cf. *bala* "spindle, pin" s. PSD B 64f. and *saḫālu*/*suḫḫulu* "to pierce".

\+ **tasīku** "powder(?)"; OA

allānū mišlum kapputūtum mišlum ta-sí-ki CCT 2, 36a: 13 "oak resin (or: acorns?), half solid, half powder(?)". Cf. *sâku*. Diff. Michel 2001b, 430.
JW/MPS/NJCK

\+ **tas/škidû** "a coat"; OB

GÚ *ta-áš-ki-du-ú*! ARM 7, 90: 8 (AHw 133, CAD T 282 s.v. *taskidūtu*); ARM 30, 123 M.5260+: 9 (among the king's garments); ib. 368 M.12814 i 8; 1 GÚ.È.A *ta-áš-ki-du-ú* ib. 359 M.6831+: 15; ^{túg}*ta-áš-ki-du-ú* (ib. 10 and pass.). Cf. Durand 2009, 123. MPS/NR

****tas/škidûtu** s. *taškidû*, above.

\+ **taskuptu** "resting place"; SB

Mayer 2017b, 233: *eperu ša* {DIŠ}*ašar šikkû tas-ku-up-tum īpuš* BM 45755: 15 "dirt from (the spot) where a mongoose made a resting place". Cf. *sakāpu* II "to rest, lie down". JW

taslīmtu "malicious talk, insult"

1. OB *ullânum* PN … *šum šarrim šanîm kêm ū kêm lū epiš ta-às-li-im-tum ina pīšu ūṣī* ARM 26/2, 260 no. 404: 31 "(he said): 'Besides PN …, the name of another king is doing just as well (lit. either way, is really made)'. Malicious talk came out of his mouth".

2. The use of *às*(AŠ) makes a derivation from the root SLM certain (pace CAD T 283) because this root is usually spelled with S-signs (for deaffricate [s]) and not with Z-signs (for the affricate [ts]). AHw 1337, in agreement with the mng. of SLM, proposes a translation "Begütigung, freundliche Rede" whereas CAD T 282 suggests to translate "malicious talk(?), insult(?)", a mng. confirmed by the ref. above (pace Joannès, ARM 26/2, 261, and Heimpel 2003, 344). A euphemistic use of SLM as proposed in CAD T 283 is currently the best suggestion.

****tasniqtu** s. *tasḫultu*

tassīstu "lamentation"

Mayer 2009, 431: OB *ta-as-sí-ís*(IŠ)-*tum* ZA 96, 201: 18 and p. 205. Cf. Westenholz 2006, 23f., 66. NR

\+ **taṣbīttu** "combat, quarrel"

1. Reiner 2007, 57: OB *bēl ta-aṣ-bi-ta-tim* PN FM 2, 112 no. 71 r. 4 "PN is the one responsible for the quarrels"; *ta-aṣ-bi-it-tam kalâšu* ... *uštaṣbitu* M.13095 ib. p. 113 n. f.

2. *taPRīSt* of *ṣabātu* D. Cf. also *tiṣbuttu*, which derives from the Gt-stem.
MPS/NR

+ taṣbītu "mattress(?)"; OB

1. 2 túg*sāq burê tá-aṣ-bi-ti* ARM 30, 123 T.525: 7 "2 (tightly) woven fabrics for a mattress pad of a *t.*".

2. 1/2 *manā ṭurru* 1 túg*sāq burê tá-aṣ-bi-ti* MARI 4, 161 T.518: 14 "1/2 a mina of yarn for 1 (tightly) woven fabric for a mattress pad of a *t.*"; cf. 1 túg*sāq burê šēʾi* in the duplicate T.519: 14 "1 (tightly) woven fabric for a mattress pad of a mattress". S. Durand 2009, 123f. NR

tašal(l)u s. *tašlu.*

tašīḫu "a plant"

Stol 2010, 173: OB *ta-ši-ḫu-um* TIM 5, 39: 1, 5 (field name). NR

tašīltu "celebration"

1. OB lit. *bīt nigûtim ša ta-ši-il-tam malû* JCS 26, 162 r. 5 "house of merry-making, full of celebration".

2. OB lit. *ana kār ta-ši-la-tim īteʾil* RA 70, 136: 23 "she undulated(?) towards the quay of celebration", s. *eʾēlu.*

3. Mayer 2009, 431, SB:
a) *Ekur ta-ši-la-tú limlāku/ka* Or. 59, 468: 23 "may the Ekur be filled with celebration for you".
b) [...*t*]*a-ši-il-ta limla* CTN 4, 190 i 5 "may [...] be filled with celebration"
c) *ta-ši-la-ti-šu-nu ēpuš* RIMA 1, 204: 21 "I held celebrations for them (= the renewed temples)". JW (1–2), NR (3)

tašīmtu "discernment, sagacity"

Mayer 2009, 431: SB *amât ta-šim-ti ludbub anāku* Or. 59, 450: 17 "I shall speak discerning words". NR

tašītu s. *tašiʾu*

tašiʾu, *tašītu*? "a container for liquids"

1. MB 3 *ḫi*!*-sí-pu ana ta-ši-ia-ti* Emar 6/3, 463: 13 "3 *ḫ*. vessels for(?) *t.*" (cit. CAD T 289 without context).

2. [...] *ta-ši-ti* [...] Emar 6/3, 488: 1 in broken context might point to a fem. var. of masc. *tašiʾu*. The word is elsewhere always attested in the fem. pl.

3. Disc. Pentiuc 2001, 178f. His derivation of the word from (NW)Sem. TŠʿ "nine" is uncertain.

taškidû s. *tas/škidû*

taškuttu, *tarkuttu* "deposit(?)"

1. LB *lū tar-ku-ut-tum lū uʾiltu lū riksu lū tuppu* CunMon. 20B, 166: 19 "neither deposit nor commitment note nor contract nor document", s. Wunsch ib. p. 200.

2. The mng. "jewellery(?)" proposed by CAD T 290 is not supported by the known refs. Cf., however, *šukuttu* "jewellery" (Stol 2010, 173). JW

tašlīmtu, *tašlīm/ndu* "payment"

Stol 2010, 173: LB *taš-lim-du* CT 49, 150: 29, after McEwan 1981b, 135 (coll.). NR

tašlīšu "third man on chariot",

1. LB lú*taš-liš* CT 44, 72: 3; CT 56, 658: 27.

2. lúKI.ZU.Ú as logogram for *t.*, cf. Stol apud Bongenaar 1997, 45 n. 76. On *tašlišū* and *kizû* in LB s. further MacGinnis 2008, 84. MPS/NR

+ tašlīšūtu "rank of third man"; NA

lú3.U_5-*u-tú* SAA 16, 68 r. 10 (broken context).

tašlu "a container?"

AHw 1339 (EA). For disc. s. Civil 1987, 156: cf. Eblaite BUR *ti-sa-la* (Pettinato 1981, 250), OB *tašal(l)u* (AHw 1338, CAD T 285), Sum. [dug]*ti-sar/sá* MSL 7, 201: 62 etc. MPS/NR

tašmētu I, + *tešmētu* "an ornament, bead"; OB

1. For add. OB ref. s. ARM 32, 55f., pace Durand 1983a, 227 who derives the word from *šamāṭu* II.

2. *ana šīm* 4 [na4]*kišadat te-eš-me-et pappardilîm* TLT 65: 3 "(1/2 mina 5 shekels of silver) as the price of 4 *t.*-necklaces made from *pappardilû*-stone", s. Vincente ib. p. 167 (a spindle-shaped bead?). JW

tašmētu II, *tešmētu* "listening, attention, reconciliation"

OB PNf [d]*Te-eš-mé-et-ma-ti* CUSAS 9, 83: 14 "Reconciliation of the land" (a deified PN(?), perhaps the wife of Gulkišar, s. Dalley, ib. p. 82).

tašnīntu "ambition, competition, contention"

On *t. ummāni* s. Koch 2005, 57f.; Lenzi 2006. JW

tašnīqu "internal disease"

Stol 2010, 173: *táš-níq šadî* AOAT 43, 319: 8; 321: 41 "*t.* of the mountain (unclear)"; s. Heeßel ib. p. 331; Scurlock 2003, 402 ("approach (*tasnīq*) of the Netherworld mountain (i.e. natural death)"). NR

tašpīltu "lowering"

Stol 2010, 173, said of field: OB *ša ana ta-aš-pí-il-tim?-ma ippušū* CT 8, 30a: 8f. "which they prepare for lowering". NR

tašrīḫū "glorification"

SB [*ē*]*pirki agê taš-ri-ḫi ša lulê* KAL 9, 4: 8 "he crowned you with a crown of glorification, laden with splendor".

tašrītu "beginning"

1. OB lit. *ilum ta-aš-⌜ri-ti⌝ balā*[*ṭi* ...] AUWE 23, 106: 2 "god of the beginning of life".

2. For the stone in MSL 10, 9: 189 and Emar 6/4, 553 annexe IV 3 s. *tasḫultu*. JW (1), MPS (2)

+ **taššīpu** "winnowing"; early OB

Mayer 2017b, 251: *ta-ši-ip* n SÌLA (*šamaššammī*) Edubba 7, 121: 16 // case 11 "(the loan will be repaid in sesame and) the winnowing of n liters (of sesame)." Cf. *našāpu* D. JW

****tāšub(ā)tu**

ARM 26/1, 466 no. 225: 10 (cf. Durand ib. n. a.; Stol 2010, 173; Mayer 2009, 432). Read *adī ša*! *šu-ba-at-ni* (thus already alternatively Durand ib.; cf. also Heimpel 2003, 264). For *adī ša* in OB Mari cf. Finet 1956, 239. MPS/NR

taʾtāmu "assembly"; Amor. lw.

For etym. s. Streck 2000, 119 (cf. Sab. ʾTM "to bring together"); also in Ebla (*da-da-mu*), s. ib. JW

tatīdu, + *tattidu* "a tree"

Mayer 2009, 432: NA *timmē* ... [giš]*ta-ti-du* (var. *ta-at-ti-du*) RINAP 3/2 p. 42: 40 (Sanh.) "(I erected) columns of (cedar, ebony, cypress, juniper, and) *t.*-wood", after Borger 1988. Cf. *sindû*. JW

tatītu s. *tatīdu*

+ tattalliku, *tettelliku* "reed box used for travelling(?)"; OB

Reiner 2007, 53:

1. 2 *amāt* PNf *ana ṣēr bēliya* 1 ^{gi}PISAN *ta-at-ta-li-ka ublānim* FM 3, 293 no. 140: 16 "2 slave-girls of PNf brought a travelling(?) box made of reed to my lord".

2. *ana* GN … *kīma šūbultiya ina* 1 ^{gi}PISAN *te-te-li-<ki->im kunukma šūbil* ARM 1, 54: 8 "seal and send (textiles and bowls) to GN in a travelling(?) box made of reed!" Cf. Durand 1997, 406 no. 258 n. a., who proposes a reading *te-te-li-kam*!

3. The tentative translation assumes that the word derives from *alāku* Gtn "to go back and forth". If correct, the word would be another example for a pattern with both *ta*-prefix and *ta*-infix, s. Streck 2012 and SAD *tartāmu* and *tattasḫuru*. But two difficulties remain: first, since the pattern with two *ta*s denotes infinitives we have to assume that ^{gi}PISAN *tattallikam*/*tettellikim*(!) is an instance of a frozen stat. cstr., only inflected at the second member. Second, *tettellikim* shows *e*-coloring which is never found with *alāku*.

MPS/NR

tattaru "a bronze item, part of a bed"; Nuzi

S. Schneider-Ludorff 2002, 137. Cf. CAD T s.v. *tutturru*. JW

+ tattasḫuru "giving constant favor, going back and forth"; OB

1. OB lit. *ešrūtum la'šūtu ta-at-ta-ás-ḫu-ru tūr panīk*[*i*] … *kûmma Ištar* Or. 87, 15 i 15 "justice, oppression, giving constant favor, changing your face … are yours, Ištar". Cf. comm. Streck/ Wasserman ib. p. 28.

2. OB lit. *šakān tēnîm padānu ta-at*!*-ta-ás-ḫu-ru kûmma Ištar* Or. 87,18 i 52 "providing a change (of clothes), the path, going back and forth – are yours, Ištar". JW/MPS

ta'û "to eat; graze"; + NB?

G 1. Mayer 2009, 432: OB *u kalī'ātīya qaqqarum i-ta-*⸢*ú*⸣ MHEO 1 p. 102 Di 450: 11 "(I am sick) and the ground is eating my kidneys (i.e. I feel the netherworld's claim on me)".
2. NB *atta at-ta-'-*[*ka*? *a*]*gâ gabbi* SAA 21, 75: 16 "you, all this is for [you(?)] to eat(?)".

Gtn Mayer 2009, 432: On K.2560: 23 quot. CAD T 301 s. var. *mu-ta-mu-ú* K.2560 [UFBG 523] + 5293: 22–23 // K.5410 A Rs. 6–7 // SpTU 2, 8 iv 2–3. S. also *tit'û*.

****D** In ARM 1, 35: 27 read, pace CAD T 301, *ú-te-e-ka*, s. already AHw 1340. The interpretation remains uncertain: Durand 2000, 163 "I will await you" (*watû* G), but the *e*-vowel is difficult. In ARM 10, 61: 5 (AHw 1340), read *ep-te-e-*[*ma*] (Durand 2000, 163; Mayer 2017b, 233).

JW (G, Gtn, D), MPS (G)

taw/me/irtu "a type of meadow, cultivated environs (of a city), irrigation district"

1. SB *ugāri rabûti qarbāti u ta-mi-ra-a-ti* MesCiv. 13, 11 r. iii 23 "the large estates, the meadows and the city environs".

2. LB *ana ta-mir-ti lā tumaššaršu* WZKM 97 p. 221 YBC 9448: 7 "do not let (the land) become *t.*" (i.e. flooded land), s. Janković ib. 226. S also Jursa 2010, 321 n. 1864. JW

tāwītu, *tāmītu* "response, speech, wording"

1. Mayer 2009, 427: *tāwītu* (CAD T 301 "mng. uncert."; but cf. the disc. ib. p. 302) derives from *awû* rather than from *wuʾʾûm*; cf. also Heimpel 1996a, 166f.

2. Mayer 2017b, 234: OB *ta-wi-it bārûtim ša bēlī īdû epšet* CUSAS 18, 4: 7 "the extispicy inquiry known to my lord was conducted".

3. OB lit. *ta-wi-*⌜*it*⌝!(text: IŠ)*-ka lūmur* ZA 108, 14 r. 2b "I would witness what you have talked about" (// [*ta*]-⌜*wi-it-ka*⌝ *lu-m*[*u-ur* …] OB Gilg. II 174, s. George ib. p. 16).

4. Denoting the end of (a paragraph in) a prayer (Mayer 2009, 427 and 435):
a) SB *ušarriḫkunūši ina puḫrikunu*! *ta*!-*mi*!-*t*[*i*]! AnBi. 12, 283: 34 // *ta*[-*mi-ti*?] BM 71621: 13 "he has glorified you in your assembly. Saying".
b) SB *tá-mì-tù* KUB 4, 47 r. 48. Del. this ref. in CAD T 442 *tû* A a4'. Cf. Beckman 2007.

5. Mayer 2009, 427: SB *kīma ta-mit bārûti …imannu* "he recites (the ritual) like a diviner's oracle question" RAcc. 42: 23 // SpTU 4, 141 r. 16.

6. On mng. "inscription" in A. 977 (CAD T 301b) s. Heimpel 1998.

JW (2–3), MPS (1), NR (1, 4–6)

\+ **tawnītum**, *tawinītum*? "deception, cheating"; OA

kīma niqīʾim šēbulim atta tù-ni-e-ma ta-aw-ni-tám taštanapparam AKT 4, 51: 21 "instead of sending me a gratuity(?), you have cheated me and keep writing me deceptive words." Cf. *wanāʾu*. NJCK

tawwertu s. *taw/me/irtu*

****tawû** s. *ṭawû* and *ṭimītu*.

tayyartu "return, forgiveness"

SB *ta-ia-a-*[*ra-tu*] KAL 5, 66: 9, s. *amertu* II.

tayyāru I "returning; relenting"

Mayer 2009, 424: LB *ta-a-a-ra-ti* SpTU 3, 76: 23 // Si. 59: 19 "you (fem.) are relenting". NR

tazkītu "clearance; purification"

Mayer 2009, 432: SB *kī ta-az-kit ezzi* DN SAA 3, 29 r. 2 "when purifying fierce DN".

tazzīmtu "complaint"

Mayer 2009, 432: SB *ta-zi-im-ta-šá* (var. *i-zi-im-ta-šá*) *upšaššûša lemnūtu ana muḫḫiša u lāniša turrū* AMD 8/1, 9.1: 44 "her complaint, her evil doings are returned to her skull and her body."

NR

\+ **tazzīqu** "vexation, anxiety"; OB

Reiner 2007, 53: OB lit. *ṣeḫrum lā īdēʾam murussu lā īdēʾam tānīḫšu ta-*⌜*a*⌝*-zi-qí-šu* YOS 11, 5: 12 "the child did not understand what ailed him, did not understand what caused him suffering and worries", s. George 1994. NR

\+ **tazzīru** "curse"; OB

OB lit. *ta-zi*!*-ru qibīt šaptī šuṣṣuru* Or. 87, 16 i 22 "cursing, guarding the uttering of the lip" JW

\+ **tazzizzu** "responsibility(?)"; OB

Stol 2010, 173: *ta-az-zi-zi nāqidim* PN *ša ina* GN *innepšu* TIM 5, 54: 8 "(sheep, brought in for shearing), responsibility(?) of the herdsman PN, that were handled in GN". Cf. CAD U 385f. *uzuzzu* 12 "to be responsible"?

MPS/NR

+ tebal (mng. unkn.); Šubrian word(?)

NA *egirtu in muḫḫiya issapar mā tebal a-da mā ṣābēku[nu] ašapparakka* SAA 5, 35 r. 11 "he sent me a letter, saying: '*Tebal ada*. I shall send your troops to you'".

tēbibtu "purification"

1. Mayer 2009, 432: *té-bi-ib-ta-šú iškuna* K.2560 (UFBG 523) + 5293: 12 // K.5410A: 5 "(Asalluḫi) has performed his purification".

2. On *t.* in Mari and Chagar Bazar s. Kellenberger 2000. NR

tebû "to get up, arise, set out"

G 1. With dative: OB lit. *mīnam šattišam maḫṣum kubbusum te-bi-kum* Fs. Stol p. 150 LB 1000: 27 "why has something beaten and downtrodden year after year (now) risen against you?"
2. OB *ina puḫur sābî i-ta-bi-a-ma umma šūma* AbB 12, 88: 21 "were he to rise in the assembly of innkeepers, he would say (the following)".
3. OB 5 *epinnū it-b[u]-nim-ma ... šerʾam iptarkū* FM 6, 465 no. 67/68: 15 "5 plow (teams) set out (?) ... and blocked the furrow", s. ib. p. 468 n. 3.
4. Mayer 2009, 432: SB *ina imniya te-bi* DN *ina šumēli te-bi* DN_2 Or. 59, 17: 20 "on my right, DN is ready; on the left, DN_2 is ready."
5. Mayer 2009, 432f.: SB *ammīni* ZI-*ta*$_5$ // *te-ba-te kīma nēši* SpTU 2, 24: 1 // BM 45755: 1 "why are you poised to attack like a lion?"
6. SB *et-bi ūʾi ušib tānīḫu* SpTU 3, 76: 14 "I rose up: (there was) woe; I sat down: (there was) wailing".
7. NA *ayya šāru ša i-di-ba-ka-a-ni* SAA 9, 1: 6 "what is the wind that has risen against you?" The form does not derive from *edēpu* (Parpola ib. p. 4 n. to l. 6).
8. On textiles *ana tabê* ("for (use in) processions") in LB s. Zawadzki 2006, 12ff. for disc. and ref.

Gtn OB *alpū ana api li-it-te-eb-bu-ú* AbB 14, 94: 23 "the oxen should regularly go up to the reed marsh", s. ib. p. 87 n. g, diff. CAD N/2, 172 s.v. *nepû*.

Š NA *ú-sa-da-bi-šu* StAT 1, 51: 21 (*usadbīšu* < *usatbīšu*), cf. Radner ib. p. 171. JW (G, Gtn), MPS (G, Š), NR (G)

tēbû "arising; insurgent"

LB *t[e]-bé-e ina ḫarrāni ana muḫḫišunu ittebû* YOS 21, 175: 9 "bandits attacked them on the way". JW

têbu "to distrust(?)"

Richter 1991: an antonym of *qiāpu*, cf. perhaps Hebr./Aram. *tʿb*. JW

tēdīqu "dress, costume"

Stol 2010, 173: NA *te-di-iq bēl arni* BIWA 151, 231 C viii 129 "dress of a penitent". NR

tegibu "a designation of copper and textiles"; Nuzi

Perhaps to be connected with Hurr. *tag-/teg-* "to be clean, bright, beautiful" (cf. *takulatḫu*, *tektumma*), s. Richter 2012, 429 with further lit. JW

teḫampašḫu "a type of payment"; Nuzi

From Hurr. *teḫambašḫe*, a type of payment (silver or payment in kind) for raising infants (Fincke 1995, 9–12). S. also Richter 2012, 457. JW

teḫiltu s. *taḫaltu*

tēḫirtu "residue, amount left over"

For disc. and further ref. s. Bongenaar 1997, 359; MacGinnis 2008, 84 BM 61271; AOAT 414/1, 64: 5. JW/NR

****teḫûtu** s. *ṭeḫûtu*

te'īqtu, *têqtu* "worry, grief"

1. LB *aḫū'a* ... *te-iq-tú lā* IB-BA-*la-a-nu* AOAT 414/1, 142: 15 "my brother must not react(?) to me in a troublesome way". For the verb cf. the comm. ib. p. 259: *apālu*?

2. Abraham/Sokoloff 2011, 54 consider a loan from Aram. unlikely because a *taPRĪS*(*t*) noun from this root is not attested in Aram. However, *taPRĪS*(*t*) is a productive pattern in Akk., and it may well be that a *taPRĪSt* noun was built on a loaned root. Moreover, form and mng. of the word as well as its occurrence only in LB fit well the suggested Aram. etymon *ʿWQ*. Therefore, *t.* is most probably an Aram. lw. in Akk. JW (2), MPS (1–2)

te'ītu s. *ti/e'ītu*

tēkītu, + *tēkūtu* "complaint"

1. OB *te-ki-tam lā nippalušu* RATL 389 no. 3 ii 14 "we will surely not reply to him with a complaint".

2. OB lit. *īhussi te-ki-ta-am* CUSAS 10, 2: 13 "he made (lit. took) a complaint".

3. OB with *rašû*: **a)** *assurri te-ki-tam tara*[*ššī*] RATL 99 no. 28: 23 "don't you complain (saying …)!".
b) *te-ki-tam lā tarašši* RA 102, 52 no. 2: 14 "you shall not complain".

4. NB var. *tēkūtu* (also ABL 1240: 7 cit. CAD T 326b):
a) *tamkāršu te-ku-tu lā išakkan* OIP 114, 81: 20 "his merchant must not complain!"
b) *enna te-ku-ú-*⌈*tu*⌉ *lā tašakkan* OIP 114, 95: 13 "now do not complain!"
c) *te-ku-ut-ka ul mur-ri-rat* OIP 114, 92: 32 "your complaint is not being examined".

5. Durand 1983a, 229f., Mayer 2009, 433 and id. 2017b, 234f. suggest to read *tēqītu* "(painted) overlay, salve" in transferred mng. "pretense, excuse". This interpretation fits in the known instances and offers an etym. Note, however, the frequent late spellings with KU and KI where *qu* and *qi* would be preferable. JW (1, 3, 5), MPS (2, 4–5)

teknītu, *taknītu* "care, solicitude; object of care"

1. Mayer 2009, 425: *bāb tak-ni-ti* DN DN_2 [DN_3] BagM Bh. 2, 97 r. 3 "gate of solicitude(?) of DN, DN_2, [DN_3]".

2. SB *ilat tak-ni-t*[*i*] SpTU 3, 75: 15 "goddess cared for". MPS (2), NR (1)

+ **tektumma** "to cleanse, to free (from obligations)?"; Nuzi, Hurr. lw.

PN *wardiya* <<⌈*ù*⌉>> *te-ek-du-um-ma ēpuš ana mārūti ana* PN *iddin* HSS 19, 48: 5 "I freed PN, my slave, and gave him to PN as a son", s. Fincke 1998, 46ff. (quot. AHw 1251a s.v. *šitektumma*, CAD Š/3 129a s.v. *šitektu*); S. also Richter 2012, 428. JW

tēkūtu s. *tēkītu*

telannu s. *talannu*

teleʾû, *teleʾāʾu* “very competent, expert”

1. Mayer 2017b, 234: OB lit. *zíb-ba-dè-eš* TUK-*a-zu*? : *te-le-i-iš nabīʾāt* CUSAS 10, 14: 51 “you are called upon as an expert”.

2. Mayer 2009, 433: SB [D]N *qitrudu te-le-ʾi-i* Or. 59, 467: 3 “DN, the courageous, the competent”.

3. SB *te-le-é-a-um* KAL 9, 35 A 8. The same spelling occurs in a hymn to Nabû (CAD T 327 *t.* a).

JW (1), MPS (3), NR (2)

tēliltu, + *tēlultu*, + *tēluttu* “cleansing, purification”

1. Lex. *sikil* = *te-lu-ul-tum*, *te-lu*!-*ut-tu* Emar 6/4, 537: 253, 255 (Sa). Diff. Sjöberg 1998, 258: *te-qú-ut/ul-tu*. For *tēluttu* s. also CAD T 328 *tēliltu* lex. sect.

2. Stol 2010, 173: *sikillu šumšu šammi te-lil-tú* STT 1, 93: 47; CTN 4, 195 r. 3 “*sikillu* is its name, a plant of purification.”

MPS (1), NR (2)

telītu “competent one”

SB *ina qibīt iqbû te-lit Ištar* KAL 7, 23 r. 3 “by the order given by the competent one, Ištar”.

JW

tēlītu “revenue, returns; outlay, expenses”

1. OB *alpī u immerātī ša nakkamātim ša qātīšunu te-li-tam kīma qātim ana* GN *lišēlûnim* AbB 13, 8: 10 “(the governors) shall bring up oxen and sheep from the stores which are at their disposal, the returns(?) in accordance with the share (that is due)”, s. Stol ib. n. b.

2. For LB s. van Driel 2002, 292 (rather “cost” than “a type of taxation”); Waerzeggers 2010, 329ff. (prebend tax).

JW

têltu “saying, proverb; pronunciation”

1. SB *ana tel-te u pīlte ina pī nišī ittaškin* SAA 3, 29 r. 9 “he became a proverb and an obscenity in the mouth of mankind”, s. Mayer 2009, 433.

2. NB *ina tel-ta šakin umma* SAA 17, 27 r. 14 “it is said in a proverb as follows”.

têlu “to pronounce (exactly)”

Mayer 2017b, 234: LB [^{kuš}*š*]*iḫ̮ṭu malā rupšu ša patri te-el šīru ša* PN Iraq 45, 189: 24 “as much (sheep-)skin as defined(?) by the width of a knife is the meat for PN”.

JW

teluttu II (mng. unkn.)

Lex. PISANxLIL? = *te-lu-ut-tum*, *nagguru* Emar 6/4, 537: 233 (Sa). Cf. *teluttu*, var. of *tēliltu*, CAD T 328 *tēliltu* lex. sect.? Cf. Sjöberg 1998, 257.

+ **temašša** “a vessel(?)”; foreign word

GA.KIN.AG 15 : *pullanza* 5: *te-ma-aš-ša* Fs. Sjöberg p. 318 RS.25138: 8 “cheese, 15 (gloss) *p.* vessels, 5 (gloss) *t.* vessels”, s. Stol 1993, 105. For Hitt. *pulla-* “a vessel for bread” s. HEG Vol. P 645.

JW/MPS

temāyu, + *tiʾāma*? “a quality of copper”; OB

1. URUDU LUḪ̮.ḪA̮ *te-ma-yu* ARM 32 p. 15 T.482: 1, T.470: 2.

2. URUDU *ti-a-*⸢*ma*⸣ BagM 21, 199 no. 140: 1, s. Reiter 1997, 168.

3. Cf. CAD T 334 s.v. *temāju*. ARM 32 p. 16 n. 40: connected to the Arab. GN Taymāʾ or a derivation from *tiʾāmtu* “sea”?

JW

temennu, *temmēnu* "foundation (document), inscription; platform; a building(?)"

1. OB (*ša*) *temenni* "a kind of personnel" (cf. CAD T 339 *temmenu* "mng. uncert."): *ša te-me-ni ina* GN ARM 26/1, 116 no. 16: 19 "the *ša t.* are in GN". Cf. Heimpel 2003, 602: "valet". S. also 2a below.

2. OB (part of) a building(?) (cf. CAD T 339):

a) *ana šipir te-em-me-nim aḫka lā tanaddī … ittī* PN 2 *sà-k[a-an-n]i* {EL KI} *elqē ša te-em-me-nim īḫuzū te-em-me-n[a]m? ša libbi ēkallim ša niṣirtim elteqē umma* PN$_2$ *te-em-me-ni šunūti awīlū lā iḫḫazū ēkallumma līḫuz* {1} *amāt bēliya te-em-me-na līḫuzā te-em-me-e[n sinn]ištim šū [m]ādiš ne-eḫ-su šūma harib iškār šattim ul ikaṣṣarū te-em-me-nu maruṣ ēkallum [l]ū ikaṣṣar* FM 9, 32 no. 3: 4–16 "do not neglect the task regarding the *t.*! (My lord instructed me thus:) 'I took two lodgings(?) from PN. The *t.*-personnel took them. I received the *t.* of the secret inner palace.' PN$_2$ said: 'Men shall not take these *t.*, it is the palace who shall take them. My lord's servant girls shall take the *t.*' This women's *t.* is very rundown(?). It is deserted. They have not assembled the work material for a year. The *t.* is in disrepair. The palace shall repair it."

b) *aššum ṭēm té-em-me-ni Elamêtim* FM 9, 120 no. 21: 6 "concerning the report about the quarters(?) of the Elamite women", s. Ziegler ib. 122. Cf. *te-em-ma-na* FM 9, 237 no. 59: 12 (in broken context).

3) OB *eqlum ina* TE-*en-nim Išḫara* RA 53, 81 no. 13: 2 "a field in the *t.* (named/of(?)) 'Išḫara'", pace Prechel 1996, 35 n. 16 and Stol 2010, 173, who both suggest a hapax *tennu* "district(?)". But cf. *ina t[e]-em-mé-nim Zababa* RA 53, 36 AO 10790 e. 3 (s. also CAD T 339 s.v. *temmenu*).

4. LB *šiddu elû* IM.SI.SÁ DA *te-me-en* BiMes. 24, 23: 3 // BRM 2, 37: 3 "upper long side, north, adjoining the foundation platform".

5. In N/LB also "foundation capsule" containing documents, for disc. s. Schaudig 2003, 455ff.

JW (1–2, 5), MPS (1, 3–4)

temēru "to cover (in earth), bury"

G OB in the expression "to bury in straw = to hide" (Mayer 2009, 433f.):

1. 1 *sinništam šâtu ina tibnim at-mi-ir-ši* FM 1 p. 82: 33 "I have hidden this woman in straw", cf. *ina tibnim it-mì-ir-[š]i* ib. 40.

2. *kīma šamaššammī … ina tibnim lā it-mi-ru-šu-nu-ti izzakar* TIM 4, 33: 28 "she declared that she had not hidden the sesame seeds in straw".

D 1. OB *kīma awât* PN *tu-um-mu-ra* ARM 26/2, 183 no. 373: 3 "(I have reported) that PN's words had been covered up".

2. NA *anāku annaka* ⸢*lu*?⸣-*tam-me-er* SAA 10, 263: 15 "I will bury (the figurines) here". JW (G, D), MPS (D)

temmenu s. *temennu*

têmtu s. *tiʾāmtu*

tenē/īštu, *tanē/īštu* "people"

1. OA *ta-ni-iš-tum lamnat* TCL 19–21, 14: 18 "mankind is corrupted", s. Michel 1991a for OA ref.

2. OB ref. in Reiner 2007, 54:

a) *[a]ssurrima ... te-ni-iš-ta-am imaš-šaʾū* ARM 26/1, 171 no. 37 r. 20 "I fear that they will plunder the populace."

b) *šumma ṣābam tanassaḫā* 10 *līmī ta-ni-iš-ta-šu-nu zikarum ana sinništim ibaššī* ARM 26/1, 167 no. 35: 18 "if you deport the people – their population is as much as 10,000, male and female" (s. Durand ib. 173 n. g).
c) 10 *līmī ta-ni-iš-tam ninassaḫamma* ARM 26/1, 168 no. 35: 26 "we will deport 10,000 people".
d) *ina* 30 *awīlī u ta-ni-iš-ti-šu-nu kâti u* GN *inaṣṣarū* NABU 1991/24 A. 2732 r. 7 "with 30 men and their people, can they guard you and GN?", s. Ziegler 1999, 498.

3. OB lit. *alik atta lū nūr te-ne-še-tim* AnSt 33, 148: 25 "go, be you the light of mankind!"

4. OB lit. [DN_f] *nabī'at te-ni-še*$_{20}$(ŠI)-*ti-im* CunMon. 8, 110: 3 "[DN_f], who is called upon by the people".

5. In MB ration lists perhaps "family members" (Sassmannshausen 2001, 123, cf. CAD T 341 mng. b).

6. S. also *tenīšu*. JW (1, 3–6), MPS/NR (2)

tenē/īšu "people"

1. Early OB *te-e-ne-i*⌈*š*⌉ *nakrišu* ZA 93, 7 ii 2 "the people of his enemy".

2. Early OB [*t*]*e-e-ne-iš* [*m*]*ātātim* Ahmed 2012, 255ff. Haladiny Inscr. i 13 "the people of the lands". JW

tenšû "a square(?) ornament made of gold or silver"

1. LB 1 *te-en-šu-ú ḫurāṣ* RA 93, 144: 61 "1 golden *t.*-ornament".

2. *ayyaru* "rosette" and *tenšû* are mentioned one after another in administrative texts. This might correspond to rosettes and squares in iconographic representations. Matsushima 1995, 175f. concludes that *tenšû* denotes a square ornament. Beaulieu 2003, 389: "sequin (made of gold)". JW/MPS (1), NR (2)

tēnû "substitute, change, replacement"

1. OB "change of clothing":
a) 3 ^{túg}*te-nu-um u kaballu* ARM 30, 124 T.365: 7 "(silver for) 3 changes of clothing and leggings".
b) 3 *te-ni-i patinnī ša uṭuplim* ib. T.341: 31 and passim "3 changes of bands made of *uṭuplu*-fabric".

2. OB "replacement of personnel" (Reiner 2007, 54):
a) *te-ne-e-em bēlī liṭrudam* ARM 26/2, 115 no. 345: 13 "let my lord send a replacement for me."
b) *mimma te-ni-e ṣābim šâti ul ikšudam* ARM 26/2, 126 no. 353: 10 "no replacements for this force have reached me." Cf. ib. 3, 7.
c) 30 LÚ *te-nu-šu-nu* ARM 26/1, 132 no. 20: 18 "30 men, their replacements".

3. OB *ištū te-ne-e-em maḫrîm* AbB 13, 75: 10 "after the previous substitute(?)". MPS/NR

** **tepēru** "to jostle" s. *epēru* III.

teptītu "opening up (land); clasp(?)"; + MB

n $^{\text{na4}}$GUŠKIN *te-ep-te-tu ana kišādi* Sassmannshausen 2001 no. 416: 25 "n golden beads, clasps(?) for a necklace"; cf. (precious stones) [*te*]-⌈*ep*⌉-*te-e-tu* PN ib. 11. Cf. SAD *pītu* I 1 and *puttu* II. Lit. "opening device(?)". JW/MPS

tēqītu "ointment, salve"

1. NA *ašhar ša te-qí-ti* SAA 8, 2324 r. 2 "*ašhar* stone for daubing".

2. NA *bīt seḫpi ana te-qi-a-te* StAT 3, 7: 4 "box for salve" (mentioned after a bed and chair).

3. LB of wax: *te-qí-tum ša* D[UḪ.L]À[L] CT 22, 225 = AOAT 414/1, 216: 8, cf. comm. ib. p. 327, pace CAD T 348a.

S. also *tēkītu*.

\+ **teqnītu?**, *teqmītu*? "right of retention(?)"; OB Alalaḫ, NWSem. lw.(?)

1. *qadu te-eq-ni-ti-šu-nu ana šīm gamer* AlT 52: 13 "(PN bought from PNf and PN_2 the village of GN) for its full price, together with their right of retention(?)" .

2. *qadū te-eq-ni-ti-šu* AlT 54: 13; 58: 8.

3. *ana té-eq-mi-ti-šu* AlT 53: 10; cf. also AlT 57: 29.

4. Cf. Zeeb 1995. In spite of Akk. *qanû* "to keep, buy" (CAD Q 91), the word might be a loan from NWSem.

JW/MPS/NR

teqrūbatu s. *taqrībatu*

terdītu, *tardītu* "addition; delivery, consignment"

1. OB "delivery": (silver rings) *te-er-di-tum ana* PN TLT 16: 3, cf. 69 r. 4; 88: 3. For add. OB ref. s. ARM 32, 3 n. 14.

2. Reiner 2007, 54: *annûtu šumū tar*!-*di-tum* Neugebauer/Weidner 1915, 59 VAT 9417 r. 20 "these lines are an addition".

JW (1), NR (2)

terdû, *tardīʾu* "secondary, following"; OA

1. As qualification of textiles s. Michel/Veenhof 2010 with disc. and add. ref.

2. 21 *gušūrū rabīʾūtum* 23 *tár-dí-ú-tum* 6 *lēʾū rabīʾūtum* 8 *tár-dí-ú-tum* AKT 5, 59: 2, 4 "21 large beams, 23 of smaller size, 6 large boards, 8 of smaller size".

3. Of son: *mēr* PN *ta-ar-dí-im* AKT 6A, 101: 16 "(before the) younger son of PN".

JW (1, 3), MPS (2)

terḫu "a beer vessel"

OB lit. *te-er-ḫi-ša* CUSAS 32, 32 r. 4, cf. SAD *darāru* N and *tarḫu*.

teriktu s. *terīqtù*

\+ **terinnatu**, + *tarnatu* "cone (of the terinnu plant)"

1. Reiner 2007, 54f.: NA *giš-še-ù-suḫ*$_5$ = *tar-na-tú* BATSH 6, 198: 6.

2. SB *te-ri-na-tú* ⸢*te-ri*⸣*-na-tú ša šeʾa malât* Iraq 71 p. 61 (A 7876) vi 28 = Maqlû V 50 "cone, cone, who is filled with seed".

JW (2), NR (1)

terinnu, + *turinnu*; pl. fem. *terinnātu* "cone; a medical plant"

1. SB *išid ašūḫi* [...]-*ḫu tu-rin*^{in}*-na-šu a-za-*⸢x x⸣ SpTU 5, 272: 16 "the root of the pine is ..., its cones are ...".

2. Cf. disc. in Abusch/Schwemer 2009, 76. However, the ref. under 1, above, shows that there is no clear-cut distinction between fem. *terinnatu* "cone" and masc. *terinnu* "a medical plant". Therefore, the ref. for fem. pl. probably belong here, and the ref. for fem. sg. are a backformation from the fem. pl. (cf. *igāru*, pl. *igārātu* > *igārtu*; *ūmu*, pl. *ūmātu* > *ūmtu* etc.).

teriptu s. *tiriptu*

terku, *tirku* "blow; (dark) spot; a method of weaving"

1. a) OB *uṣûm rabûm ša ter*$_4$*-ki-im* ARM 30, 124 T.407 iv 9 "a big *uṣû*-fabric in *t.*-technique(?)".
b) S. *tarāku* D "to beat textiles" CAD T 205 *tarāku* 4.
c) S. also AHw 1349 *terku* 2 "ein Teil des Schuhs" und CAD T 426 *tirku* 3 "a supply for travellers"; Veenhof 1972, 44f. and Durand 2009, 175 suggest that

these ref. belong to a word *dirku* "packing sack". Since the verb *darāku* "to pack" is only attested in OA this suggestion remains uncert.

2. On *tirik šadîm* "dawn" in Mari s. Heimpel 1997; Streck 2017, 606 (lit. "strike (of the light) in the east").

3. SB [*ni*]*kkas u* 15 *ubān ti-rik sungin-nišina* JCS 66, 82: 310 = Gilg. SB V 290 (cf. CAD T 426 *t.* 1a) "3 half-reeds and 15 fingers (long) were the wood-chips (thrown up by) the strokes (of their axes')". JW (2), MPS (1, 3)

terru II "a type of grain or an offering made of grain"

OB 4 BÁN ^{še}*te-er-rum* CUSAS 9, 142: 1 "4 seah of *t.*"; ⸢$^{\text{še?}}$*ti*$^{?}$⸣*-rum ša ilī* MU.DU *ana ēkallim*!? ib. 78: 1 "*t.* for the gods, delivery for the palace"; ⸢^{še}*ti*$^{?}$⸣*-rum* (followed by a list of deities) ib. 84: 1; (^{še})*ti-rum* ib. 409 ii 1, 419 vii 1, 422 vii 1, 424 vii 1. According to Dalley ib. 77 ad 78: 1 "possibly a type of offering of barley rather than a type of grain", also in MB texts from Elam (cf. CAD T 356 *terru* "an offering?").

terṣu, *tirṣu* "stretching out, extension; (ritual) preparation; a garment"

1. OB in adv. acc. "directly, immediately" (Reiner 2007, 57; Mayer 2009, 435):

a) *anāku te-er-ṣa-am-ma appa*[*lšu*] ARM 10, 139: 23 "I will answer him immediately" (coll. Durand 2000 p. 383 n. 198).

b) *ṣābam muṣlālamma te-er-ṣa*!*-am*! *meḫretišunu aṭrudma* ARM 28, 19 r. 11 "it was at noon that I sent the troops directly against them".

c) *ribīt* GN *te-er-ṣa-am ireddûši* FM 9, 282 no. 71: 29 "(they seated the woman on a mule and) led her straight along the main street of GN."

d) *ana* [...] *te-er-ṣí-im-ma usaḫḫir* ARM 2, 24+A.1234: 19 "I sent (them) straight back to [...]" s. Durand 1998, 224 n. 451.

2. *ina te-er-ṣí-im nuqabbaršu* ARM 6, 37 r. 13 (CAD T 428 mng. 2b3') "do we bury him in outstretched position?", s. Heimpel 1996b.

3. Ritual preparation of meat (Stol 2010, 174): OB *te-er-ṣum* AOAT 25, 229 r. vii 12; Fs. Alp p. 94 iii 15, p. 96 iii 24f.

4. A garment (CAD T 428 *t.* 4, Stol 2010, 174): OB *ti-ir-ṣum* BIN 9, 470: 5; ^{túg}*ter-ṣum* YOS 5, 94: 9; 207: 55; Riftin 52: 12; ^{túg}*te-er-ṣum* YOS 5, 96: 7; ^{túg}*ter-ṣ*[*um la*]*-ḫa-ri-tum* ib. 224: 6. MPS/NR

tertītu "spoke (of a wheel)"

Balkan 1954, 128–130; Waetzoldt 2006–2008, 216 § 1.4. MPS/NR

têrtu "instruction; office; omen"

1. Reiner 2007, 55: OA *lū ana šīmim ana ēkallim iddin lū té-ra-at ēkallim ukallim lū našīma* AKT 5, 1: 17 "whether he has already sold (the *amūtu* metal) to the palace or has shown it to the office of the palace or is still carrying it with him".

2. Mayer 2017b, 235: OB *aššum šê te-er-tim* ARM 28, 141: 32 "concerning the ordered barley"; cf. (barley) *rēḫat* [*t*]*a-i-ir-tim ša šaddaqdim* AbB 12, 169: 7 "the remainder of last year's order".

3. With det.: OB ^{uzu}*te-*⸢*re-e*⸣*-tim* CUSAS 29, 206: 21, s. *beʾru*.

4. *šūt tērēti* "officials" (CAD T 368): OB lit. ^{lú}*šūt te-re-(e)-tim ša Nippur* "officials of N." CUSAS 10, 17: 8, 16, 66, 77.

5. *bēl tērēti* "chief administrator": OB *mimma ana bēl te-re-tim u ḫalṣim elîm kanikātīka itaddunim u awīlūtī šūṣîm uwaʾʾerka* FM 6, 390 no. 50: 18 "have I in any way instructed you to give your sealed orders repeatedly to the chief administrator and the upper district to let the staff leave?", cf. ib. 26 and ARM 1, 61: 29.

JW (5), MPS (2–4), NR (1–2)

tērubtu "entry, entrance, entrance-ritual"

1. Stol 2010, 173: OB *ina te-ru-ub-ti šeʾam … ana karê ušērib* BE 6/2, 52: 9 "during the entrance-ritual(?) I brought barley into storage".

2. MA *ina* UD 6^{kám} *te-ru-bat bīt* DN Chuera 80: 1 "on the 6th day 'entrance'(-ritual) into the house of DN".

3. MB *kurummat immerī marûti te-ru-ub-ti* CUSAS 30, 212: 13 "fodder for fattened sheep for the entrance-ritual".

MPS (2–3), NR (1)

teslītu, *tešlītu* "appeal, prayer"

Mayer 2009, 433: OB *šēmī te-eš-li-tim* OECT 11, 1: 4 "he who hears the prayer"; cf. SB *še-mu-ú te-eš-l[i-ti]* K. 3416+9069: 9. NR

tēṣābu, *tēṣābītu* "leftovers(?), addition(?), follower(?)"

1. The OA refs. concerning a textile probably do not belong here, s. *TiSāBu*.

2. SB [*māra*]*t ili u té-ṣa-bi-šá* // ⸢*te*?⸣-*ṣa-bi-tum ay iṭḫē*[*ka*] KAL 9, 36: 43 "may [the daught]er of god and her follower(?) not approach [you]". S. the disc. of Jakob ib. p. 82. JW (1), MPS (2)

\+ **teṣbû** "admiration"

Mayer 2009, 433: (*ṣalmu ša*) *ina šipir nikiltim ša mārūt ummiʾānūtim te-eṣ-bi-i-iš epšu* BagM 34, 148 xiii 9 "(a statue, which) has been fashioned by the skill of professional craftsmanship for admiration". Cf. *ṣubbû*. NR

tēṣētu "quarrel, contest"

OB lit. *te-ṣe-et eḫzišunu* CUSAS 10, 14: 28 "the quarrel about their knowledge".

****tešê** s. *tišē*

tešēnu, *tušēnu* "a wild animal?"

On ref. cit. CAD T 373 cf. Lion 1991. Possibly identical with *tišānu*, s. also *ditānu*. JW

\+ **tešêšri** "nineteen"

Reiner 2007, 55: LB ⸢*te*⸣-*še-eš-ri* NABU 2004/56, YBC 8057: 9. JW

****tešiā** s. *tišē*

tešmû "attention, listening (to each other)"

1. Mayer 2009, 433: logogram ZU.ZU, s. SB *bēlet téš-me-e* CTN 4, 168 iii 51 // *b*[*ēlet*] ZU!.ZU BMS 33: l.

2. Cf. Kouwenberg 2010, 398: reciprocal mng. "concord, harmony".

NJCK (2), NR (1)

\+ **teštû** "a wooden part of a door(?)"; SB … ^{giš}*te-eš-tu-šu* SpTU 5, 257: 22 "its *t.* is a …". From *retû* D (*tertû* < *teštû*?) "to set doors in doorways"?

tēšû "confusion, chaos"

1. Mayer 2009, 434: SB *ina te-še-e naspanti ummassu liḫalliq* Sumer 38, 125 v 6 "he shall destroy his forces in devastating chaos".

2. Mayer 2009, 434: SB [*i*]*na qereb te-še-e ašar šatât anuntu* STT 70: 2 "amidst chaos, where battle is woven". S. Mayer 1992, 21. NR

****tetēlu** s. *tattalliku*

tettelliku s. *tattalliku*

teʾû I "covered"; + OB

OB lex. *te-e-ʾu*$_5$ IGI UET 7, 93: 33 "covered with respect to the eye". S. Sjöberg 1996, 228f.

teʾû II "to cover"

G OB *šê* ... [*ša*] *e-te-ú-ma šipassīya addû* CTMMA 1, 70: 6 "the barley … which I covered (in storage) and put my sealed bullae upon".

+ **Gt** OB lit. *nurbi šammī dīšātim te-et-te-i* MesCiv. 7, 212 no. 14 iv 10 "with the succulent portion of the abundant grass you bedecked yourself". Since the text elsewhere only uses pret. an N-stem (Mayer 2017b, 235) is less likely.

Disc.: Mayer 2017b, 235 analyses the verb as *teʾû* rather than *têʾu*. JW/MPS

****tēʾu** s. *teʾû* I, ****têʾu** s. *teʾû* II

teʾûtu s. *ti/eʾûtu*

tezû "to excrete; to shit"

G Mayer 2017b, 251: OB lit. *i-te*$_9$*-zi* (// *be*$_9$*-be*$_9$) *illak* Fs. Wilcke 142 BT 9: 13 "he/she shits and walks" (list of insults and profanities). JW

+ **ti-?** "to speak"; Hurr. word in MB Qaṭna

kī anāku ana bēliya : *ur-ḫu tu-uk-ku* QS 3, 5: 59 "that I do not (gloss) speak(?) truly to my lord". Cf. disc. ib. p. 74. S. Richter 2012, 453ff.

tiʾālu, *tiyālu*, *tiʾāru*, *tiyāru* "a type of tree; wood of the *t.* tree"

1. OB *iṣṣī pasrī ša īnāt magarrī* [*qa*]*dūm ti-ia-ri-šu-nu iksānim* ARM 26/1, 580 no. 280 r. 15 "cut the wood for the poles for the wheel naves together with their *t.*!", s. Durand ib. p. 581 g (referring to bark or branches?); Heimpel 2003, 283 ("axle housings"). S. also ARM 32, 158f.

2. OB ^{giš}*ti-ia-ri lišābilamma ana šūrub-ti niqî* DN *magarrī mādūtimma lušērib šumma lā kīʾamma* [*k*]*ūm ti-ia-ri ša ṣarbatim*[*ma*] *inneppešū kīma ti-ia-ru lā* .[..] PN *ana ṣēr bē*[*liya*] *uwaʾʾer* ARM 26/2, 16 no. 285 r. 26–30 "may he send *t.*-wood to me, and I will bring in many wheels for the contribution of the offering of DN. If that is not so, they will be made of poplar rather than of *t.* As *t.* are not .[..], I have sent PN with instructions to my l[ord]".

3. OB 36 ^{giš}*ti-ia-ri damqūtim* 14 ^{giš}*ti-ia-ri* … ŠU.NÍGIN 50 ^{giš}*ti-i*[*a-ri*] ARM 26/2, 533 no. 540: 14–16 "36 good *t.*, 14 *t.* … together 50 *t.*"; cf. ib. p. 532 no. 540: 8. The reading 14 *t. terdennū-šunu* "14 *t.* of second quality" (Marti 2001) is uncertain because the construction (nom. pl. in *-ū* with suff.?) is without any parallel.

4. OB [...^{g}]^{iš}*ti-ia-ri ša* ^{giš}GIGIR ARM 26/2, 533 no. 541: 20 "*t.*-wood for a chariot" (quot. in part in CAD T 399b as ArOr. 17/1 329 B 130 r. 4).

5. OB 20 ^{giš}*ti-ia-ri* ARM 26/2, 532 no. 539: 20, cf. ib. 22.

6. Cf., perhaps, Hurr. *tiari/tiyari* (Bogh., Ugar.) "spindle" and Hitt. ^{giš}*tiyarri/a* "chariot", s. Richter 2012, 456f. for lit. JW (1, 6), MPS (2–5)

tiʾāmtu, *têmtu*, + *tiʾāmetu*, +*tiwīʾatu* "sea; lake"

1. Mayer 2009, 428: *kakkī ša ittī te-em-tim amtaḫṣu addinakkum* MARI 7 p. 45: 3 "I gave you the weapons with which I have fought the sea".

2. OB *ina te-em-tim ša* GN ARM 26/2, 134 no. 358: 4 "(they occupy the area) in (the region of) the lake of GN".

3. OB lit. pl. *ti-a-me-tim* CUSAS 10, 1: 40, cf. *tīru* I.

4. OB lit. *šārum ti-me-a-tim uṣīma u ti-a-me-tum ippallassum* [*im*]*ḫās uruḫ* [*ti*]*-wi-a-tim* CUSAS 32, 7 I 19–22 "the wind went out (upon) the sea and the sea looked at it. It beat the sea's hair". Cf. George, ib. p. 152: "The spell appears to play with variants of the Sea's name". The verbal form *ip-pa-al-la-súm*, if not to be corrected with George to *ip-pa-al-la-*<*sà*>*-šum*, indicates that all these forms are sg.

5. NA ⸢*ēta*⸣*nabbir nārāti u tam-tim*^{meš} SAA 9, 9: 9 "I cross over rivers and oceans".

6. Mayer 2009, 428: Correct *ti-a-mat* OECT 6, pl. 10 to *ti-*GÉME (Maul 1988 pl. 39).

7. On the topographical designation *t. elēnītu* in NA (CAD T 155 mng. 9') s. Yamada 2005.

JW (2, 7), MPS (3–5), NR (1, 6)

tibbû s. *timbuttu*

tibku, Ass. also *tikpu* "outpouring, deposit, layer"

Mayer 2017b, 235: MA n *te-ek-pi* AN.TA Numoto 2009, 94: 3 "(the wall) was 80 courses (of bricks) high". JW

tibnu "straw, chaff"

1. OB lit. *kīma zābil šaḫar*[*ri*] *ša ti-ib-ni-im luqqutāt kabattī* ALL no. 1 ii 5–7 "like a carrier of a net for straw you have plundered my interior".

2. OB IN.NU.DI *eqlim* 5 GUR *ša* 1 IKU *eqlim* CUSAS 36, 167: 7 "the straw of the field is 5 kor per 1 iku of field".

3. Mayer 2009, 434: OB in the expression "to bury in straw" = "to hide", s. *temēru*. JW (3), MPS (1–2)

tibûtu "rise, attack"

OB lit. *ti-bu-ti erbîm lū tetebbīʾam ina ṣabrišu* YOS 11, 6: 10 "you must rise a locust's rise in its clittering". Cf. Mayer 2009, 434. JW/MPS/NR

tidugaru in *tidugarumma epēšu*; "to attack each other, to fight"

Cf. Hurr. *tid-* II "to attack", s. Richter 2012, 464f. with further lit. JW

****tidūku B** (CAD T 396), s. *dâku* Gt

tigidlû, *tingitallu*, *tigitallu* "a musical instrument"

1. Reiner 2007, 55: OB *ṭāti ša … sinništi ti-in-gi-ta-li-im* WZKM 86, 481 M.8426+ : 6 "the payment for … the woman (who plays) the *t.*"

2. Reiner 2007, 55: *ti-gi-tal-li* YOS 10, 59: 9, a formation on the exta, cit. CAD T 398 s.v. *tigitallu* and CAD N/1 89 s.v. *nadû* 3b1', probably belongs here.

3. For disc. s. Shehata 2007, 524 (a type of lyre).

4. For CAD *tigidlû* 1 (a bird) s. *tigil*(*l*)*û*. JW (3), NR (1–2, 4)

+ tigil(l)û "a bird"

OB *ti-*⌜*gi*⌝*-lu-um*[mušen] Edubba 7, 100: 25 (in list of birds). Black/Al-Rawi 1987, 124 read *ḫu-la-lu-um*, but the first sign was copied as a clear *ti*. Al-Rawi/Dalley 1987, 105 read *ti*?-⌜*la*⌝*-lu-um*. For the *ti-gi-lá*/*ti-gi-il-la-*/*ti-gi*$_4$*-lu*-bird in lex. texts s. AHw 1356 s.v. *tigi(l)lû* 2 and CAD T 397 s.v. *tigidlû* 1. The name is identical with the name of the plant *tigilû* "a squash" CAD T 397. S. also *tigidlû*.

tigitallu s. *tigidlû*

tignu s. *tiqnu*

tigû I "a lyre, stringed instrument"

SB [..]. *nârī u ti-gi-i ūmišamma urtaṣṣanū ina pani Ḫumbaba* JCS 66, 76: 25 (Gilg.) "… of singers and *t.* instruments daily resounded before Ḫumbaba".

tigû II, fem. *tigîtu* "lyre player"

Mayer 2009, 434: OB (PNf) *ša bīt tege-tim* FM 4, 9 vi 30; 30 iv 7; 32: 11 "(women) from the house of lyre players". S. further Ziegler ib. 94–96 and ead. 2007, 79. NR

ti/eʾītu, *tiwītu* "nourishment"

1. Lex. *mur* = *te-i-tum* Emar 6/4, 537: 62 (Sa), s. Sjöberg 1998, 245.

2. OB lit. *ti-wi-ti-iš mātim* CUSAS 10, 2 i 4 (Atr.) "for the nourishment for the land" (cf. George ib.).

3. Cf. *ti/eʾûtu*.

tikātu s. *tikku*

tikiltu II s. *takiltu* I

+ tikizaraʾu, *tikzarû*? "a stone?"; MA, NA?

Reiner 2007, 56:

1. MA 35 MA.NA *ti-ki-za-ra-ú* SAAB 13, 7 no. 3 BM 108943: 2 "35 minas of *t.*" (beside *pu-ru-tu* and *sammuḫu* stones).

2. NA uncert.: [UD]-26-KÁM ⌜*ša ilu*⌝ *ana* É.KAŠ *illaku bīt iḫrû* DN *ša ti-ik*(-)*za-re-e iqabbû dīki anun*[*ti*] SAA 3, 40 (LKA 73): 11 "the 26th day, when the god goes to the brewery, (is) where they dug DN and which is called *t.* (or: a drop (*tīk*) of the progenitor?) (meaning) stirring up bat[tle]".

JW (1–2), MPS (2)

tikku, pl. *tikkānu*, fem. pl. *tikkātu* "neck; bank; pl. reins(?)"

1. Mayer 2009, 434: SB *asḫar kīma nalšu u imbaru lamâ ti-ik-ki* SpTU 2, 24: 28 "*asḫar*-stone, like dew and mist, surrounds my neck."

2. MacGinnis 2008, 84: LB [*a*]*tānu peṣītu ša* LÚ *ina muḫḫi ša ti-ik-ki u ṭurru* WZKM 87 p. 231 no. 4: 2 "a white female donkey that has 'LÚ' on its neck and rump".

3. LB as a cut of meat:
a) [uzu]*ti-ik-ka-nu ša immeri* BiMes. 24, 5: 2, cf. 7 "sheep necks".
b) *ti-ik-ka*[meš] *ša alpi* ib. 2: 2 "bull necks".
c) [uzu]*ti-ik-ka* ib. 7: 6, [uzu]*ti-ik-ku* ib. 9: 6.

4. LB 3 DANNA [*qaq*]*qaru ina ti-ik-ki* [*itt*]*alak* AOAT 414/1, 93: 6 "he went a distance of 3 miles on the river bank".

5. The refs. for *tikkātu* "reins(?)" (CAD T 400 *tikātu* A) belong here (Mayer 2009, 434 and already AHw 1357, s. Durand 1987a, 208). Or fem. sg. *tikkatu*? MPS (3–4), NR (1–2, 5)

tikpu "dot, spot"

On the body (as a symptom of disease): **1.** SB *ti-ik-pi* SpTU 5, 253: 19 r. 1, s. *takāpu* N.

2. *epēssu ša ti-ik-pi* ib. 22 "its (the medicine's) preparation for spots".

3. *u ti-ik-pi* SIG$_5$ ib. r. 5 "and the spots will become good".

tiktu s. *diktu*

tīku "(rain)drop, shower"

On LKA 73: 11 (CAD T 405 *t.* b1') s. *tikizaraʾu* 2. For SpTU 2, 24: 28 s. SAD *tikku* 1. JW

tilgūtu "hugeness(?)"

Cf. SAD *tullugu*, below. No loan from Aram., s. already Abraham/Sokoloff 2011, 55. JW/MPS

tilim(a)tu "a drinking vessel"

1. Mayer 2009, 434: SB $^{\ulcorner\text{dug}\urcorner}$*ti-lim-dù ní-ba kaš* ⸢*dé*?⸣*-a-ĝu*$_{10}$: ⸢*ti-li-ma*⸣*-ti ša ina ramāniša šikara imlâ* BagM 37, 95: 21 "my *t.* which filled with beer by itself".

2. Stol 2010, 174: LB (beer) *ša* 1-*en* TI.LIM.DÙ *ša* DN OECT 12 A 170: 1 "for 1 *t.* vessel for DN" NR

tillāniš "into tells, into ruins"

SB *māti lā manūtu til-la-niš limni* SpTU 4, 141 r. 10 "may he turn countless land(s) to ruins".

tillaqurdu "a medicinal plant"

Mayer 2009, 434: OB *ti-la-q[u-ur-dam]* BagM 4, 393: 23 (among med. ingredients). NR

tillatu I "help, support; reinforcement"

1. OB *ṣābaka u ṣāb šarrī ti-la-a-tim ṭurdam* ARM 28, 1 r. 8 "send me your troops and the kings' support troops!"

2. OB *bēlī aššumika til-la-a-at mātim kalîša irkusma* ARM 26/2, 391 no. 468 r. 11 "my lord bound the auxiliaries of the entire land because of you".

3. Reiner 2007, 56: LB *ana ti-il-la-a-t[a] ša abulli*! MacGinnis 1995, 141: 6 (coll. M. Weszeli) "(reed bundles) for the support troops of the city gate."

MPS (1–2), NR (3)

\+ **tillišu** "into a ruin"; OA

Lit. *bētam šāgimam tí-li-šu taškun* kt 94/k 520: 7 "she has turned the lively house into a ruin" (incant., s. Barjamovic/Larsen 2008, 145). Corresponds to Bab. *tillišam* in *bītam šāgimam ti-li-ša-am iškun* ZA 71, 63: 11). NJCK

tillu I "tell" s. *tīlu*

tillu II "(military) equipment"

Mayer 2017b, 236: SB *til-li kabtūti kakkī [ēsiḫš]u* K.2387+ r. 7 || K.5022+ r. 13 "I assigned to it (the figurine) heavy equipment and weapons". JW

tillu III "a quiver"

LB among household utensils: 1 ^{kuš}*ti-il-lu* dubsar 7, 39: 19. JW

tillû "a garment; appendage, trappings"

1. OB in descriptions of jewelry: *tiṣbu-tā ša til-le-e* ARM 21, 247: 7 "(golden beads) linked in a *t.*", cf. *ti-il-le-e* ARM 32, 435 M.6875: 7, s. ib. p. 100.

2. MB 3 ^{túg}*til-lu-ú kī* 12 KÙ.BABBAR MBLET 74: 9 "3 *t.*s for 12 (shekels of) silver".

3. MB: CUSAS 30, 374 lists altogether 14 *t.* garments: *til-le-⌜e⌝ aḫi* l. 3 "with sleeves"; *mūši* l. 2 "for the night"; *karrūtum* ll. 5, 11 "?"; *karrūtum ubānu* l. 9 "?, finger"; *adi ša s[ū]nāti* l. 12 "with trimmings(?)". JW (1–2), MPS (3)

tillūtu "(military) assistance"

SB *ana ilki u til-lu-ti* Iraq 44, 74: 26 "(they summoned the people to) *ilku* service and to service in the *tillatu* troops", pace van Driel 2002, 292 (*qēme til-lit-tum* Ash F2, cit. ib. 293, rather belongs to *tēlītu*). JW/MPS

tilmu I s. *talīmu*

+ **tilmu II** "desire(?)"

Mayer 2009, 434; Stol 2010, 174: OB lit. (PN) *ša bēlum* DN *ana ti-li-im libbišu irdûšuma* BagM 34, 140 iv 1 "(PN) whom lord DN led to his desired goal(?)". For the etym. cf. *talīmu* "beloved brother". MPS/NR

tilmuttu, + *talmuttu* "a musical instrument"; + SB

Lex. ŠÀ.TAR-*s*[*a*!-*ús*!] // MIN (= ŠÀ.TAR)-*sa-ús* = *ta-al-mu-ut-tu*, *sa-ús* = *ta-al-mu-ut-tu* Emar 6/4, 545: 407f. (Ḫḫ).

tilpānu, *talpānu* "(composite) bow"

1. OB NINDA *ti-il-pa-na-a-tum* CUSAS 9, 100: 9 "bread (shaped as) bows".

2. For add. OB ref. s. ARM 32, 127f.

3. Mayer 2009, 434: SB *ṣabīta ina* GIŠ.RU SÌG$^{?!}$-*aṣ-ma* SpTU 2, 12 iii 23 "he beats (or: shoots?) a gazelle with his *t.*-bow."

4. On mng. "composite bow" (rather than "throwing stick") s. Postgate 2003–2005, 457 with prev. lit.

JW (2, 4), MPS (1), NR (3)

tīlu I, *tillu* I "ruin mound, tell"

1. Lex. *du*$_6$-*gi*$_4$-*gi*$_4$ = MIN (= *sāḫirat*) *ti-li* Emar 6/4, 602: 355 (Lu) "(woman) roaming the tell" (in list of prostitutes).

2. OB lit. *šarrum ašar illa*[*ku*] *panūšu ālum wurkassu ti-lu-um* CUSAS 18 p. 290: 35 "the king, wherever he goes: before him, a city; behind him, a ruin mound."

3. LB logogr. DU$_6$.DU (DU$_6^{du}$?), s. Jursa 1995, 36 (on nos. 8, 23, BM 60757).

S. also *tillišu*. JW (3), MPS (1–2)

timbuttu, + *timbuʾtu*, + *tubbu*, + *tibbu* "harp"

1. Lex. ^{giš}*balag-di* = *ti-im-bu-ʾ-*[*tum*] = [*t*]*ù*!-*ub-bu* Emar 6/4, 545: 381 (Ḫḫ), cf. Cohen 2010, 830.

2. OB lit. *kirissam si*-IB-*tam uḫḫa ti-ib-ba našī zikru* Or. 87, 19 ii 7 "the man carries a hairpin, a *s.*, an *u.*, a harp".

JW (2), MPS (1),

timiraš "a (color-) designation of horses and bovines"

1 GU$_4$ *ti-mi-ra-aš ša* PN UM 29-15-209: 6, 11 "1 *t.* ox", s. Brinkman 1996 with further ref. JW

timminu s. *temennu*

timmu, + *tēmu*, pl. *timmānū* "post, pillar"

1. Lex. *dim* = *te-e-mu* Emar 6/4, 537: 434 (Sa), s. Sjöberg 1998, 265.

2. OB 1 ^{giš}*ti-im-mu ša bīt eleppētim* ŠÀ.BA 4 *iḫzū ša kaspim* ARM 21, 253: 18 "1 wooden pillar for the boat house, with 4 silver settings".

3. Reiner 2007, 56: LB *gabbi tim-ma-a-nu ša galāla* Fs. Steve 278: 17 "all the columns of dressed stone".

4. LB *šallaṭu itti ti-im-⸢mu⸣* dubsar 3, 86: 15 "leather scabbard with stakes(?)".
JW (2, 4), MPS (1), NR (3)

timru I "embers"; + OB

1. Lex. *te* = NE = *ti-im-r*[*um*] Emar 6/4, 537: 306 (Sa).

2. Said of a bird baked in hot ashes or embers: OB lit. *šumma iṣṣūram ana ti-im-ri-*[*i*]*m taṭabbaḫma* YOS 11, 26 ii 21 "when you slaughter a bird for *t.*".

3. Var. of *tumru*. For further ref. s. CAD T 419 *t.* lex. sect. (pace AHw 1346 "ein Kultmahl"). CAD T has a single lemma *timru* "embers(?); burying(?)", but we probably have to distinguish two lemmata. MPS (1–3), NR (2)

timru II, *temru* "burial"; + OB, + SB, NA

1. OB *ana te-em-ri-im ša Dumuzi* FM 12, 139 A.4540: 4 "for the burial of D.", with Jacquet ib. (pace AHw 1346 not "Kultmahl", and pace CAD T 419 *t.* 1 not "embers").

2. SB *ana* IM.LIMMÚ.BA *tim-ri tu-tammar* Schwemer 2001 p. 679 K. 151: 15 "you bury (materials for the ritual) at the four cardinal points" (Reiner 2007, 56).

3. NA, s. CAD 419 *t.* 2. Probably not related to SAD *timru* I, above.
MPS (1, 3), NR (2)

timšak s. *mašāku*

tim'u s. *dummû*

tindû "a lyre"

Lex. *za-an-*MÙŠ (var. *á-za-an-*MÙŠ) = *ti-in-du-u* Emar 6/4, 545: 393 (Ḫḫ).

tinūru "oven, tandoor"

1. Lex. *é im-šu-rin-na* = *bīt ⸢ti⸣-nu-ri* CUSAS 12 p. 40 ii 50 (Kagal) "house of the oven".

2. SB [*a*]*ttama šar ilānī ti-nu-ri* KAL 2, 30 r. 4 "you are the king of the gods, my kiln!".

3. NA ⸢É⸣ IM.ŠU.RIN.NA StAT 3, 69: 7 "kitchen (lit. oven house)" (in house sale contract).

4. LB *u'il*[*tu*] *ša maškanūtu ša anāku ašṭuru … ina* É IM.ŠU.RIN.NA *šaknat* OECT 12 AB 253: 12 "a debt note, concerning a pledge, which I have written, it lies in the kiln (for burning)".
JW (2), MPS (1, 3–4)

+ Ti-pa-tum "a stone"; OB

OB ⸢4 NA_4⸣ *ti-pa-tum* Haradum 2, 8: 7 (among precious stones and ornaments). JW

tiqmītu s. *teqnītu*

tiqnu, + *tignu* "proper equipment, ornament, insignia"

1. SB *illabbiš ti-qin-šú-ma* //|*ti-gi-in-šu-ma* Jiménez 2017, 252: 37 "he puts on his insignia".

2. For the var. with *g* s. also CAD T 199 *taqānu* 3. In fact, no writing **ti-qi*/*qí-in-* is attested so far, so that *ti-qin-* must perhaps rather be read *ti-gin*$_x$-.

3. For ref. cit. CAD *tiqnu* mng. 2 s. *teqnītu*.

tiqqûtu "a color designation (esp. of eyes)"

Mayer 2017b, 236: SB *ana ti-qú-ut šemerī urêšu ana ti-qú-ut ḫi-x*[...] *ana ti-qú-ut inṣabtī, ana ti-qú-ut šá ṣa-ba-ba* ... VS 24, 90 r. 17–19 "concerning the *t.* of the metal rings of his team of horses, the *t.* of […], the *t.* of the earrings, the *t.* of …". JW

tīrānū I, + *tarnu* pl. tant. “coils”; + OA

1. “intestines” (in omina):

a) Mayer 2009, 434: OB *ti-ra-an šuginêm kīnūtum* YOS 11, 23: 71, 130 “the normal (number of) intestine coils from the daily offerings”, s. Starr 1983, 33, 36.

b) OB *ti-ra-nu waṣbū* ARM 26/1, 284 no. 117: 12; 306 no. 142: 11 “the coils were bloated”.

2. As décor on vessels:

a) OA 10 *šaplātum ša tí-ra-⌜ni⌝* OACT p. 77 kt h/k 87: 1 “10 grooved(?) stands”.

b) OB 1 *šušmarû ša ti-ra-ni* ARM 31, 85: 6 “1 basin with *t.*s”; cf. 1 ŠU.ÚŠ.GAR.RA *ta-ar-nim* ARM 31, 185: 1, s. Guichard ib., 139f.

JW (2), MPS/NR (1)

+ **tirdu?** (mng. unkn.); OB

Reiner 2007, 57: *ana ti-ir-di-im uṣīma išpura[mma] ana ṣērisu ūṣī* FM 7, 163 no. 48: 10 “he(?) left to (or: for) *t.* and sent word here, and I(?) left to (go to) him”. GN? MPS/NR

tirḫu s. *terḫu* and *tarḫu*.

+ **tiriptu**, *teriptu* “discoloration; blemish”; OA, OB

1. Reiner 2007, 57: OA *šumma zakûmma* <<*ma*>> *pūṣum ù tí-ri-ip-tum lā īšū šīmšu gumrā* NABU 1991/54, Ankara 9-245-87: 7 “if (the lapis lazuli) is clear and has no white spot or (other) discoloration, pay the full price for it!” Cf. Michel 2001a, 349 kt 87/k 387.

2. OB *mimma ḫiṭītum u te-ri-ip-t[um] ul ibaššī* ARM 26/2, 205 no. 386 r. 11 “there is no wrong or blemish(?)”. Cf. Heimpel 2003, 334; however, he derives the word from *erēpu*.

3. *t.* is referred to in CAD T 207 s.v. *tarāpu*, the lemma is, however, actually missing in CAD. MPS (2–3), NR (1)

tirku s. *terku*

tirratu “halter” s. *dirratu*

tirratu “an affliction; trembling” cf. *tirru* II

+ **tirru II** “tremors, trembling (?)”; OA

kīša B*i-ru-um lamnum kīša šittum abiktum tí-ru-um* kt 94/k 520: 4 (inc.) “truly – a malicious *B.*-disease! Truly – carried away sleep! Trembling!” (after Barjamovic/Larsen 2008, 147f.), cf. *tarāru* “to tremble”; cf. perhaps *tirratu* “an affliction” (SB). NJCK

tirṣu s. *terṣu*

tīru I “a courtier”; + OA

1. OA **a)** *ana tí-ri ⌜ēkallim⌝ ... itadna[nni]* AKT 6A, 109: 33 (// 110: 29) “he handed me over to the palace officials”.

b) *a-tí-ri ēkallim igmur* AKT 9A, 8: 25 “he settled (it) with the palace officials”.

2. Stol apud Mayer 2009, 435: OB *ti-ir bīt* DN AUCT 5, 160 r. 6 (already cit., without ref., in CAD T 429 *t.* A c).

3. OB lit. *ti-i-ru tiʾāmētim ti-i-ru-ú-šu* CUSAS 10, 1: 40 “are (not) his courtiers courtiers of the seas?”

4. On Sum. *tiru* “eunuch(?)” s. George 1997. Further disc. Peled 2016, 252–256. JW (1), NR (2, 4), MPS (3)

tīru II, *tēru* “coil (of silver); loop (of a river)?”

1. Coil (of silver): **a)** OA (here I showed *ašīʾum*-iron to the king) *ana anneqē* 1 1/3 MA.NA^{ta} KÙ.BABBAR *uka’’il ana té-re-e* 1 1/2 MA.NA^{ta} *uka’’il* CUSAS 34, 2: 7 “for the rings he offered 1 1/3 minas per piece, for the *t.* he offered 1 1/2 minas per piece”; cf. *té-re-e* EL 34: 2; KBo. 9, 3: 2 and *té-e-re* kt k/k 19: 2 (quot. Veenhof 1989, 523). This passage suggests that *té-ri* refers to the form of the silver and contradicts its interpretation as a stamp on metal (CAD Ṭ 113b s.v. *ṭīru* A; AHw 1392b s.v. *ṭīru* IV) or as a reference to an official weighing system (Veenhof 1989, 522f. and 2014, 391). Compare OA *kaspum šawerū* “silver (in the form of) rings”. For the use of silver in the form of coils as a means of payment alongside rings (Sum. *ḫar*), s. Powell 1978.

b) OA 3 1/6 GÍN KÙ.BABBAR *kibsātim ša té-re* PN *uṣaḫḫeram* CUSAS 34, 35: 2 “PN deducted for me 3 1/6 shekels of silver as compensation(?) for the coils”; cf. *té-re* TPAK 1, 110: 1.

c) For disc. s. Veenhof 1989, 523 and 2014, 391; Dercksen 2005a, 22. Cf. SAD *ṭīru* IV. S. also *tīrānū* I.

2. Loop (of a river)(?):

a) OB *ana šūmī ša ina te?-ri i-pu-šu* AbB 13, 79: 18 “for the garlic which he/they planted in the loop (of the river)(?)”.

b) Further OB ref. AHw 1361 *t.* V, CAD T 430 *t.* D. MPS (2), NJCK (1)

+ TI-ru-KU “a type of sesame(?)”

Stol 2010, 174: *ti-ru-ku* OECT 15, 219: 2 (followed by *gurnu*). NR

TiSāBu “an Anatolian textile”; OA

S. CAD T s.v. *tēṣābu*, AHw 1361 s.v. *tisappum*. For disc. and add. ref. s. Michel/Veenhof 2010, 245; AKT 8, 269: 4; AKT 10, 23A: 8 JW

tiṣbutu “linked”

In OB said of beads for jewelry, s. ARM 32, 100f. for add. ref. and disc.

JW

tišanni “ninth”; MB Ekalte

ina MU.KAM *ti-ša-an-ni* WVDOG 102, 28: 4 “in the ninth year”, s. Mayer, ib. 101 (Akk. ordinal number with Hurr. suffix *-anni*). NR

tišānu “a type of (wild?) sheep; a wild animal(?); + SB

1. Lex. *a-lim* = *te*!(copy: *li*)-*šá-nu* Emar 6/4, 551: 46 (Ḫḫ XIV 144a; MSL 8/2, 18). Pace Kogan 2005, 296, this favors an equation of *ditānu* and *tišānu*. For phon. disc. s. Streck 2000, 216–218.

2. 200 $^{\text{udu.ḫá}}$*ti-ša-né* ARM 26/1, 107 no. 11: 24 “200 *t.*-sheep”.

3. OB 1 *ti-ša-na-am ušāb*[*il*]*am ti-ša-nu-um šī sin*<*ni*>*šat u māram ulid* NABU 1988/15 M 6974 “I brought you 1 *t.*, it is female, and it bore an offspring”, s. for further ref. and disc. Durand ib.; cf. Lion 1992, 361 n. 36.

4. OB lit. *rīmī ti-*⌜*ša*⌝*-nu* Gilg. OB VA+BM i 1 “aurochs, *t.*” in broken context.

5. The ref. BWL 277: 11 (now Streck/Wasserman 2018a, 248–251), quot. CAD T s.v. *tišānu* belongs here.

6. OB PNf *Ti-ša-na-tum* AbB 9, 50: 3. Cf. Streck 2000, 216 and ib. 314 for similar names (Amorite or Akk.?).

7. Perhaps var. of *ditānu* (s. above 1) and of *tešēnu* “a wild animal” (CAD T 373, s. Lion 1991 and Kogan 2005, 296). On Ebla ref. s. Conti/Bonechi 1992 (zoomorph jewellery?).

JW (2–3, 7), MPS (1, 4, 6)

tīšāʾu s. *dīšāyu*

tīšāyu s. *dīšāyu*

tišē, *tešē* "nine"

With Streck 1995, 44 n. 104, the form *te-še-e* in RA 70, 117 cit. CAD T 373 belongs here ("nine" rather than "ninety", Reiner 2007, 55; Mayer 2009, 433). NR

+ **tištu** "willow(?)"; SB

Lex. ŠID.GIM = *ḫilāpu* = *ti-iš-tu* Emar 6/4, 545: 516, cf. DCCLT MB Ura 04 and Pentiuc 2001, 182.

tišû s. *tišanni*

+ **tišuḫula?** (mng. unkn.); Hurr. word in MB Qaṭna

6 ^{giš}: *pí-iš-ri* : *ti-iš-u-ḫu-la ša ṣubātī* QS 3, 14: 15, cf. 18 "6 *p.* implements for *t.* of cloths". Cf. disc. ib. p. 91 and SAD s.v. *pišri*.

titennu I, + *tetannu* "four-pronged pitch-fork used for winnowing"

1. Lex. *al-zú*-4 = *te-tá-nu* Emar 6/4, 545: 183 (Ḫḫ).

2. OB *te-te-nu* ZABAR ARM 25, 274 = ARM 32, 325 M.7091: 2; ARM 25, 328 = ARM 32, 330 M.11969: 6, s. ib. p. 144.

3. Borger 2010, 347: [^{giš}*al-zú-*]*4 -gin*$_7$: [*ki-ma ti-t*]*i-in-ni* CT 17, 10: 51.

JW (2), MPS (1), NR (3)

tittu "fig (tree)"

1. OAkk. *ti-na-tim* Subartu 2, 98 ii 3.

2. "brick of figs", a fig cake, s. Stol 2010, 174:

a) OA *libittam ša tí-na-tim* FAOS Beih. 2, 14: 12, s. Dercksen 1991, 180.

b) SB 14 SIG$_4$ ^{giš}PÈŠ^{meš} Emar 6/3, 387 no. 388: 8.

3. OB *ti-na-tim Amurrêtim* FM 7, 101 no. 26: 49 "Amorite figs".

4. Stol 2010, 174: MA 2 BÁN PÈŠ^{meš} *ḫappuʾātu* MARV 3, 32: 2 "2 seah of crushed figs" (s. AoF 19, 312).

5. MB n *ti-it-tum* CUSAS 30, 300: 23, cf. 1. JW (1–3), MPS (5), NR (2, 4)

+ **titʾû** "to be(come) twins"; SB

Gt SB *it-tu-ú-ni* (Etana), quot. CAD T 301 and AHw 1340 s.v. *taʾû* "to eat, graze", denom. of *tūʾû*, *tūʾamu* "twin", s. Streck 2003, 15 no. 48; 26 no. 25.

JW

titūru, *titurru* "bridge"

1. OA: On bridge tolls (payments *ana*/*ina t.*) s. AKT 8 p. 201 with add. ref.

2. OB lit. *ētiq ti-tu-ra-am* CUSAS 32, 27a: 1 "it(!) crossed a bridge".

3. OB [*ana*!] *ti-tu-ri-im ibêt* ARM 26/1, 285 no. 119: 17 "(the troop) will stay overnight [by] the bridge".

4. Stol 2010, 174: in YOS 5, 94: 19 (CAD T 438a *t.* d) read MU.TÚM ÌR!-*ti-tu-ri-im.* JW (1), MPS (2–3), NR (4)

ti/eʾûtu, + *tem/wûtu* "nourishment"

1. Mayer 2017b, 234: SB *adī ti-ʾu-ú-ti-ša* BBS 7 i 15; cf. *te-ʾ-ú-*[…]? SpTU 4, 131: 3.

2. SB *kīma Nissaba ana māti aparras te-mu-tú* Jiménez 2017, 248: 13 "like Nissaba I distribute nourishment to the land".

Cf. *ti/eʾītu.* JW (1), MPS (2)

tiyāru s. *tiʾālu*

tû I "incantation(-formula)"; + OA

1. Mayer 2009, 435: OA *bēl šipātim u bēl tí-i-i*[*m*] PIHANS 100, 398: 22 "lord of incantations, lord of the spell".

2. Mayer 2009, 435: OB lit. *ittaṣīʾakkum tu-ú ša awīlūtim* YOS 11, 16a: 3 "the spell of mankind has come out towards you" // *attadī-ku ta-a ša awīlūti* YOS 11, 77b: 13 "let me cast the spell of mankind on you".

3. Mayer 2009, 435: SB *tu-ka bulṭu lipitka šulme* Finkel 2000, 201f. 2 (ms. A, B, C) "your (= Gula's) incantation is healing, your touch is well-being."

4. Mayer 2009, 435: SB *tu-ú-ka ša balāṭi qīšamma* AulaOr. Suppl. 23, 78: 35 "bestow your invigorating incantation upon me!"

5. SB *ša tu-ú-šu* // *it-tu-šú itbû* Jiménez 2017, 254: 47 "he for whom an incantation had risen". The var. *ittu*(*š*) "whose sign" is perhaps corrupt.

6. Mayer 2009, 435: SB *ša ina šipti u tu-e* SpTU 3, 100: 21 "(according to a saying) which is from an incantation text or formula".

7. Mayer 2009, 435: In KUB 4, 47 r. 48 (CAD T 442 *t.* a4') read *tá-mì-tù*, s. *tāwītum* 4b, above.

8. On etym. s. Röllig 1996.

MPS (5), NR (1–4, 6–8)

tūʾamu, *tūʾimu*, fem. *tūʾa*/*i*/*umtu* "twin"

1. OA PN *tù-i-mu-um* TPAK 179: 22 "PN, the twin".

2. OB lit. *ašar tu-a-mi iṭṭul* CUSAS 18, 26: 34 "(if a weapon-mark on the liver) looks towards the place of the twins"; cf. George ib. p. 183.

3. OB a type of vase:

a) 1 *tu-im-tum ša* 10 SÌLA ARM 31, 240: 8 "1 twin-vase of 10 liters", s. Guichard ib. p. 315.

b) (oil) *ana tu-ḫi-ma-tim ša bīt ilātim* FM 3, 252 no. 108: 4 "for (the ritual of) the twin-vases of the temple of the goddesses"; cf. FM 12, 163 M.10601: 3 and ib. p. 80.

4. Of animals: SB [*ša en*]*zi tu-ʾ-a-mi-ša* Lamaštu Ug iv 10 (Farber 2014, 262) "[the go]at's twin".

5. Cf. SAD *titʾû*, above.

JW (1, 3), MPS (2, 4, 5)

+ **tuʾānu II** "bathhouse"; NA, Aram. or Sum. lw.(?)

1. Reiner 2007, 58: *tu-a-ni adī gušūrīšu adī dalātīšu … uppišma…ilqē* StAT 2, 53: 5 "he contracted for and purchased a bathhouse, together with its beams and doors", cf. É TU_5 *šuʾāte* ib. 11 "this bathhouse"; cf. PN *bēl tu-a-ni* ib. 4 "PN, the owner of the bathhouse".

2. On the supposed Aram. etym. s. Cherry 2017, 261ff. with prev. lit. (cf. OffAr., JBA, Palm., Nab., Syr., *twn*, *twnʾ* = *tawwān*, *tawwānā* "chamber, room"). However, the Aram. etyma never mean specifically "bathhouse". Rather lw. from Sum. tu_5?

MPS/NR (1), MPS/JW (2)

tubāqu, *dubāqu* "(elm) glue, bird-lime"

According to Cherry 2017, 263–265, a lw. from Aram.; this remains, however, uncertain. JW/MPS

tubarru s. *tabarru*

+ **tub/pazzigu** "a vase made of silver or gold"; OB, Hurr. lw.

1. OB [gal]*kannu ša tu-ba-zi-gi-im* KÙ.BABBAR ARM 25, 517: 4 (Reiner 2007, 58); ARM 31, 34 r. 7; *tu-[b]a-zi-gi* 237 r. 10; *tu-pa-zi-gi-im* 231: 15; 236: 4; [gal]*tu-[p]a-zi-gu* KÙ.GI 168: 8; 237: 14.

2. In Hitt. texts [dug]*du-pa-an-za-ki-*, s. Guichard ARM 31 p. 316–320 for disc.; cf. Richter 2012, 472. JW/MPS

+ **tubbu** (*tūbu*?), *tumbu*? "a type of blanket or upholstery(?)"; LB

1. Reiner 2007, 58: *ša tu-bu kuttuntu* Joannès 1989, 355: 11 "(a bed of *musukkannu* wood) that was covered with *t.*"; cf. (a *musukkannu* wood chair and table) *ša tu-bu* ib. 12 and 13, s. Roth 1989, 86.

2. *ana tum-bi u ṭimâta ša pišannu* OBO 206, 388: 14 "(3 minas of wool) for *t.* and yarn for the *p.*-bag".

3. Reiner 2007, 58: *ša ana tu-bu šanṭatu* Jursa 2003 p. 232 BM 82760: 2 "(a bed of *musukkannu* wood) that was stripped(?) for *t.*", s. ib. 233f.

4. Cf. *tumbu* "plank(?)" (CAD T 471)? JW (2), MPS (4), NR (1, 3)

tubkinnu, *tubqinnu* "refuse heap"

1. Stol 2010, 174: *ina tub-ki[n-na]-a-te ḫuṣāba ammīni taššâni* BAM 6, 510 iv 36 "why have you lifted the piece of wood from the refuse heap?", s. Geller 1984, 297.

2. SB [ÉN *atti t*]*ub-kín-ni māhirat kalā* <*lā*> *damqu* van der Toorn 1985 pl. 3, 79-7-8.71: 7 (Šurpu) "incantation: You, refuse heap, which receives everything evil"; cf. [É]N *atti túb-kín-n*[*u*] LKA 153, r. ii 4 (Reiner 1958, 12). S. Simons 2017, 14.

3. S. also Biggs 1993, who suggests *e-pi*<*-né*>*-et* in Ištar's Descent 104 is a hearing mistake for *t.* Cf. Malul 1993; Worthington 2012, 101 n. 352 (with reservations). FJMS (2), JW (3), NR (1)

tublu I, *dublu* "pilaster"

1. SB DUB.LÁ *āṣû* SpTU 4, 220 ii 9 "projecting pilaster"; DUB.LÁ *qatnu* ib. iii 5 pass. "shallow pilaster".

2. On mng. "pilaster" rather than "foundation trench", s. George 1995, 183ff. JW

+ **tub/plu II** "a plant"; SB

Stol 2010, 174: *šuruš* [giš]*tu-uB-li* Tsukimoto 1999 p. 192: 13 "*t.*-root" (among other plants). NR

tubqu, + *dubqu*, pl. *tubqātu* "corner, recess"

1. OB lit. *šumma rēʾûm ana mārakišu 4-šu tu-ub-qa-tim ušēlīma* CUSAS 18 p. 297: 25 "if the shepherd has grown corners in four places along its length".

2. Stol 2010, 174: OB PN *Mār-Tu-ub-qum* Scheil, Sippar 13 r. 2 "Son of the corner".

3. LB 2 *dannu ina du-ub-qa* CTMMA 3, 72: 6 "2 *dannu*-vats in the corner", s. Jursa 2001/2, 224; s. also *du-ub-qá-at* VAB 4, 164 B vi 5 (other var. *tu-ub-*, Nbk. inscr.). JW (2–3), MPS (1, 2)

tūbu s. *tubbu*

+ **tubuqqatu** "corner"; SB, MB Nuzi

1. SB *tu-bu-uq-qá-a-ti ana tu-bu-uq-qá-a-ti iṣṣ*[*anabbat*?] Lamaštu MB 20 (Farber 2014, 122) "she [keeps] hi[ding?] in one corner after another".

2. The Nuzi ref. cit. CAD T 449 *t.* B b belong here, cf. Farber 2014, 248.

3. Cf. *tubqu* and *tubuqtu*. JW/MPS

tubuqtu "corner"

1. OB *a-na tu-bu-uq-ti gallābī* YOS 14, 73 r. 1 "for the corner of the barbers"; cf. Simmons 1961, 83; Stol 2010, 174.

2. ^{lú}GÌR.SIG$_5$.GA^{meš} *ša tu-bu-uq-tim* ARM 21, 398: 39 (CAD T 449 *t.* B a) "attendants of the corner" (part of the palace), cf. Durand ib. p. 523–525.

****tubuqtu II** (mng. uncert.; CAD T 449 *t.* B) s. SAD *tubuqqatu* 2 and *tubuqtu* 2.

tûdalu s. *tuwadalu*

+ **tu-da-nu-nu-um** "a weapon"; OB

Stol 2010, 174: OB *pāšātum šukurrū tu-da-nu-nu-um pāšū kibirrū* BM 28887 "adzes, lances, *t.*, axes, *k.*-weapons" (cit. Sigrist/Zadok/Walker 2006 p. 194). JW

tudittu, *dudittu* "a (women's) dress-pin, toggle-pin"

1. OA lit. *tù-dí-tám* OA Sarg. 62, cf. SAD *edēdu* D, a verb with which the scribe seems to connect *tudittu* etymologically (s. also Kouwenberg 2015).

2. OA (if the wife is impudent) *ina šiḫiṭ tù-dí-tim tuṣṣī* AKT 10, 41A: 14 "she will leave by tearing off the dress-pin.", s. ib. p. 91. Add. OA ref.: ib. 8, 164: 1, 355: 14; 9A, 39: 7.

3. OB, with head in shape of *arzallu*: ARM 32, 74 M.11532: 34–37; cf. ib. p. 268 M.18472: 10f.

4. MB Ekalte [*t*]*u-di-it-tum*/*tu* (of silver) in testaments WVDOG 102, 19: 12; 95: 12.

5. Mayer 2009, 435: SB [*t*]*u-di-it-tum ša qaqqad kusarikki* BagM 37, 94 i 8 "dress-pin with a bison's head".

6. SB *mušṭu pilaqqu du-di-tú* Farber 2014, 276: 24 "comb, spindle, dress-pin".

7. SB *du-di-na-a-šá* Lamaštu I 140 (Farber 2014, 86) "her two dress-pins."

8. SB 1 *du-di-it ḫurāṣi ina guḫalṣi ḫurāṣi ṣabtat* NBC 4894: 73 (Beaulieu 1999) "1 dress-pin of gold held by golden filament", s. ib. 150 with add. ref.

9. For gen. disc. s. Green 1998 and ARM 32, 101f. with add. ref.

JW (2, 7–8), MPS (4, 5), NR (1, 3, 5, 6, 9)

tugānu s. *dugānu*

tugguru s. *Tuqquru*

+ **tugsiqqû**, *tugsiqqāʾu* "good garment"; Sum. lw.

Lex. *túg-sì-qu-u* // ⸢*túg*⸣*-sì-qá-ú* = *ṣubātu damqu* AOAT 50, 410: 42 (malku) "good garment = good cloth". Cf. Hrůša ib. p. 263: < Sum. *túg-sig*$_5$.

tuḫallu, + *tuḫullu*? "palm-leaf basket"

Stol 2010, 174: SB [*ep*]*er tu-ḫu-ul-la-ti* Tsukimoto 1999, 192: 5 "dust from a palm-leaf basket(?)". MPS/NR

+ **tuḫbal** "delivery(?)"; Nuzi, Hurr. lw.

1. n GIG^{meš} *tù-uḫ-bal-šá* HSS 14, 507: 8 "n wheat, her delivery(?)".

2. *i*?*-na*? *tù-uḫ-ba-al-šu nadû* HSS 13, 412: 32 "(barley is given to PN,) it is deposited in(?) his *t.*"

3. Cf. Schneider-Luddorff 1998, 206ff.; Reiner 2007, 58; Richter 2012, 466.

JW

tuḫḫu "residue, waste product; bran, draff"

1. OB lit. *uttēr tu-uḫ-ḫi-ki ana minûtim* CUSAS 32, 32: 13 "I returned your spent grain to the reckoning".

2. For *ba-tab tuḫ-ḫu-um* s. *batabtuḫḫu*.

tuḫlu "a medicinal plant"

Stol 2010, 174: *tuḫ*-LAM and *tullal* are used in parallel with *maštakal* BagF 18, 130: 23; 134: 87, s. Maul ib. p. 63 n. 42. Cf. Mayer 1976, 270 n. 72. JW

tuḫlulu "a plant"

S. Kinnier Wilson 2005, 5: from Sum. *duḫ-làl*, "honeycomb"? JW

tuḫnu s. *duḫnu*

tuḫru "part of the heel, achilles tendon; a lyre string"

1. OB "a lyre string": [*sammûm nīš t*]*u-úḫ-ri-im* [*šumma sammûm nīš tu*]-*úḫ-ri-im* UET 6/3, 899: 9–10 "the lyre is 'rise of the *t.*'; if the lyre is 'rise of the *t.*', (you play [...])" (tuning text); cf. *nīš* GABA.RI in CBS 10996 i 11, KAR 158 viii 50, and perhaps RS 19.164 (Ugaritica 5, 477ff.); ⌜*nīš*⌝ *tu-uḫ*-[*ri-im*] UM 29-15-357 r. i 9, s. Mirelman/ Krispijn 2009, 48f.

2. SB *šumma tuḫ-ri imittišu ištanaḫḫiṭ* AfO Bh. 27 p. 265 (TBP 22+) 19, cf. 20 "if his right tendon moves jerkily".

3. CAD considers this word a variant of *šaḫūru* B (Š/1, 109; T 455). However, both terms appear on the same tablet in AfO Bh. 27 (cf. *šu-ḫar-šú* p. 269 l. 62). S. Mirelman 2008 for further disc. The reading of GABA.RI as either *t.* or *meḫru* is not always clear from the context. JW

tuḫšu s. *dušû*

tuḫtuḫannu "a festival"; OA, Hitt. lw.

A deified object after which a festival was named, perhaps to be connected with Hitt. *tuḫtuḫḫiya-* "to swing" (s. HEG III 414). For prev. lit. s. Dercksen 2007, 38. JW

tuḫullu s. *tuḫallu*

+ **tuḫušḫu** (mng. uncert.); OB, Mari

ša ana tu-ḫu-úš-ḫi ARM 30, 356 M.11604: 3 "(belts and *massilātu*-blankets), which are for *t.*"; cf. Durand ib. p. 125.

tūʾimtu s. *tūʾamu*

+ **tukītu?** "a rite or sacrifice"; OB

(1 sheep) *ana tu-ki-tim* ARM 23, 303: 1 (coll. MARI 5, 381), among sacrifices (s. Jacquet 2011, 66). JW

+ **tūkīyu** "inner"; Ugar., Ugar. lw.

i-na ᵘʳᵘ*Ga-li-li-tu-ki-ia* PRU 6, 78: 9 "in Inner Galīlu" = alphabetic *gll*(.)*tky* del Olmo Lete/Sanmartín 2004, 298f. Cf. Huehnergard 1987, 185: /*tūkīyu*/ nisba adj. from Ugar. /*tōku*/ "centre, middle". MPS/NR

tukku I "alarm, warning, rumor"

1. OB *ūm tu-uk-ki wāṣî*[*šu*] *nišemmû* ARM 26/1, 341 no. 168: 22 "when we hear a rumor of [his] coming out".

2. OB *aššum tu-uk-kum iššemmû* ARM 26/1, 341 no. 168: 25 "because a rumor might be heard".

3. OB *adī tu-uk-ki ṣābim annî*[*m*] *iššemmû* ARM 26/1, 352 no. 172: 20 "until the rumor of that troop will be heard".

4. OB *tu-uk-ka-ša ašar šanîmma ittanaddû* ARM 26/2, 183 no. 373: 36 "they keep spreading rumors that they are (directed) to another (king)".

5. SB *i niškun tuk-ka* JCS 66, 76: 33 (Gilg.) "let us spread a warning".

6. SB *tuk-ka lū uššuṭ sikr*[*īya*] ORA 7, 322: 68 "rumor has made [my] spee[ch] hard". Or *tukku* II "oppression"?

7. SB *kīma tu-uk-ka ummānāt bēliya* PN […] MesCiv. 13 p. 156 i 7 "when PN [heard] the rumor about my lord's troops". JW (7), MPS (1–6)

tukku II "oppression, persecution"; Aram. Lw.

1. NB *ištēn* ⌜*tu-uk?-ku-ú šarru lā umaššaranni*⌝ SAA 17, 135 r. 9 "may the king not abandon me [to(?)] a single (act of) oppression".

2. On etym. s. Cherry 2017, 265–267 (cf. Syr. *tkk*, *twk*). JW (2), MPS (1)

tukku s. also *tuqqu*

tuklu I "help, trust, safety"

On *bīt tukli* in Emar (CAD T *tuklu* C) s. Pentiuc 2001, 185. Instead of 370: 80' (CAD T 459 *tuklu* C) read 340: 80'.

tuklu II, *dug/klu*? "a commodity, an implement"

OA *a-tù-uk-li* Prag 624: 2 "(1 shekel 15 še) for *t.*"; s. also OIP 27, 55: 30 (// Prag 429: 25); AKT 6B, 333: 27 and 335: 18. NJCK/NR

tukpītu s. *takpītu*

tukrišû, + *tukrišītu* "Tukriš-style (in vessels, wool); a stone"

1. OB 4 *šiqqātum tu-*[*uk*]*-ri-še-a-tum* ARM 21, 222 = ARM 31, 9: 28 "4 Tukriš-style flasks"; cf. 1? *šiqqatum ša* ^{na4}*tu-uk-ri-ši-im* ib. 13 "1? flask of *t.*-stone".

2. OB [1 GAL *tu*]*-uk-ri-ši-tum* ARM 31, 161: 41 "1 *t.* vessel" (made from 1/3 mina 9 shekels of silver).

3. For disc. s. Guichard ARM 31, 320–324; Richter 2012, 467. JW

tukšû "(leather) shield"

Mayer 2009, 436:

1. OB 20 *tu-uk-šum* Mayer 2003, 368: 5 (list of military equipment).

2. SB DNf *tuk-šu allallu* AfO 50, 21: 14 "DNf, strong shield". NR

tuktû "revenge"

NB *ul itti* ^{lú}*tuk-te*^{meš} *ma-a-šá-t*[*a*] SAA 21, 131: 14 "you are not forgotten(?) by vengeful men". Parpola ib. p. 131 derives the stative from *māšu* "twin" and translates "you are not twinned".

****tuktukkû**

In Ludul I 25 read after Ms. F (Iraq 60, 188f.) *ú-tuk-ku ra-ʾi-i-bu*, "the *utukku*-demon of the *r.*-disease", s. Oshima 2014, 181ff. JW

tukultu "support; trust"

Reiner 2007, 59: logogr. GIŠ.TUKU, in NB PNN also BÀD/BAD.MAḪ, s. *Nabû*-BAD.MAḪ CTMMA 3, 15: 4, s. Jursa 2001/2, 224.
S. also *takaltu*. NR

tukumma "come on, then"

Mayer 2009, 436: Gilg. X 250 (cit. CAD T 464) read with George 2003 [*ana*]*-ku um-ma*. NR

tullal "a soap plant, 'you purify'"

Stol 2010, 174:

1. ^{ú}*tu-lal mu-lil-tu ša* x x x BAM 3, 244: 61 "*t.*, cleanser of …"

2. *tu*$_x$*-làl* (DUḪ.LÀL) Finkel 2000, 149 no. 1: 6 (and pass.) S. also *tuḫlu*. NR

tullugu "huge (?)"

OB lex. *lú al-maḫ-maḫ* = *tu-ul-lu-gu-um* CUSAS 12 p. 163: 5 (OB Lu). Cf. Civil ib., 164: lw. from Sum. *til-lu-ug* "elephant"(?).

tullultu, *tallultu* “trappings”

NA (silver) *ana salṭānī ana tal-lul-te* SAA 11, 27: 8 “for bow-and-arrow cases for trappings”.

tûltu “worm, maggot”; + MB Emar

1. PN *Tu-ul-ti* Emar 6/3, 52: 14, 26, 50 “My worm”.

2. SB *ammēni* tul_5*-tu ša libbi zê ikkalanni yâši* Stadhouders 2018, 175 n. 46 (P417297): 13 “why is a maggot hatched in dung tormenting me?”.

3. For disc. s. Streck 2016; Stadhouders 2018, 175 (“maggot” rather than “worm” in toothache incantations).

FJMS (2–3), MPS (1, 3)

tulû I “breast, teat”

1. OB lit. *mēlil tu-li-i-ni* PRAK 1 B 472 i 14 “play with our breasts!”

2. OB *ištēniš tu-li-a-am nīkul* AbB 10, 3: 15 “(he is not a stranger), we fed together at the breast” (lit. “ate the teat”, cf. NB ABL 920 r. 9).

3. OB oil rations *ana ša tu-li-a-tim* CUSAS 8, 85: 8 “for that of the breasts(?)” (unclear, between *malāḫu* “boatman” and *uḫūlu* “alkali”).

4. OB “spout, funnel”: *ṣuršu bābūšu išissu u tu-lu-šu u sugūnšu* KÙ.GI GAR.RA ARM 25, 347: 7 = ARM 31, 401 no. 80 “a *ṣ*.-vase, its outlets, its base, its spout and its *s*. gold-plated”; s. ib. r. 4.

5. OB “a vessel” (with a prominent spout?):

a) Reiner 2007, 59: *anūmma* … 1 *tu-la-am zikir šumika* … *ušābilakku* Durand 2001 p. 122 A.2881: 14 “herewith I am sending to you … 1 *t.* as a present for you”; cf. 1 IŠ+IL *tu-la-am* ARM 13, 101: 28 (coll. Durand 1983b, 158).

b) 2 *tu-lu-ú* ARM 31, 85: 16; 2 ^{gal}*tu-lu-ú* ib. 231: 9; $^{gal.pap}$*tu-l*[*u*]*-ú* ib. 154 e. i 3. Cf. Guichard ib. p. 324 “vase en forme de sein”.

6. Round lump or boss attached to the lower end of a punting-pole (cf. the disc. in George 2003, 285f. and 872): SB *kupurma šukun tu-la-a* Gilg. SB X 161 (cf. also 167) “trim and equip (the poles) with a teat!” Cf. AHw 1370 *t.* 3 (“Schale”) and CAD T 469 *t.* 1e end (“obscure”). *t.* replaces older *ṣerretu*: *šukun ṣerrētim* Gilg. OB VA+BM iv 28 “equip (them) with teats”.

7. SB *tu-li-šú* AulaOr. Suppl. 23, 42: 35 (Gilg.), cf. *birītu* I.

8. Cf. also SAD *rimmānu*.

JW (2, 4–5, 8), MPS (1, 3, 5–7)

tumāgu “a kind of flour”

Lex. […]*-làl* = *tu-ma-gu* Emar 6/4, 560: 104 (Ḫḫ). MPS/NR

tumāru “a textile, a type of band or belt”

1. OB 8 ^{gú}*tu-ma-ru* ARM 30, 208 M.5681 iii 31; 1 ^{túg}*tu-ma-ru* ib. 206 i 40; 208 iii 30; ib. 514 M.18222 ii 11.

2. Pl.(?) OB ^{túg}*tu-ma-ra-tum* GÍD.DA/ LÚGUD!.DA (ÚS) T.423: 12, 15 (unpubl., s. ARM 30 p. 126) “long/ short *t.* (of second quality)”. According to Durand ib. p. 125f. a fem. sg. *tumāratu*. Same text as “T 332” cit. in CAD T 470?

+ tum(m)āḫu “a big dove; a fish”; Sum. lw.

1. Lex. *tu-maḫ* = *tu*/*tù-ma-ḫu* = *girribu* Emar 6/4, 555: 72 (Ḫḫ) “big dove = crow”. Cf. Cohen 2010, 818.

2. Lex. *tu-maḫ*^{ku6} = *tu-um-ma-ḫu* Emar 6/4, 555: 35 (Ḫḫ)“big-dove-fish”.

tumru, + *tūru* "cinder, ember"

1. SB *tu-ú-ru ana* 1 DANNA[àm] *napāḫu* Gilg. SB V 104 "to blow on the embers for a double hour".

2. *ina šupālu āli attadi tu-ú-ru* SpTU 3, 74A i 16 (= Maqlû III 23) "I threw the embers into the lower city".

JW (2), MPS (1)

tumurtu "buried thing"

Mayer 2009, 436: On mng. "buried thing" rather than "ant eggs" s. Heeßel 2007, 89. MPS/NR

+ **tun-** "to perform"; Hurr. word in MB Qaṭna

: *eḫ-le-ši* : *du-ni-iu-áw*(AB)-*wu* QS 3, 4: 49 "I perform saving". Cf. disc. ib. p. 64. S. Richter 2012, 469 for bibliogr.

+ **tunimmu** "a kind of leather"

NA *qersē damqūte ša* NIM.[MA] ⸢túg?⸣GADA *ša* KI.TA kuš⸢*tu*?⸣-*nim-me* SAA 5, 152 r. 11 "good carts, (furnished) with linen above, with *t.* leather below".

tunšu, + *tuzzu* "a ceremonial garment, drapery"; + MB Emar

1. Reiner 2007, 59: MB Emar 1 *ereqqu qadu* túg*tu-zi-ši* CunMon. 13, 21: 21 "1 wagon together with its *t.*-cover".

2. LB túg*tu-un-šú ša eli erši ša* DN OBO 260, 13: 2 "*t.*-fabric for covering the bed of DN". Cf. tu_9-*un-šú* ib. 14: 2.

JW (2), MPS/NR (1)

tupninnu "box, casket"

Rare spelling *tu-up-* instead of DUB-: SB *pitēma tu-up-ni-in-na ša erēni* AulaOr. Suppl. 23, 42: 22 (// *tupšenna* SB Gilg. I 24). MPS

tuppanuri, + *tuppātnura/i* "an official, chief scribe(?)"

tup-pa-at-nu-ri/ra RSO 14 p. 260f. RS 92.2007: 4, 15; *tup-pa-*⸢*at*?⸣-*nu-ri* in PRU 4 p. 42 RS 17.227: 30. For disc. and ref. s. Arnaud 1996, 58–61. JW

tuppaššu s. D*uppaššu*

tuppu I "(clay) tablet, document, letter"

1. OA *mīnam i*-DUB-*pè lušamʾid* OA Sarg. 63 "why should I make numerous (words) on tablets?"

2. OA *i–tù-pì-im* AKT 6A, 267: 17, 27, 30, 64.

3. OB syll. spellings which show /t/ instead of /ṭ/ (cf. Streck 2009a, 137f.):
a) *tu-up-pa-am* CUSAS 36, 147: 7, *tu-up-pi-im* ib. 9. The text writes *ṭù* in *li-ba-al-li-ṭù-ka* ib. 5, *ta-aš-ṭù-ra*(*-am*) ib. 22, 25, 31.
b) *tu-up-pi-im* CUSAS 36, 194: 20. The text writes *ṭù* in *li-ba-al-li-ṭù-k*[*a*] ib. 5, ⸢*ip*⸣-*ṭù-ra-ak-ku-šu* ib. 12, *ú-ba-al-la-ṭù-k*[*a*] ib. 15.

4. Further OB syll. spellings: [*tu-u*]*p-pa-am* CUSAS 36, 13: 16; *tu-up-pi* ib. 104: 5; *tu-up-pu* ib. 133: 13. *tu-up*(*-pi*) ib. 201: 8, 18. *tu-up-pi-I* ib. 215: 6.

5. With determinative NA_4 "stone" in the mng. "seal": OB 11 GÍN *kaspam ina* na4DUB-*pí šumiya aknukma* ARM 28, 97bis: 5 "I sealed 11 shekels of silver with a seal with my name".

6. Mayer 2009, 438f.: OB DUB-*pu-um* (*u*) *siḫtum ša* PN *ḫe-pí* Sumer 51 p. 8 Si 103a: 12 // 103b (case): 13 "the tablet and case of PN are to be destroyed" (not: *ṣiḫtum*, s. already CAD S 240a).

7. Mayer 2009, 438f., *bīt tuppi*: MA *ana pī tuppi* ⌜*ṣabi*⌝*tte ša* É DUB-*pa-a-te ētašrū* MARV 2 (VS 21), 6: 2 "(four people) have verified (the previous entries) according to the wording of the tablet kept at the tablet-house."

JW (2), MPS (1, 3–5), NR (6–7)

tuppu II "mark on skin, mole(?), wart(?)"; + OB

CAD *ṭuppu* B.

OB lit. *ina irtišu tu*[*p*]-*pu lā mādum* CUSAS 18, 21: 21 "a not extensive mole(?) on his breast".

****tuppû** (CAD T 476) s. *tappû* II

tuppussû s. *duppussû*

tupšarratu "female scribe"

OB lit. *Nissaba* DUB.SAR-*ra-at* CUSAS 10, 14: 23 "N. is scribe".

+ **tupšarrû**, fem. *tupšarrītu* "scribal (in name of a canal)"; OB

Stol 2010, 176: *nārum* DUB.SAR-*ri-tum* CT 8, 15a: 6 = MHET 2/3, 436; CT 4, 17b: 6 "scribal canal"; cf. ÍD DUB.SAR CT 4, 7b: 5 = MHET 2/3, 437, cit. CAD Ṭ 161b *ṭupšarru* e. JW

tupšikku, + *tapšukku* "hod, basket"

1. Mayer 2009, 436: OA *marrīkina u ta-áp-šu-kà-tí-ki-na liqēʾānimma* Michel 2004 p. 396 Kt 90/k 178: 12 "take your spades and earth baskets", s. ib. p. 407; s. also CCT 5, 50: 12 (JEOL 44, 141f.).

2. OB UN.ÍL (CAD T 479b) is perhaps *kinattu* (AHw 1568a).

3. On *t.* as "corvée" s. Stol 1995a. NR

tuptu "a footstool(?)"

SB *tu-*⌜*pat*⌝ *burāši* KAL 2, 15 ii 35 // 4R 14 r. 10 (s. CAD T 480) "a footstool made of juniper wood". JW/MPS

tuqqu "a workshop(?), an administrative building(?)"

S. Pentiuc 2001, 184f. with prev. lit. In OB Mari, a work shop(?) associated with leatherworkers and carpenters. In MB Emar, an administrative building.

NR

tuqqunu "appropriate" s. *taqānu*

Tuqquru, pl. *Tuqqurātu* "a type of house"; NWSem. lw.

1. Selected spellings in addition to CAD T 450f.: TU-KU-*rum*/*ri* CunMon. 13, 5: 24, 30, 37; 7: 25; pl. É TU-GU-*ra-tu*^{meš} ib. 22: 2. Thus the first syllable is mostly wr. with TU (once TUM) and the second syllable with GU, KU or KUM.

2. Disc.: Arnaud 1991, 12: root WGR "tumulus", hence "maison à étage"; unlikely, s. Pentiuc 2001, 46. Pentiuc 2001, 46: *duggūru* (cf. Hebr. DGR "to gather together" etc.). Westenholz 2000, 19: sold together with fields and vineyards, once with a well and once with a foundation; also on size and price. Ikeda 2003, 270: ref.

3. Emar 6/3, 253 uses *gu* (*i-ra-gu-um* l. 14), but has [*t*]*u-ug*-KUM-*rum* l. 29. Emar 6/3, 144: uses *du* (*qa-du* l. 2), but has *tu-ug*-KUM-*rum* ll. 1, 8, 13, 15, 23. Emar 6/3, 115 uses *du* (*qa-du* l. 1), but has TU-GU-*ru* l. 1, TU-GU-*ra* l. 11. CunMon. 13, 22 uses *du* (*qa-du* l. 11), but has TU-GU-*ra-tu* l. 2. All this, combined with the spellings under 1, above, favors /t/ or /ṭ/ as first and /q/ as second consonant.

tuqumtu, + *taqumtu* "battle"

1. OB var. *taqumtu*:
a) Reiner 2007, 59f.: OB *ki-še-eš-bi* URxUR = *ašar ta-qum-*⌜*tim*⌝ ZA 83, 4 r. i 14 "battle field" (school exercise).
b) OB lit. ⌜*ta*⌝*-qum-tam* Gilg. OB III 150, contra CAD T 482a *t.* b 1'. Cf. George 2003, 211.

2. OB lit. PN *rīm tu-qú-um-tim* FM 14 i 1 "PN, wild bull of battle".

3. OB lit. *ittanpaḫ tu-uq-ma-tim qere[b māti]m* FM 14 iii 29 "inflamed with battles was the center of the land".

4. OB lit. (Marduk) *bēl tu-qú-um-tim* RA 86, 8: 6 "lord of battle".

JW (2–4), MPS/NR (1)

+ tur- "to run"; Hurr. word in MB Qaṭna

GN *ana ṣābika* : *du-ra* QS 3, 2: 42 "GN defects to your troop". Cf. disc. ib. p. 52. S. Richter 2012, 475.

tūra, *tūru*, + *tūr* "again"; + MA, + OA

1. OA: **a)** *tù-ur-ma ammala tuppim ša ālim awātam ana* PN *dí-na* Fs. Alp 26 kt c/k 283: 16 "respond again/for the second time to PN on the basis of the tablet of the City".
b) *tù-ur-ma umma anākuma* BIN 4, 33: 48 "I spoke again".
c) Grammaticalization of *tuʾāru* "to return" in hendiadys with the following verb, parallel to *turram* in SB (CAD T 488a s.v.), *tūra* in NA (ibid. 483 s.v.).

2. MA *tu-ur ūmū ikaṣṣû* BATSH 4, 6: 11 "it will become cold again".

JW (2), NJCK (1)

turāḫu "wild goat, mountain goat, ibex"

Reiner 2007, 60: 63 *qarnātu ša tu-ra-ḫi* MDOG 134, 75 Ass. 2001.D-2218: 4 "63 ibex horns (for bows for the king)", cf. ib. 10, 16, 22, 27. NR

turāšu, *turēzu*, *turazzu*, + *turīšu*? "harvest"; + SB?, + MB?, + NA?

1. Lex. *al-zú-4* = *tu-ra-šu* Emar 6/4, 545: 184 "pitch-fork =(?) harvest".

2. MB Emar ^{d}INANA (*ša*) *tu/tù-ri-ši* Emar 6/3, 373: 94; 383: 4; 460: 25 "Ištar of the harvest(?)". Cf. von Soden 1987, followed by Pentiuc 2001, 183.

3. NA *tu-ri-su maḫir* StAT 2, 230: 5 "he has received his *t.*".

MPS (1–3), NR (2)

turatannu s. *tartānu*

turatānu s. *tartānu*

****turāʾu** s. *duraʾuʾannu*

turazzu s. *turāšu*

turba(l)lû "bare ground"

Stol 2010, 174: Cf. *burubalû*, s. Charpin 1980, 163. NR

turbuʾtu s. *tarbuʾ(t)u*

turbuʾu s. *tarbuʾ(t)u*.

****turdu** "a type of flour"

Reiner 2007, 60: for the ref. in CAD T 486 s. now MARV 3, 16 (4 SÌLA ZÍD *sím-du*). NR

turēzu s. *turāšu*

turi/ennu I "kiln(?)"; + MB Emar

1. [É-*t*]*um* : *tu-re-en* DUB Emar 6/3, 186: 4 "building : kiln(?) for(?) tablet(s)".

2. É-*tum* : *t*[*u-re-en* ...] Emar 6/3, 187: 36.

3. Neither the form with ending /-inn/ nor the OA attestation favor a WSem. etym. /dōr-/ as proposed by Pentiuc 2001, 46f. The transl. "kiln(?)" follows

Civil 1973, 172–175 who suggested to connect *turinnu* with Sum. *šu-rin* = Akk. *tinūru* "oven"; note especially the glosses *du-ru-un*/*-na*, *di-li-na* (Diri, Ea) CAD T 420.

turinnu II s. *terinnu*

+ **turittu**, pl. *turinnētu* "a component of the tiara"; LB

1. 7 *tu-ri-in-né-e-ti* Beaulieu 2003 p. 323f. YBC 11390: 14; cf. ib. 389.

2. PN: [f]*Tu-rin-né-tum* SpTU 5, 291: 9 pass. (pl.?).

3. Cf. Beaulieu 2003, 389. Perhaps to be connected with *turunnu* "a setting for jewellery" (attested in Qaṭna inventories). JW

turiš s. *warāšu* II

turīšu s. *turāšu*

+ **turmedīsu** "part of a deity's apparel made of silver"; LB

MacGinnis 2008: LB *ana tur-me-di-su ša* DN *ana* PN *nappāḫi nadna* BM 64017: 2 "(1/2 mina 4 shekels of silver) given to PN the smith for the *t.* of DN". MPS/NR

turru II, *durru*, *ṭurru*? "binding, knot; corner angle; an astronomical feature"; + OA

1. Ur III(?) lex. *dur gìš-ĝu*$_{10}$ = *tu-ru-um ša išariya* CUSAS 12 p. 157 ix 19 (Ugumu) "frenulum of my penis".

2. Lex. *tu-ur-ru* = *zamû* AOAT 50, 368: 27 (malku) "band = outer corner". Cf. Hrůša ib. p. 235.

3. Lex. *tu-ur-ru* = *sippu* AOAT 50, 368: 130 (malku) "band = jamb".

4. OA "yarn, twine": (PN is bringing you n textiles of good quality and Subarean make) *mūdeʾam … ṣabatma tù-re-šu-nu lušaddidma annibrārē lussi-makkuššunūma* AKT 8, 80: 15 "take on an expert from … and let him stretch their yarns and make them suitable for you as *nibrārum*-textiles".

5. OB DÚR-*ru* ARM 30, 155 T.518 pass. (unpubl.); DUR-*ru* ib. 6; [siki]DUR T. 519: 21 (unpubl.). Durand ib.: a fleece, strands of fibres? Perhaps "skein".

6. OB lit. *du-ur-ri naṣrapti ītiq* CUSAS 18, 26: 14 "(if a weapon-mark) passes the corner angle of the dyeing vat"; cf. George ib. p. 182 and George 2008.

7. SB *tu-ur-ra ana tu-ur-ri ittanamzaz* Lamaštu MB I 18 (Farber 2014, 120) "she keeps stopping at corner after corner" (Zomer 2018, 182f. pace Farber 2014, 248: "time and again").

8. Mayer 2009, 439:

a) SB *iḫṭīṭū*! DUR!-*ra-a-ti* Tn-Ep. V ("II") 39 (after von Soden) "they checked the bindings".

b) In PBS 15, 80 i 22 (CAD Ṭ 165) read *ku-du-ur-ru* (s. Schaudig 2001, 347).

9. LB [*i*]*na tur-ru kitê ṣabt*[*i*] PTS 2950: 30, cf. 13 "held on a linen string". The syll. spelling suggests the reading *turru* rather than *riksu* for the logogram DUR when it denotes a string of beads (Beaulieu 2003, 237; 389).

10. Corresponds to CAD Ṭ 164–166 *ṭurru* A–C; AHw 1397 *ṭurru*, *turru* II. Cf. George 2008, 223; Hrůša ib. p. 235. For the reading *turru* or *durru*, rather than *ṭurru*, s. Streck 2009a, 139f. On *turru* as an architectural feature ("corner angle", CAD *ṭurru* B) s. George 2008. On *t.* as a designation of birds in MB Alalaḫ s. *turru* III.

JW (7), MPS (1–3, 6), NJCK (4), NR (5, 8–10)

+ **turru III** "(turtle) dove"; MB Alalaḫ

200 *tu-ur-ri*$^{\text{mušen.ḫi.a}}$ AlT 48: 10, 13 "200 doves (as interest)", pace AHw 1397 s.v. *ṭurru* 4, CAD Ṭ 165 s.v. *ṭurru* A e. NWSem. lw.(?), cf. Hebr. *tōr*, Ugar. *tr* II (DLU 473), Latin *turtur*. Disc. and prev. lit. s. Militarev/Kogan 2005, 293; Niedorf 2008, 370. JW

turrupu s. *tarāpu*

turšummu I "a prebend(?)"

Mayer 2009, 436: OB *tu-ur-šu-mu-šu* AUCT 5, 127: 4; s. Charpin 2005, 418f. NR

turtannu, *turtānu*, *turtennu* s. *tartānu*

tūrtu "turning, reversion"

1. OB lit. *meḫiṣ panim tu-ú*[*r*?-]*ti īnim* ZA 75, 198: 10 "blow on the face, 'turning the eye'". Cf. CAD T 491 *tūrtu* A 4 for *tūrti īni* "an eye disease?" and Fincke 2000, 173.

2. MB *tūrti qāti* "turning of the hand" =(?) "out of control", e.g. *tur-ti qāti* PN CUSAS 30, 91: 26 "out of control of PN(?)". Cf. the expression *qāt* PN *turru* "to undo the control of PN(?)", s. the disc. van Soldt CUSAS 30 p. 31f.

3. SB *balāṭa kalāšu* ⌜*tu-ur-ti*⌝ *īnimma* (// ⌜*igi*⌝ *nigin*/*nígin-na*-(⌜*a*?⌝)-*kam*) Ballad of Early Rulers Ugarit I 12 "the whole of life is just a glance (lit. turn of the eye)"; s. Sjöberg 2003, 259.

4. SB (offerings) *inaššûmi ina tu-ur-ti* [*išakkanū*?] Emar 6/3, 373: 200 "they lift up (the offerings) and [place (them)] in return", s. Fleming 2000, 71f.

5. *aban tur*-⌜*ti*⌝ [...] CT 51, 89 iii 5 "stone of turning (away the evil)" (an amulet stone).

6. NA *tur-ti amāt ša aḫīya lušmēma* SAA 19, 202 r. 1 "let me hear my brother's answer".

JW (4–5), MPS (1–3, 5–6)

****tūrû** (CAD T 492) cf. SAD *tarbuʾtu* 2

turubu "a kind of bread"; Hurr. lw.

Cf. Hitt. *tu-ru-up-pa-aš* and Hurr. *turubi*-, s. Pentiuc 2001, 184 with prev. lit. MPS/NR

turuḫtānu "a container for beer"

Reiner 2007, 60: OA *tù-ru-ùḫ-ta-nam*/*num* KAŠ Prag 682: 4, 18 "a *t*. container of beer". MPS/NR

turu(n)nu II "a setting for jewellery"

Cf. Wilhelm 1999, 415ff.; Durand 1990c, 155f. Cf. *turittu*? NR

+ **turunus** "throne"; Gk. word (< θρόνος) in LB

kussû ša šarrim … ša šumšu yamanāya tu-ru-nu-us Astronomical Diaries 3, -124 B r. 15 "the royal throne (…) whose Greek name is 'thronos'", reading after van der Spek 2000, 436.

JH/JW

turuʾu "a cry"

Stol 2010, 175: mng. "a cry" with AHw and Stol 2007, 241 pace CAD ("a medicinal plant?"). NR

tusinnu s. *tuzzinnu*

tūṣātu "offspring, descendants; escapee"; + OB

Reiner 2007, 60:

1. OB *ilū annûtum mal*[*a*] *piriʾ šumiy*[*a*] *ù tu-ṣa*-[*ti*] *liḫalli*[*qū*] Fs. Garelli p. 26 M.6182: 19 "may these gods destroy all my offspring and my descendants".

2. OB *dawdâm ša nakrim … adūk tu-ṣa-tam ul uwaššer* ARM 10, 122 +M.15083: 9 "I defeated the enemy, I allowed no one to escape", s. Durand 1987b, 622; 2000, 317f.

3. Both ref. show that the word is sg. (noun pattern *taPRāS*, derived from the separative Gt). MPS/NR

tuša "it could have been that; it was as though; apparently"

1. OB *tuša ṣābum mādum ittīšu* ARM 26/2, 90 no. 323: 4 "apparently, (there were) many troops with him".

2. Cf. Wasserman 2012, 95–114 with prev. lit. JW

tūšaru "desert, battlefield"

SB [*ana*] *tu-šá-ar ništakan qīšta* JCS 66, 82: 303 (Gilg.) "we turned the forest into a battlefield".

+ **tūšīru?** "a qualification of textiles, loose weave(?)"; OB

^{túg}NÍG.BÀRA *ša tu-ši-ri-im* ARM 30, 127 T.383: 12f. "a *uṣû* cloth of *t.* Further ref. and disc. s. Durand ib. p. 127f. Derives from *wuššuru*? JW

+ **tušmu** (mng. unkn.); NA

n *Gurrāya ... adakanni lā tú-uš-mu* SAA 19, 195: 11 "the n Gurreans have not been *t.* … until now".

tušru "a plant"

Stol 2010, 175: *tuš-ru* BAM 4, 322: 33; *tuš-ra* BAM 6, 543 i 17. JW

tuššu "slander, malicious talk"

1. Lex. *kúr-da-ga-daḫ* = *tu-uš-šu-um* CUSAS 12 p. 252 iv 12.

2. Mayer 2009, 437 and 2017b, 236: *ēpiš tuš-ši tuballa* K. 7263: 4 // CTN 4, 180 iv 4 "you eradicate the one who 'makes' evil talk".

3. NB *tu-uš-šú iqbi* SAA 17, 27 s. 1 "he said an insult". JW (2), MPS (1, 3)

tušu (mng. uncert.)

Reiner 2007, 61: Dietrich 2001b, 650f. suggests a meaning "grant". JW

tušuʾû "ninth; nine-year-old"; + LB

LB *imēru* 9-*ú* TCL 13, 127: 1 "a 9-year-old donkey". Cf. *rubuʾû* "four-year-old".

tuttu "mulberry (tree)"

MacGinnis 2008, 85: LB 3 GUR *tu-ut-tum ḫarpū*[*tu*] BM 54242: 1 "3 kor of early mulberries". NR

tuttubû, *tuttubāʾu* "a garment"; + OA, + MB Qaṭna

1. OA *tuttubāʾu* :

a) Reiner 2007, 61: 3 *tù-tù-ba-a-tim* 2 1/4 GÍN KÙ.BABBAR *šīmšina* PN *ublakkum* Prag 429: 42 "PN brought to you three *t.*-s valued at 2 1/4 shekels of silver."

b) *ša tù-tù-ba-a-tim* kt 94/k 122 and 175 "the maker of/dealer in *t.*-s", s. Veenhof 2003, 35.

c) Durand 2009: 112: *tuttubû* is a nisbe from GN Tuttub and a luxurious garment. If correct, *tuttubāʾu* is unlikely to be identical with *tuttubû*: the OA form with *ā* can hardly be a nisbe, and the price of less than 1 shekel of silver per piece is lower than that of almost any other kind of textile (Kouwenberg, forthc. 191). Judging by their contexts, it is not certain that the two OA instances refer to textiles.

2. OB **a)** In ARM 9, 20: 18 read *tu-ut-tu-ba-tum* (coll. Durand 2009, 112).

b) ^{túg}*tu-tu-ba-u* GAL ARM 30, 111 T.525: 1.

3. MB **a)** 8 ^{túg}*ṣubātu* : *tù-tù-be-na* QS 3, 12: 14 "8 garments (gloss:) *t.* cloaks".
b) 5 TÚG^{me} : *tù-ut-tù-bi* QS 3, 13: 3 "5 garments (gloss:) *t.* cloaks".
c) 2 *ta-pal* TÚG : *tù-ut-te-we* QS 3, 12: 25 "2 pairs of garments (gloss:) *t.* cloaks".

4. MA 1 ^{túg}*tu-ut-tu-bu*^{meš} MARV 10, 14: 10 (for royal beds).

JW (2), MPS (3–4), NJCK/NR (1)

tutturru "granule, bead"

1. For *ša tutturrī* in OB s. ARM 32, 69f. with add. ref.

2. According to Arkhipov, ARM 32, 43, *dadurru* "a cylindrical bead" (spellings *da-du-ur-ru/ri*, *da-du-ru/ri*, *du-du-ru*, interchangable with *kunukku*) might be a separate word.

3. For *t.* in Nuzi s. *tattaru*. JW

tutummu s. *šutummu*

tutunu "a vessel"

Pentiuc 2001, 184: cf. Hittite *duddu-* "measuring vessel"? NR

tuʾu "room, cella, chamber"

Both CAD and AHw consider this a variant of *diʾu* II "platform". After Röllig 1996, it can be considered a separate lemma, connected to WSem. *tw*(*n*) "room". S. *tuʾānu*? JW

tuʾʾumu II "to reconsider, ponder(?)"

D Reiner 2007, 61: cf. *mutaʾʾimu*, *muteʾʾimu* (CAD M/2 319f. s.v. *muṭeʾemu*), which corresponds to Old Pers. *framātar-* "commander"; *t.* corresponds to Old Pers. *framānā-* "to command".

NR

\+ **tuwadalu?**, *tûdalu*? "a tool or vessel made of bronze"; MB Emar

1. 1 *tu-wa-da-lu* ZABAR Emar 6/3, 283: 16 (inventory of implements and vessels).

2. 1 *tù-da-lu* CM 13, 27: 7 (inventory).

MPS/NR

tuwaššu "a type of bread"; Hitt. lw.(?)

SB ^{ninda}*tù-a-šu* Emar 6/3, 472: 78. Cf. Pentiuc 2001, 45. NR

tuzinnu s. *tuzzinnu*

tūzu s. *tunšu*

tuzzinnu "a field tied to a type of service obligation; persons responsible for the performance of this obligation"; OA, Hitt. lw.

1. Persons:
a) *šumma mamman lū tù-zi-nu-um lū bēl ḫubullišunu ana bēti ituwwar* Hecker 1997 p. 171 kt 87/k 312: 11 "if anyone, be it the *t.* or their creditor, raises a claim for the house".
b) PN *u* PN$_2$ *bēlū tù-zi-nu-um izzizzū* ib. 17 "PN and PN$_2$, lords of the *t.*, were present"; cf. AKT 10, 17A: 10; 50A: 4; 55A: 4; 58A: 7; 59A: 11; 61A: 11; 64A: 8.

2. A type of service field:
a) *inūmi rubāʾum ana tù-zi-nim eṣādim errubu* ArAn 1, 59 kt 88/k 90: 11 "when the king will enter to harvest the *t.*"
b) *šumma ana tù-zi-ni-im ša abīšu* PN *ituwwar* 3 *manā kaspam u bētam ana* PN$_2$ *u* PN$_3$ *iddan šumma ana tù-zi-ni-im ša abīšu lā ituwwar bētum bē<tu>-šu u ṣuḫārū mērʾūšu* PIHANS 100 p. 161 kt 87/k 39: 7, 15 "(we purchased PN today. We gave him our house. He accepted the *arḫālum* of the king (and) accepted the house of the king). If PN

returns to the *t.* of his father, he will give 3 minas of silver and the house to PN_2 and PN_3. If he does not return to the *t.* of his father, the house will be his house and the servants will be his sons."

c) *bētam u tù-zi-nam* PNf *u* PN *mēraša ilqēʾū* Hecker 1997 p. 168 kt 87/k 285: 15 "PNf and PN, her son, accepted the house and the *t.*" (same PN as 87/k 39).

d) *tù-zi-nam kilallānma ukallū* Hecker 1997 p. 169f. kt 87/k 253: 14 "(PN and PN_2 are brothers, they divided (the household.)) The two of them hold the *t.*"

e) *tù-zi-n[u-um] ša rabī sikkātim* Belleten 53 p. 52 kt a/k 1263/b: 4 "(PN bought the house of PN_2). The *t.* is of the *rabi sikkātim.*"

f) PN *zi-tù-šu u tù-zi-nam ša rabī simmilte ilqē* kt 91/k 282 (Veenhof *apud* Dercksen 2004, 163): 8 "PN took his share and the *t.* of the Chief of the Staircase" (division of estate).

3. Disc.:

a) Etym.: Likely to be connected with Hitt. *tuzzi-* "army" (s. already Bilgiç 1945–1951, 18 n. 133; id. 1954, 48; Starke 1993, 25; HEG III/10 T. D/3, 501; Müller/Marzahn 2000, 300f. and n. 56; Dercksen 2007); *t.* can sometimes refer to military service (s. below). Cf. AHw 179 *d/tus/ṣinnum*; CAD T 493f. *tusinnu.*

b) Mng.: The dicts. give a mng. "seller with right of pre-emption, redeemer" (CAD) based on texts where *t.* refers to persons. Based on additional evidence where *t.* is a commodity, more specifically a type of agricultural land (2a), Dercksen 2004 proposed to understand this term as "agricultural land whose tenant has to perform a (military) obligation" and, respectively, "persons in charge of the performance of the service obligation". A military aspect is suggested by an unpublished ref. to "*t.* of the bow" (s. ib. p. 148). JW

Ṭ

ṭābātu "vinegar"

Lex. *é a-ĝeštin-na* = *bīt* ⌜*ṭa*⌝*-ba-ti* CUSAS 12 p. 40 ii 60 (Kagal) "house of the vinegar".

\+ **ṭabbuʾu** "a qualification of copper"; OA

20 *manā ḫušāʾē elīʾātim* 4 *manā ṭá-bu-ú-tim ana* GN PN *ubilšum* n/k 524: 12 (Dercksen 1996, 76) "PN brought 20 minas of scrap copper in the form of *elītum*s (and) 4 minas of *ṭ*. to him in GN". NJCK

ṭābiḫu "slaughterer, butcher; a weapon, ornamental dagger"

1. OB lit. *ṭa-bi-ḫi* Westenholz 1997, 166: 182 (in list of professions).

2. Borger 2010, 347: pace CAD Ṭ 8a read ^{dingir}*bi-ṭu-ḫi-du-gul* in BagM 21, 461: 19.

3. Pl. *ṭābiḫūtu*:

a) MB *bītāt ṭá-bi-ḫu-te*^{meš} *annû ša ēkalli* QS 3, 50: 7 "houses of the butchers. These belong to the palace".

b) MB *bītāt ṭá-bi-ḫu-tum annû ša bītāt : ta-aḫ-a-ka-še-na* ib. 15 "houses of(!) the butchers. These belong to the houses of the men".

4. For the (ornamental) dagger in Mari s. Arkhipov 2012, 128 with add. ref. In this mng. *ṭ*. is synonymous with *ḫubūsu*. There are no grounds for parsing it as *ṭabīḫu* (pace CAD Ṭ 6).

JW (4), MPS (1, 3), NR (2)

****ṭabīḫu** s. *ṭābiḫu*.

\+ **ṭābtiš** "pleasantly(?)"; SB

ṭàb-tiš ātamū Ludlul I 118 "(I sweetened my lips but they were hard as a lance,) I spoke pleasantly(?) (yet my conversation was a hindrance)", diff. George/Al-Rawi 1998, 197 and Oshima 2014, 219 ("like salt = sharply"). S. also *daʾīmu*. JW

ṭābtu I "salt"

1. OA 2 *ḫa-*PI*-ru ša ṭá-áb-tí-in* AKT 6B, 467: 5 "2 *ḫ*. of/for salt", s. Barjamovic/Larsen 2008, 153; cf. AKT 5, 60: 4 and ib. p. 120f. (ad 31).

2. OB lit. *bēlaki? epšetki ina* ⌜*ṭa*⌝*-ab-tim lā tašakkanī* CUSAS 10, 10: 37f. "don't put your lord, your task, in salt!" (sexual metaphor).

3. LB 10 *manā* MUN$^{\text{ḫi.a}}$ *ina sattukki ša* MN *ša bīt* DN AUWE 5, 87: 1 (cf. ib. 88: 1; 89: 1) "10 minas of salt from the regular offering in the temple of DN".

JW (1), MPS (2–3)

ṭābtu II, pl. *ṭābātu* "goodness, goodwill, good deed(s)"

OA *ṭābātu* (pl. tant.) "friendliness, willingness":

1) *šumma ṭá-ba-tum kaspam liddin* Günbattı 1999, 392 no. 397: 14 "if there is willingness (on his part), let him give the silver; (if he starts a quarrel, let PN and PN_2 lead him (to court))".

2) *šīmam ša tēpušu ana ālim ṭá-ba-tum-ma* AKT 6B, 319: 13 "the purchases you made (are destined) for the city, (they are an act of) kindness".

3) *aḫātki ištē maḫātīʾa ṭá-ba-tum-ma* AKT 3, 79: 6 "your sister is friendly with my *maḫātu*".

4) (PN has seized your slave girls) *i-ṭá-ba-tim amātim punuʾāma luššerūnekki-nāti* CTMMA 1, 78A: 14 "appeal (to him) in a friendly way that they release the slave girls to you"; cf. kt h/k 20: 6 (Sever 1998, 529).

5) *šumma i-ṭá-ba-tim kasapša laqāʾam lā tamūʾa* Farber 2001, 139: 22 "if she refuses to accept her silver willingly".

6) *ṭābātu* corresponds in use to Bab. *ṭūbātu*, *ṭubbātu*, s. CAD Ṭ 114f.

NJCK

ṭābu "good, sweet"

1. said of health (CAD Ṭ 25 *ṭ.* m): OA *raminī lā ṭá-áb-ma* AKT 6B, 423: 15 "I am not well myself (therefore I shall send you my servants)."

2. In *kī ṭābi* in Ugar. "correct, proper, according to regulations", s. Malbran-Labat 2010, 92. JW

ṭâbu s. *ṭīʾābu*

ṭābūtu "goodness"; + LB

(silver) *ša* PN *ana ṭàb-bu-ú-{nu}-ti? iddinu* Joannès 1989, 256 L 1672: 11 "which PN amicably gave".

+ **ṭaḫānu** "to injure"; OB, Am. lw.

G Stol 2010, 175: OB 300 *Ḫanê ša warkassu<nu> ṭá-aḫ-nu aklāma* ARM 2, 25 r. 4 (Durand 1998, 229 n. d) "I detained 300 Ḫaneans, whose rear(?) was injured".

D Stol 2010, 175: PN *idukkū u šanêm ú-ṭá-⌜ḫi⌝-nu* M. 6159 (cit. Durand 1998, 229) "they killed PN and injured another".

Disc.: For etym. s. Streck 2000, 119.

EZ

ṭaḫdu "abundant"; + OA

In OA only as a qualification of silver:

1. *kīma kaspum ṭa-aḫ-du-um ina* GN *inneppušūni u libbaka iḫadduʾu epuš* AKT 5, 19: 13 "act so that abundant silver can be earned in GN and your heart will rejoice!"; cf. AKT 3, 39: 11.

2. [*kīma*] *kaspam* (sic?) 1 *manā ṭá-aḫ-d*[*a-am*] *illakanni epš*[*ā*(*ma*)] AKT 5, 16: r. 26 "do (pl.) your best that … at least a mina of 'abundant silver' comes my way"; cf. *ina* 10 *manā kaspim ṭá-aḫ-dim* 89/k 355: 22 (part. cit. CAD Ṭ 44b s.v. b, without transl.).

3. "Abundant silver" fits the instance in (1), but fits poorly with the mention of an explicit quantity in (2). Veenhof, AKT 5 p. 109 suggests "at least" for these. Elsewhere, *ṭaḫdu* qualifies rain and inundation, offerings and food.

NJCK

ṭamû s. *ṭawû*

ṭapālu "to scorn, treat with disrespect"; + OA

G OA *aḫiʾūtum i-ṭá-pu-lu-kà* AKT 6A, 287, 28 "outsiders will speak of you disapprovingly".

D "to slander, to defame": OA (PN has disclosed confidential matters of yours) *u šumka damqum ṭá-pu-ul u anāku ištēkama ṭá-pu-lá-ku* AKT 5, 18: 6f. "your good name has been besmirched and I have been besmirched together with you".

+ **N 1.** OA *ammākam awātam šaḫiltam mimma ē tēpušma ē ta-ṭí-pì-il*$_5$ AKT 3, 88: 55 "do not do any … matter at all there, lest you should be criticized".
2. OA *u atta kīma lā ta-ṭá-pu-lu-ú-ni ina libbika atallakma alē wasmatni malā lā ni-ṭá-pu-lu epuš* RA 59, 170:

19, 23 "and you, think carefully so that you will not be criticized and where it is proper, make sure that we will not be criticized (either)"; cf. CCT 3, 30: 32.
NJCK

+ **ṭaparu?** "wooden board"; SB

Lex. ^{dur}DÚR = *ki-iš-kàr-rum* = TA-*pa-rum* Emar 6/4, 545: 267. Pentiuc 2001, 187 relates the word to Ethiopic *ṭafar* "roof, wooden floor". Cohen 2010, 817 connects it with *dabāru* CAD D 14: DA-*ba-rum* = *iṣṣ*[*u*] Malku VIII 157A (s. AOAT 50, 146) "D. = wood".
MPS/NR

****ṭapāru** "to press towards" (AHw 1380)

For G s. *epēru* III Gt, for D s. *dapāru* "to go off".

ṭapultu, *ṭapiltu*, *ṭupultu* "slander, denigration"

1. Mayer 2009, 437: OB *tuppāt ṭá-pí-il-ti*[*m*] Fs. Garelli 334: 11 "tablets (about) defamation".

2. OB *ša* ... *ṭú-pu-ul-ti-ia lā šakānim epuš* ARM 27, 46 r. 11 "act so that I am not slandered! (lit. that my insult is not placed)". EZ (1), MPS (2)

ṭarādu "to send off"

D LB "to protest" s. *ṭerdu* 2.

ṭarīdu "exile"

1. Abstract: OB *ina* GN *ina ṭá-ri-di-im amūtam allak* CUSAS 36, 38:5 "I work as a slave-girl in GN, in exile".

2. SB *alpī ṭa-ri-du-ti* CUSAS 30, 448: 12 "driven out oxen". Prob. not a form of *ṭardu*.

ṭarīdūtu, *ṭardūtu* "exile, banishment; dispatchment"; + LB

Var. *ṭardūtu*:

1. OB lit. [*ša*] *ṭa-ar-du-ú-*[*ta illaku*] *ana ālišu iturra* CUSAS 18, 27: 4 "[one who is in] exile will return to his city".

2. LB [*ina pa*]*n ṭar-du-ti* [*ša*] *ṣēnū* dubsar 3, 210 (= CT 22, 232): 12 "before the dispatching of sheep", coll. ib.
JW (2), MPS (1)

ṭarpaʾu "tamarisk"

A tree-like species of *tamarix*, chiefly *tamarix aphylla* (MB, SB, NA). The same tree is called *bīnu* in OAkk. and Bab. (Streck 2004, 253f.; 2011–2013a, 428 § 2). JW/MPS

ṭarpu s. *tarwu*

ṭātu "bribe, baksheesh, a gift, a tax or toll"

1. OA a type of transaction levy:
a) *annakam šalmam balūm ṭa-tim u taššīʾātim išaqqal* AKT 8, 301: 49 "he will pay the full amount of tin without fees and transport cost"; cf. AKT 9A, 59: 7.
b) OA *šāqil ṭa-tim* AKT 5, 1: 3 etc. (cf. index ib. p. 207 s. v. *šāqil dātim*).
c) S. Dercksen 2007a, 189f. for disc.

2. OB as a qualifier of bronze (*ṭa-tum*/*tim*), s. ARM 25 p. 277 and Reiter 1997, 339f. with ref.

3. OB a type of tax, s. disc. Villard 1990, 677–681; for further ref. s. de Boer 2016, 597ff.

4. NB *ṭa-aʾ-ti šulmānu* OIP 114, 35: 9 "(give me) a gratuity (or) present"; cf. ib. 17.

5. LB *ṭa-wa$_6$-ti-šú* Iraq 56, 117: 7/9, s. MacGinnis 2008, 118.

6. Borger 2010, 348: in BWL 132, 98f. // Si 832 quot. CAD Ṭ 64 read NÍG.PEŠ$_4$ instead of NÍG.ŠÀ.A (coll.), s. MesZL 446.

EZ (5–6), JW (1–4), MPS (1)

ṭātūtu "present"; + NB

NB (bread) *ša ṭa-tu-tu nadānašu ukinnu* SAA 18, 123: 5 "which I had guaranteed to give as a present"; Reynolds ib. p. 97 and 180 *datūtu* (mng. unkn.).

ṭawû, *ṭamû* "to spin, plait"

G 1. Mayer 2009, 432: OB *lu-uṭ-wi-ma ṭimītī* RA 36, 10: 8 "I shall spin my yarn" (pace AHw 1341a and CAD T 302 s.v. *tawû*, ib. 440 s.v. *tīwītu*).
2. SB *ušandû ana gišparrišu i-ṭa-am eblu* Jiménez 2017, 250: 21 "the birdcatcher plaits the rope for his trap".
3. MB (wool) *ana ṭa-me-e* CUSAS 30, 307: 11 "for spinning".

+ **D** Mayer 2009, 437: MA *ana ṭa-a-ú-⌜e⌝* MARV 8, 85 r. 3 "for spinning(?)"

+ **N** Stol 2010, 175: [*šu*]*tûm li-iṭ-ṭa-wi* BagM 23, 151 no. 186 r. 8 "the *š.*-textile shall be woven".

Disc.: For mng. "to twine" s. Farber 1977, 159.

EZ (G, D, N), MPS (G)

ṭebû, + *ṭepû* "to sink, submerge"

G + OA **1.** *ilippum li-iṭ-b*[*u-m*]*a* ... [*mim*]*ma ḫuluqqāʾum ša iḫalliqūni* ... *lū tumalliʾāni* Günbattı 2004, 257 kt 00/k 10 ii 14 "if a boat sinks …, you will pay full compensation for all losses that occur".
2. OA "to be declared invalid" (passive to D 2, s. GOA § 21.2.5): *tuppū paniʾūtum lū ṭá-bi$_4$-ú* KTS 2, 7: 51 (= AKT 1, 22) "let the previous tablets be declared invalid".
3. OB *šubultu ṭe$_4$-bi* ARM 27, 101: 18, 24 "the ear is submerged".

D 1. "to cause to sink": OA *ša* [*nēb*]*erim ina sartim u lamuttim lā tušaḫḫazānima ilippam lā ú-ṭá-bu-ú-ma unūtam lā uḫalluqūni* Günbattı 2004, 257 kt 00/k 10 ii 13 "you shall not fraudulently and maliciously instruct a ferryman to make the boat sink and cause the loss of the goods"; for *ša nēberim*, s. Veenhof 2008, 199 n. 848.

2. OA "to declare invalid, to erase, to waive (interest)":
a) *alkamma tuppēka* 3 *lū nu-ṭá-bi$_4$-ma tuppam* 1 *ša naruqqika lū nilput* KTS 1, 34a: 5 "come, let us declare your 3 tablets invalid and write a single tablet of your *naruqqum*".
b) *kīma ālum qātam šakānam ú-ṭá-bi$_4$-ú* TC 3, 42: 17 "since the city has declared 'the laying of a hand' (i.e. a claim) invalid".
c) *tuppam ša šumī laptu šumī ṭá-bi$_4$-ma šumi* PN-*ma luput* CCT 2, 50: 22 "(on) the tablet on which my name is written, erase my name and write PN's name".
d) *ina šaqāl* URUDU *ṣibtam ú-ṭá-ba-ma mimma ulā iqabbīʾam* CUSAS 34, 4: 13 "at the payment of the copper I will waive the interest, so that he has nothing to say (i.e. to protest) to me".

3. OA "to withdraw, to remove" (often with *ina*):
a) KÙ.GI n *ša iqqātīʾa ú-ṭá-bi$_4$-ú-ma šumša alputuma* Anatolica 12, 135 Ka 423: 21 "(for) n gold that I withdrew from my share and booked in her name".
b) (after the sons of PN had died, our brothers arrived) *lū ana bikītišunu lū akkussiʾim ša ummišunu ṭá-bu-im* AKT 8, 184: 11 "both to bewail them and to remove their mother's chair".
c) (PNf has received 20 shekels of silver as the price of PNf$_2$) *ina maḫīrim* PN *ú-ṭá-bi$_4$-ší* ArAn. 3, 161 kt 87/k

287: 11 (Hecker 1997) "PN (= the buyer) has taken her away from (i.e. purchased on?) the market".

4. "to hide": OA *ašar tuppē tù-ṭá-bi₄-i-ni mamman lā emmarki* Veenhof 2015c, 276 kt 91/k 563: 14 "let no-one see where you hide the tablets"; sim. CCT 5, 8b: 25, s. Dercksen 1996, 75.

5. OA with *awātam* "to clear up, to eliminate" (an affair): (unfortunately, PN has died here) *lāma* PN *imūtuni awāssu nu-ṭá-bi*(*-ma*) CCT 4, 24b: 7 "before PN died, we cleared up his affairs"; cf. AKT 3, 80: 18 and BIN 4, 38: 29.

6. Referring to the treatment of copper: OA *ana* URUDU *ṭá-bu-e-em* TC 3, 163: 8 "(I paid n silver) in order to 'submerge' copper", s. Dercksen 1996, 75; perhaps a different verb, s. also *ṭabbuʾu*.

Dt SB *narātu limlâ agammu li-ṭe-e-pi* (// *li-ṭe-pi*) *mû ṭa-ap/b-a-ta lišēlâ* (// *lišēṣâ*) *rikis lumniya* SpTU 5, 248: 15 r. 7 "may the rivers become full, may the swamp become submerged, may the water in which you submerge yourself remove the bond of my evil". Both the change *b/p* in *liṭēpi* and the form with strong /ʾ/ in *ṭab/pʾāta* are Ass. Pace von Weiher ib. p. 62 not the verb *ṭepû* "to extend". MPS (G, Dt), NJCK (G, D)

ṭeḫû "to come near, approach"

G Early OB *ana šarrim iṭ-ḫa-ma* AS 22, 19: 5 "(PN) had an audience with the king"; cf. ⸢*i*⸣*-ṭe₄-ḫe* AS 22, 33: 3 (broken context).

Dt *uṭ-ṭá-aḫ-ḫu-ú* FM 3, 68 no. 4 ii 6 "(the meal for the gods) will be brought" (cit. CAD Ṭ 79b without transl.), s. Streck 2003, 114. JW

ṭēḫu "immediate vicinity, adjacent (place)"

Mayer 2009, 437: In absolute use: SB *kirû ina ṭa-ḫi azqup* BagM 21, 345 iii 28 "I planted a (fruit) orchard in (its) vicinity". EZ

ṭeḫûtu "clientele, associates; attachment (as part of clothing)"

1. MB [*naḫl*]*aptu ṭe-ḫu-tum* CUSAS 30, 372: 11 "[cl]oak with attachment(?)".

2. MB (wool) *ana ṭe-ḫu-ti* CUSAS 30, 375: 8 "for an attachment(?)".

3. Stol 2010, 173: for *teḫûtu* (CAD T 325b) read *ṭeḫûtu*, s. Krebernik 2004, 230 i 9; 233. EZ (3), MPS (1–2)

ṭēʾinu, fem. *tēʾintu* "miller; grinder"

Mayer 2009, 437: LB *ṭe-e-in-tu* Or. 57, 72: 3 "grinder(?)" (in list of implements). EZ

ṭēmānû "sensible, intelligent"

NB *ana ṭè-man-ni-i niptaraska* SAA 131: 14 "we considered you an intelligent man".

ṭēmu, + construct state *ṭeʾam* "(fore)-thought, plan(ning), understanding, instruction"

1. OB lit. *ana kibrāt erbêm ṭe₄-em-šu ispuḫ* FM 14 i 21 "he frustrated his (enemy's) plan throughout the world" s. Guichard ib. 36; cf. ARM 28, 63: 17f.

2. OB *aššum ṭe₄-a-am* … FM 9, 130 no. 25: 7, 11 "concerning the report about …".

3. MB Ekalte *ṭe₄-ma-tum anniʾam rubbāma ul ṭe₄-mu* WVDOG 102, 36: 32f. "the orders are replaced with respect to this(?), and there is no order any more".

4. Stol 2010, 175:
a) *ṭēmu gamru* can be used for the past "full report" (s. CAD Ṭ 86f.) and for the future "detailed instructions" (s. CAD Ṭ 90 sub 2).
b) *kī ṭēmu* "what is the situation?" (CAD Ṭ 86a): *lū kī ṭe*$_4$*-mi* FM 1, 127: 10 "what could be my decision?" (i.e. "what should I do?"); cf. ib. 140: 48

EZ (4), JW (1–2), MPS (3)

ṭēnu, fem. *teʾintu* "ground, milled"

1. MA *šeʾu u ṭé-in*!*-tu* MARV 1, 9: 34 "barley and flour", cf. *šeʾu u* ŠE.ÀRA Subartu 14 p. 84 no. 5: 9, 6: 9; cf. ib. p. 80 no. 2: 10, p. 94 no. 13: 7.
2. Mayer 2009, 437: *teʾintu* in MA as collective, specifically for *ḫašlātu*, *kurmišu* and *kuddimmu*, s. Freydank 1974, 80. EZ

ṭênu "to grind"

G 1. OB *ḫargalû ša ana ṭe-e-ni amātu ēkallim imḫurā* CUSAS 9, 372: 1 "*ḫ*.-grain which the servant-girls of the palace received for grinding".
2. MA pres. *i-ṭé-an* also in Chuera 81: 13.

ṭepû "to extend, apply, add"

G 1. Stol 2010, 175: OB *lipīʾam e-ṭe-e-pe an*[*ad*]*dī* YOS 11, 26 i 67, cf. ib. 10 "I add (a piece of) fat and throw (it into it)" (recipe), s. Bottéro 1995, 222.
2. LB *ta-ṭi*!*-pi*!*-an-ni* AOAT 414/1, 141: 8 "you added me". Cf. *i-ṭì-pi-iʾ* ib. 38: 27. EZ (1), MPS (1–2)

ṭēpu s. *dēpu* II

ṭerdu "protest, resistance, obstacle; name of gatekeeper of the underworld"

1. LB ⸢*ṭer-di*⸣ PN *kī ú-ṭar-ri-du* dubsar 3, 114 (BIN 1, 73): 17 "as soon as PN protested".
2. Name of the gatekeeper of the underworld, cf. Krebernik 2014–2016.

JW (1), MPS (2)

+ **ṭerittu** "expulsion"; SB

Mayer 2009, 437: *lū* MAŠKIM *ṭe-ri-it-ti* CTN 4, 106 ii 14 "be it the lurker of expulsion" (list of demons). EZ/MPS

ṭerītu I "mud, silt"; + OA

1. OA (I wanted to enter GN but) *ṭí-ri-tum ittaškanma ištū šapa*[*t*] GN *nārim urkātēʾa attūwar* kt 93/k 94: 8 "there was mud deposited, and I had to turn back from the bank of the river GN" (cit. Michel 2008, 251 n. 56f.; interpretation after Barjamovic 2011, 328 with n. 1362: "there was too much mud").

2. OB *ṭe*$_4$*-ri-ta-am iṭrûma* MHET 2/5, 595: 3, s. *ṭerû* G 1. MPS (2), NJCK (1)

ṭerû, + *ṭarû* "to penetrate, rub into; to beat; to dredge?"

G 1. Stol 2010, 175: OB *ṭe*$_4$*-ri-ta-am iṭ-ru-ma* MHET 2/5, 595: 4 "he dredged(?) mud".
2. Var. *ṭarû*: MB *abnī gabba ištu šamni u damī i-ṭar-ru-u* Emar 6/3, 373: 32 "they rub all the stones with oil and blood". The parallel ib. 58 has [*ipaš*]*šašū* "they anoint".

D S. CAD Ṭ 167a *ṭurrû*.

EZ (G, D), MPS (G)

ṭēru, *ṭīru* "mud, silt; a tree"

Lex. [^{giš}*ma-nu lù-a*] = *ṭi-ru* = *in-*[*za-ḫu-re-tu*] CTN 4, 215: 8 "[muddy *manu* tree] = mud (tree) = a red dye" (s. DCCLT CTN 4, 215, Murgud). The lex. ref. quot. AHw 1392b s.v. *ṭīru* I and CAD Ṭ *ṭīru* C belong here. JW

ṭīʾābu, *ṭâbu* "to be(come) good"

G NB of road: *ḫarrān* ⸢*ka*⸣-*da*-⸢*na*⸣ *ul ṭa-a-bi amīltu ul ašapparakka pan ludgulma aššâ ḫarrānu ta-aṭ-ṭi*$_5$(NE)-⸢*bi*!⸣ *ul a-kel-le-šú* OIP 114, 34: 24 "the road of the watches is not good. I will not send the slave girl to you. I want to wait, and when the road has become good, I will not hold her back"; cf. Jursa 1997/1998, 422.

+ **Gt** OB lit. *ūm ti-ṭù-bi-im rēqū* CUSAS 10, 14: 14 "days of feeling excellent are distant".

D 1. OA "to refine (oil)":

a) *ana bēt* PN *erbīma šamnam ṭá-i-bi*$_4$ AKT 9A, 74: 12 "enter PN's house and refine the oil!"; cf. AKT 6B, 303 r. 8.
b) *šamnam ša ina bētim ṭá-ú-bu ublūnim* AKT 3, 84: 32 "they have brought the oil that had been refined in the house".
c) *sardam liqēma ṭá-i-bi-šu* POAT 31: 17 "take olive oil and refine it!".
2. OB *aššum ana* GN *alākiša iltu ú-ṭa-ab-ši adī ana* GN *illaku murussa ul uṣṣī* ARM 26/1, 222 no. 83: 13 "the goddess will make her healthy when she travels to GN. Until she goes to GN her illness will not leave". Durand, ib. p. 222f., suggested to derive the verb from *daʾāpu*, Heimpel 2003, 209 thinks of a mistake for *udabbabši*.
3. OB *ana a(b)būt bītišu ú-ṭà-ba-an-ni* ARM 26/1, 259 no. 93: 14 "he flatters me in order that I become the 'father' of his house"; cf. ARM 2, 130: 8.

MPS (G, Gt, D), NJCK (D)

ṭīdu, *ṭiddu* "clay, mud; a kind of beer"

1. OA *anāku ṭi-dam ša ālim ina šutebbulim agdamar* "I have used up the clay of the city in sending (letters) all the time" AKT 4, 30: 28, s. Veenhof 2008/9, 195.

2. OA *ulā qēmam ulā ṭí-da-am mimma ulā ilmad* AKT 9A, 18: 33 "neither flour nor clay, he has learned nothing" (i.e. he does not know how to trade anything), s. ib. p. 49.

3. Mayer 2009, 438: SB *ša ina nāri imluʾu* IM-*a-a* Maqlû II 183 "(oh witch), who has taken out clay (for a figurine of me) from the river"; cf. *ša imlû* IM-*a-a ina nāri* KAL 2, 26 iv 4 // Akkadica 130, 106 iii 7.

4. Mayer 2009, 438: with terminative (CAD Ṭ 109):
a) Of vermin: SB [*lī*]*mû ṭi-de-eš* George 2010, 98f. K. 2629: 9 "may they turn to clay".
b) SB [...*k*]*ullati tušemme ṭi-id-diš* CTN 4, 180 iv 3 "you turn [a]ll ... to clay".

5. NA 2 SÌLA *ṭi-i*!-*di* StAT 3, 8: 6 "2 liters *ṭ*. beer". Pace Faist, ib. p. 29, and Gaspa 2012, 182 and 187, not fig (*tittu*) beer. Cf. AHw 1392 *ṭīdu* 8, CAD Ṭ 114 *ṭīṭu*.

EZ (3–4), JW (2), MPS (2, 5), NJCK (1)

ṭikmēnu s. *diqmēnu*

ṭimītu s. *ṭiwītu*

ṭīmu "yarn, thread"

1. LB ^{siki}*ṭi-me ša pišanni ana ṣīpi* OBO 260, 544: 1 "yarn of a *pišannu*-bag for dying", cf. (stone) *ana ṣīpi ša ṭi-me ša pišanni* ib. 10.

2. LB n GÍN *ṭi-im* PN ... *ittadin* OBO 260, 632: 1 "n shekels of yarn: PN has delivered". JW

+ **ṭimūtu** "a type of yarn"; LB

1. *gabbû ana ṭi-mu-tum ša* DN OBO 260, 609: 2 "alum for *ṭ*.-yarn of DN". Cf. ^{siki}*ṭi*-⸢*mu*⸣-[*tu*] OBO 260, 631: 1.

2. Cf. *ṭīmu* and *ṭiwītu*. S. Zawadzki 2006, 31 for disc. JW

+ **ṭīpānu** "person responsible for *ṭīpu*-obligation"; LB

In documents concerning bow- or *ilku*-obligations:

1. *ilki ša* PN … *u ṭi-pi-ni-šú* BM 30261 = Bertin 2836: 1f. "the *ilku*-obligation of PN … and his *ṭ*."

2. *qašt*[*i ša*] PN … *u* ^{lú}*ṭi-pa-ni-šú* BM 30589 = Bertin 2619: 4f. "the bow-obligation of PN … and his *ṭ*.-people"; cf. Bertin 2235 and 2836.

3. (n persons) ⸢*ṭi-pa*⸣*-ni ša* PN VAT 6, 295+296 = AfO Bh. 30, 202: 8.

4. For further ref. Jursa 1999, 106 n. 447 (erroneously read *qīpāni*).

5. Disc. s. van Driel 2002, 240f. n. 59; Baker 2004, 74f. JW

ṭīpu "addition, application"

1. LB "Annex" (CAD Ṭ 112f.): ⸢^{giš}*ṭi*⸣*-pi ša* [… *l*]*ibbū itê ippu*[*šū*] Hackl 2013, 74: 15 "they will built a wooden annex that […] corresponding to the neighbors".

2. LB "additional payment (associated with a bow-obligation)", s. van Driel 2002, 240f. n. 59 and Baker 2004, 74f. with prev. lit.:

a) *ana ṭi-pi ša qašti* VS 4, 96 = AfO Bh. 30, 201: 1 "(silver) for the additional payment of the bow-obligation", sim. Bertin 2621.
b) S. also *ṭīpānu*. Both terms have hith. been read *dīku* (CAD D s.v. *dīku* 1) or *qīpānu*, respectively.

3. Passages quot. CAD Ṭ 113 a2 ("a feature of the exta") belong to *dēpu* II.

JH/JW/MPS (1), JW/NR (2)

****ṭīru I** (AHw 1392b, CAD Ṭ *ṭīru* C) s. *ṭēru*.

ṭīru IV, *ṭirru* (mng. uncert.)

AHw 1392b *ṭīru* IV; CAD Ṭ *ṭīru* A, *ṭīru* B

1. For all OA and MA ref. qualifying metal s. *ṭīru* II.

2. Del. CCT 4, 47a: 32, read *ana* URUDU *Tí-ri-ta-ra-im* "for copper from Tiritar" (Dercksen 1996, 44f. with prev. lit.).

3. Only one MA ref. remains: 1 ME ANŠE^{meš} ŠE-*um*!(SU) *ṭí-ri aban bīt āli* KAJ 47: 3. JW (3), NJCK (1–2)

ṭīrûtu "beating up"

Mayer 2009, 438: LB *ṭi-ru-ú-tu* AS 27, 212f.: 8; 214f.: 8, 17, 20; *ṭi-ru-tum* 214f.: 15; all in connection with *batāqu rittu* and *miḫṣū*. EZ

ṭîtu s. *ṭiwītu*.

ṭiwītu, *ṭîtu*, *ṭimītu*, *ṭebētu* "yarn, twine"

1. Mayer 2009, 432: pace CAD T 302a s.v. *tawû* read *lu-uṭ-wi ṭì-wi-ti* RA 36, 10: 8 "may I spin my yarn."

2. OB 7 *manā turru* ^{siki}*ṭì-i-it* 2 GÍN^{ta} T.518: 21f. "7 minas of wool skeins(?), (with strands of) yarn (weighing) 2 shekels each"; *ṭì-i-it* 10 1/3 GÍN^{ta} T.525: 9; *ṭì-i-it* x GÍN^{ta} T.525: 5, s. Durand 2009, 154f.

3. MA *ṭé-be-ta lēṭa ša* ⸢GAD^{meš}⸣ *šēbila* BATSH 4, 7: 17 "send me yarn (for?) linen *l*.-cloth"; 130 GÚ.UN *ṭé-be-tu ša* GAD ib. 23.

4. LB 3 *mana ana tum-bi u ṭi-ma-a-ta ša pišannu* OBO 206, 388: 14 "3 minas (of wool) for *t*. and yarn for the *p*.-bag". S. Zawadzki 2006, 29f. for further LB ref. S. also *tubbu*.

EZ (1), JW (2–4), NR (2)

ṭūbātiš "cheerfully, peacefully"; SB

lūrub ina šulmema ṭu-ba-ti-iš (var. *-tiš*) *lutūra* Stadhouders/Panayotov 2018, 630: 9 "let me enter safely and return well-pleased". JW

ṭūbātu "happiness; friendliness"

ina/ana ṭ. "willingly" (Stol 2010, 176): **1.** OB n *akalam ina ṭú-ba-ti-šu ukāl* YOS 13, 198: 4 "he willingly holds on to n bread".
2. MB *ana ṭu-ba-tim u mitgurti ina bērišunu* DamM 1, 250: 9 "willingly and mutually between them". EZ

ṭuBBuru "an implement" s. *DuBBuru.*

ṭūbu, *ṭubbu* "goodness, happiness, prosperity, free will"

1. Var. *ṭubbu* already OB lit.: *ṭú-ub-bu-um* Westenholz 1997, 198: 51, cf. *šumu.*

2. *ina ṭ.* "graciously, willingly" (CAD Ṭ 117 e, f, cf. *ṭūbātu*): OB n *immerātim ittī Ḫanê ina ṭú-bi-šu-nu-ma [up]aḫḫir-ma* FM 6, 129 no. 7: 9 "I gathered n rams from the Hanaeans with their consent". JW (2), MPS (1)

ṭūdānu "a tree (lit. 'at the road'(?))"

MacGinnis 2008, 85: LB *ṭu-da-nu* BM 68140: 2. NR

ṭuḫḫû "a qualification of silver"

For disc. and prev. lit. s. Jursa 2010, 483f. n. 2633 (inferior(?) silver not normally used for transactions). JW

ṭulīmu "spleen; pancreas"

1. OB lit. *ṭù-li-ma-am* CUSAS 10, 12: 16 (in enumeration of insults?)

2. OB lit. *šumma* ⌜*ṭù*⌝*-li-ma maḫiṣ* CUSAS 18, 16 vii 26 "if he is stricken in the spleen".

3. For mng. "pancreas" s. Westenholz 2010, 19 ("spleen": *erru ṣalmu*). JW (3), MPS (1–2)

ṭullumāʾu "liar, cheater"; Aram. lw.

On etym. s. Cherry 2017, 267f. JW

ṭumânu "a fine thread or fabric"

1. LB *ana batqa* ⌜*šá*!⌝ *ṭu-ú-nu* YOS 17, 104: 4 "(wool) for repair of *ṭ.* fabric". The spelling reflects a pronunciation /ṭuwânu/.

2. For add. LB ref. s. Zawadzki 2006, 31f.; for disc. ib. 25. JW (2), MPS (1)

ṭuppaššu s. *Duppaššu*

ṭuppi "(within) timespan of; one-year period"

1. Mayer 2009, 438: Cf. Freydank 2007, 225–236 ("in addition, moreover, otherwise").

2. For *ṭuppišu* in AKL "last year(?)" s. Janssen 2007 for disc. and prev. lit.

3. N/LB *adi ṭuppi ṭuppi* (and variants) means "for a one-year period", s. Baker 2010. S. also Hackl in Jursa 2010, 713 n. 3686. Etym. uncert. EZ (1), JH/JW (2–3)

ṭuppu s. *tuppu*

ṭuppuru "to expel; expelled" s. *dapāru* D; "an implement?" s. *DuBBuru.*

ṭupšar-… s. *tupšar-…*

ṭupullû "slander; suspicion"; + SB

1. Mayer 2009, 439: SB *ṭú-pu-u[l-l]a-a ay aršī* Or. NS 59, 450: 19 "may I not suffer an insult".

2. SB *ṭú-pu-ul-lu-ú šakinšu* K. 2289: 6 "suspicion is placed on him" (omen apodosis, court. H. Stadhouders). EZ (1), JW (2)

ṭupultu s. *ṭapultu*

\+ **ṭurdānu** "dispatched group of workers"; OB

ṣābam ṭù-ur-da-na-am ana ṭarīdim YNER 4, 28: 3 "worker(s): *ṭ.* for dispatch(?)". JW

ṭurru I (AHw *ṭurru, turru* II; CAD *ṭurru* A–C) s. *turru*

ṭurru II, *durru* "rectum, anus"; Sum. lw.

1. Lex. *ṭú-ur-ru = ṭú-ur amēli* AOAT 50, 368: 129 (malku) "*ṭ* = rectum of a man". Cf. Hrůša ib. p. 235.

2. LB *ultu du-ur-ri-šú lā uṣṣâ* SpTU 1, 36: 18 "it does not flow out of his rectum".

3. Corresponds to CAD Ṭ 166 *ṭurru* D. For the reading of this word as *durru* or *ṭurru* s. Streck 2009, 136–140.

JW (2), MPS (1), NR (3)

ṭūru, *ṭurû* "an aromatic (perhaps opopanax or galbanum)"; + MB

1. MB:

a) 1 (p) ⌜2 (b)⌝ *ṭú-r[u-ú]* MBLET 27: 12 "1 bushel 2 seah of *ṭ.*".

b) 2 (b)!⌝ *ṭú-re-e* ib. 27 r. 10 "2 seah of *ṭ.*".

c) 1 GUR *ṭú-ru-ú ab-lu-ú* ib. 52: 3 "1 kor of dried(?) *ṭ.*".

d) 2 (p) 4 (b) *ṭú-ru-ú* ib. 52: 18 "2 bushel 4 seah of *ṭ.*".

e) 30 *laḫtan* ⌜*ṭú*?⌝*-re-e* ib. 51: 11 "30 *laḫtannu*-vats for/of(?) *ṭ.*".

f) Note that Gurney 1983, 91 reads *durû* (elsewhere unattested) and thinks of a cereal.

2. SB *ṭu-ri šadê* SAA 3, 28 r. 10 "*ṭ.* of the mountains".

3. *ṭ.* is also attested in SB medical and LB economic texts, where it is either weighed or counted, and the amounts are usually rather small (several shekels or up to 60 plants, s. CAD Ṭ 167 *ṭūru* a), but once, in a LB text, we find two talents of *ṭūru* (s. CAD Ṭ 167 *ṭūru* b).

4. S. Jursa 2009, 166.

\+ **ṭuwāb(u)** "an official(?)"; MB Emar

^{mí}É.GI$_4$-*ia ana* ^{lú}*ṭù-wa-ab ana muḫḫi* PN *u* 2 *aḫâtišu lā iraggumu* AulaOr Suppl. 1, 76: 15 "my fiancée should not raise claims before a *ṭ.* against PN and his 2 sisters". For disc. s. Arnaud 1991, 11 (*qutāl* of ṬWB?); Pentiuc 2001, 187. JW/NR